Family in Mission

Dr Reimer is asking an overarching question: when it comes to the current scholarly discussion regarding mission and evangelism, why is it that our families are not included whatsoever? Considering my experience as a pastor and theologian in Latin America and all the biblical and theological insights Dr Reimer presents here, it is puzzling and somewhat shameful that we haven't given the attention this crucial issue deserves. The Christian family is God's trinitarian gift, his intelligent design for the salvation of the world, and the most natural place for mission. Thus, Dr Reimer is right – family and mission belong together. What does a "missional family" look like in theory and practice? I highly encourage you to read and savour this book to find out the answers.

Rubens Muzio, PhD
Missionary, SEPAL, One Challenge International
Professor, Faculdade Teológica Sul Americana (FTSA), Londrina, Brasil

Professor Reimer is to be congratulated for offering a superb account of the holistic calling of the family to be the most important channel of experiencing the reality of God's kingdom within and outside the church; to share the good news with those closest to the faithful by being the light "to all in the house" (Matt 5:15). Thoughtful, scriptural, and thought provoking, this accessible book is brimming with theological and practical insights. It is a breath of fresh air in mission literature by looking at the family as the indispensable missional unit of the church and advocating for its place of primacy in the evangelistic outreach activities of the whole people of God.

Parush R. Parushev, PhD
Rector, St Trivelius Theological Institute, Sofia, Bulgaria
Associate Director for Academic Development,
Langham Partnership Scholars' Programme

Dr Johannes Reimer's book *Family in Mission: Theology and Praxis* is a long overdue work on the important subject of family. It is a must-read for every Christian and especially those in leadership of churches and mission organizations who have shifted the emphasis of faith and praxis to the individual. Dr Reimer has provided both a strong biblical foundation and an impressive narrative of possible missional applications of the theme. I deeply appreciate the inclusion of study and reflection questions at the end of the chapters. My hope and prayer is that this book would cause a radical shift to consider family as the basic and essential unit of faith and practice.

CB Samuel
Theological Advisor,
Evangelical Fellowship of India's Commission of Relief (EFICOR)

Johannes Reimer's book *Family in Mission: Theology and Praxis* is an incredibly important piece containing the author's thoughts and deep insights about relations between God's mission, church and family. Dr Reimer has a gift of incorporating contemporary issues and problems of the global church with relevant answers in the Holy Scriptures, understanding *missio Dei* and emphasizing the role of local churches. The author "lands" high notions of missional church to missional families and their daily praxis. I recommend this book for every Christian to understand the depth of God's mission, and also for every preacher and church teacher.

Vladimir Ubeivolc, PhD
President, Beginning of Life NGO
Senior Pastor, Life to the World Church, Chisinau, Moldova

Family in Mission

Theology and Praxis

Johannes Reimer

© 2020 Johannes Reimer

Published 2020 by Langham Global Library
An imprint of Langham Publishing
www.langhampublishing.org

Langham Publishing and its imprints are a ministry of Langham Partnership

Langham Partnership
PO Box 296, Carlisle, Cumbria, CA3 9WZ, UK
www.langham.org

Published in partnership with Micah Global

Micah Global
c/o Christ Church, Christchurch Road, Winchester, SO23 9SR, United Kingdom
www.micahglobal.org

ISBNs:
978-1-78368-810-4 Print
978-1-83973-004-7 ePub
978-1-83973-005-4 Mobi
978-1-83973-006-1 PDF

Johannes Reimer has asserted his right under the Copyright, Designs and Patents Act, 1988 to be identified as the Author of this work.

All rights reserved. No part of this publication may be reproduced, stored in a retrieval system or transmitted, in any form or by any means, electronic, mechanical, photocopying, recording or otherwise, without the prior written permission of the publisher or the Copyright Licensing Agency.

Requests to reuse content from Langham Publishing are processed through PLSclear. Please visit www.plsclear.com to complete your request.

All Scripture quotations, unless otherwise indicated, are taken from the Holy Bible, New International Version®, Anglicised, NIV®. Copyright © 1979, 1984, 2011 by Biblica, Inc®. Used by permission. All rights reserved worldwide.

Translations from non-English sources are the author's own.

British Library Cataloguing-in-Publication Data
A catalogue record for this book is available from the British Library

ISBN: 978-1-78368-810-4

Cover & Book Design: projectluz.com

Langham Partnership actively supports theological dialogue and an author's right to publish but does not necessarily endorse the views and opinions set forth here or in works referenced within this publication, nor can we guarantee technical and grammatical correctness. Langham Partnership does not accept any responsibility or liability to persons or property as a consequence of the reading, use or interpretation of its published content.

Contents

Preface ix
Abbreviations xi
1 A Surprising Discovery 1
2 Family and Mission: Laying a Biblical Foundation 17
3 Families in Mission 59
4 Family and Church 75
5 Growing Family-Centred Churches 91
6 Becoming a Missional Family 117
7 Family Mission in Practice (1) 159
8 Family Mission in Practice (2) 183
9 Families in World Mission: A Unique Challenge 211
Epilogue: The Family Is the Path of the Church 227
Bibliography 229
Index of Names 243
Index of Subjects 245
Index of Scripture 247

Preface

I owe this book to my Indian friend and teacher CB Samuel, who spoke on "Family and Mission" at the International Christian Community Development Conference (ICDC) that took place in May 2014 in Schwäbisch Gmünd, Germany. His lecture on the intrinsic meaning of family in mission, his passion and his biblical insight touched me deeply. Yet nothing he said was really new to me: for years I had observed people finding faith mostly in, through and by their families. However, I was moved by Samuel's words and started to search my memory for books I knew on family and mission. I couldn't think of a single one. When I asked the speaker, after his lecture, which titles he could recommend, he told me the same – there are none. My subsequent research brought nothing helpful to light. It seems that hardly anyone takes notice of this topic and correlation. However, if we are to take seriously the statistics and figures which show how people get to know Christ, we need to put the main focus in mission on families.

George W. Peters, a missiologist in the USA, is one of the very few experts on mission who refers to this topic. Having observed and studied the correlation of mission and family he concluded that the evangelization of whole families is the primary biblical and cultural approach to mission.[1] Peters made this statement in 1970, more than four decades ago. What has happened since? Mission in families has not really been invigorated. On the contrary, collectivist societies today demand that mission's focus be on evangelizing all sorts of other groups – social clusters and ethnic groups.[2] Although you can find a wide range of literature on church planting and strategic mission, and even though the individualistic Western world has claimed back the private home as a target group, as yet, little has happened. Not even the Lausanne Consultation of Pattaya, Thailand, which demanded that evangelism focus more on non-traditional families, has brought real change.[3]

---

1. George W. Peters, *Evangelisation: Total, durchdringend, umfassend* (Bad Liebenzell: VLM, 1977), 164.

2. Take, for example, the Lausanne Occasional Papers (LOP): Lausanne Committee for World Evangelization, "Christian Witness to Muslims," Lausanne Occasional Paper (LOP) 13, 2–4, 1980, accessed 19 January 2015, http://www.lausanne.org/content/lop/lop-13.

3. Lausanne Committee for World Evangelization, "Non-Traditional Families: Reaching Families with the Good News," Lausanne Occasional Paper (LOP) 36, in *A New Vision, a New Heart, a Renewed New Call: Lausanne Occasional Papers*, ed. David Claydon (Pasadena, CA: William Carey Library, 2005), 438–491.

When I found this out, I was drawn to do more research on this correlation. I hope that my conclusions will help our churches to open their eyes to see families as agents and instruments of effective mission and to start family ministry wherever possible. In order to prioritize family ministry, the church has to stop thinking in traditional "ghetto" paradigms to take the social reality seriously.

I dedicate this book to all families who pursue their relatives, intercede for them and do everything they can to reach them for the gospel. May the Lord our God bless them richly. I also pray for families who dare to leave their comfort zones and reach out to other, less-privileged families. I seek to encourage you and I offer practical ideas on how to do that.

This book would not have been written without the support of precious people by my side. First, my good friend Wilhelm Faix carefully read the draft and made helpful comments to refine its content. Nina Krämer translated the book from German into English. My beloved wife, Cornelia, listened carefully as I discussed the book's progress with her, making objective comments while we went on countless walks in the splendid Lee Valley Park near London. The Ewersbach University of Applied Arts, Germany, facilitated our research project by scheduling a whole research semester. All Nations Christian College, UK, was of great support, enabling us to stay at their wonderful college site in Easneye, Ware, and giving us access to its great library. Again and again they ordered books I needed. And lastly, I must highlight all the colleagues, missionaries and evangelists I contacted who gave me precious counsel, including information I was able to find out only through them. Thank you so much!

Johannes Reimer
Bergneustadt, Germany
Spring 2020

Abbreviations

AOK	Allgemeine Ortskrankenkasse (Local public health insurance company in Germany)
EN	*Evangelii Nuntiandi*: "Apostolic Exhortation of His Holiness Pope Paul VI to the Episcopate, to the Clergy and to All the Faithful of the Entire World."
FC	*Familiaris Consortio*: "Apostolic Exhortation *Familiaris Consortio* of Pope John Paul II to the Episcopate, to the Clergy and to the Faithful of the Whole Catholic Church on the Role of the Christian Family in the Modern World."
FCC	Family-centred church
FFE	Family-to-family evangelism
FIC	Family Integrated Church
GS	*Gaudium et Spes*: "Pastoral Constitution on the Church in the Modern World *Gaudium et Spes* Promulgated by His Holiness, Pope Paul VI on December 7, 1965."
LOP	Lausanne Occasional Paper
SOLA	Sommer Lager (German summer camps)

1

A Surprising Discovery

In What Context Do People Come to Faith?

The gospel is good news for all the world. Unlike any other philosophy, ideology and religion, the gospel meets all the needs of all people in all cultures and all contexts. Therefore Christians, the church of Christ, are called to "take the entire Gospel to all the world."[1] Yet how do they do that effectively? Where, how and by whom do people come to believe in Jesus Christ? Which methods of evangelism and mission are best to achieve this goal?

Most would say it is done above all by great ministries and famous evangelists. And yes, we should be very thankful for every person who was led to Christ by those anointed servants of God. Far be it from me to minimize the significance of national and international evangelism ministries in any way. Thank God we have them! But even though our libraries are full of the biographies of these great men and women, we need to recognize that it is not through them that most people come to know Jesus Christ.

Perhaps it is through pastors and their local churches, at least those with special gifting in evangelism, those who have a certain evangelistic DNA? Surely they are supposed to lead most people to Jesus? There are masses of books, manuals and seminars on church and evangelism. Yet, while such gifted churches are really important, it is not through them that most people come to faith either.

Worldwide, we see that it is rather through relatives and family members that most people come to believe in and follow Christ. However, hardly any research has been done on this. The few examples that exist only underline the conclusion just stated.

---

1. Charles van Engen, *Mission on the Way: Issues in Mission Theology* (Grand Rapids, MI: Baker, 1996), 168.

According to the research of C. B. Samuel, a church founder and mission leader in India, nine out of ten Indian converts come to follow Jesus through their families or their friends' families.[2] Such figures are confirmed by Jakob Zweininger, who studied Muslim converts in Kyrgyzstan, Central Asia,[3] as well as by Heinrich Klassen, who researched conversions in the former Soviet Union.[4] The Anglican Archbishop of Kenya, David Gitari, described a great spiritual awakening among the people of Gabra in Northern Kenya due to mission focused on local communities and families.[5] The same was said by Arnell Motz and Donald Posterski to be true for Canada. They evaluated empiric surveys demonstrating that only 8 percent of people came to believe in Christ through church events, while 67 percent of the people interviewed stated that their faith stemmed from personal relationships with family and friends.[6] The situation is similar in Germany: it is predominantly family members and close relatives who tell seekers first about the saving gospel. Elmer L. Towns, a missiologist and leading specialist on church growth in the USA, claims that all the statistics on evangelism leave no doubt that most new converts find Jesus through the testimony of family members or close friends.[7]

To the surprise of some, Catholic Church dignitaries and theologians express an opinion on this too. Pope John Paul II, who was a passionate advocate of a new evangelization of Europe, stated that "family is the first target of evangelism."[8] Other dignitaries speak of the family being the nucleus of faith

---

2. Lecture at CCDI Conference in Schwäbisch Gmünd, Germany, May 2014. Others confirm Samuel's figures, such as D. W. Fowlkes and P. Verster, "Family (*oikos*) Evangelism for Reaching Forward Caste Hindus in India," *Verbum et Ecclesia* 27, no. 1 (2006): 321–338.

3. Jakob Zweininger, "Allah oder Christus? A Missiology Case Study on the Reasons Why Kyrgyz People Convert from Islam to Christianity" (unpublished DTh diss., University of South Africa, 2009), 269–292.

4. Heinrich Klassen, *Mission als Zeugnis zur missionarischen Existenz in der Sowjetuinon nach dem Zweiten Weltkrieg* (Nürnberg: VTR, 2003).

5. David Gitari, "Kenya: Evangelism among Nomadic Communities," in *One Gospel, Many Clothes: Anglicans and the Decade of Evangelism*, ed. Chris Wright and Chris Sugden (London: Regnum, 1990), 60–70.

6. Arnell Motz with Donald Posterski, "Who Responds to the Gospel and Why?," in *Reclaiming the Nation: The Challenge of Evangelizing Canada in the Year 2000*, ed. Gerald Kraft et al. (Richmond: Church Leadership Library, 1990), 142.

7. Elmer L. Towns, ed., *Evangelism and Church Growth: A Practical Encyclopedia* (Ventura, CA: Regal, 1995), 210.

8. John Paul II, "Brief Papst Johannes Pauls II. an die Familien" (Letter to families by Pope John Paul II), 1994, 16, accessed 1 September 2016, http://w2.vatican.va/content/john-paul-ii/de/letters/1994/documents/hf_jp-ii_let_02021994_families.html.

and the *home of gnosis* – the very place to get to know God.⁹ Curial Cardinal Emeritus Walter Kasper of Germany even declared the family to be inherent to faith.¹⁰ That's very explicit: family and evangelism appear largely to depend on each other. This correlation can thus be found in all kinds of testimonies by people with very different cultural, national and spiritual backgrounds.

The question that arises then is *how* exactly do people get to know God within their families? Let's take Sebastian as a typical example. He was the first in his family to get to know Jesus. In an interview he told me, "From day one I kept praying for my family. Whenever possible I shared my faith with them. But it wasn't easy. My parents had been raised as communists. There was no place for God in their *Weltanschauung*. Yet they must have observed my life, and being touched they stopped resisting. So one day, they went to church with me. Right after the service both decided to come back again. Today my parents are true and loyal followers of Jesus." Sebastian's parents then began to pray for their close relatives. More of their family members were converted. These converts in turn started to pray for their families and shared their faith. Now, several years later, Sebastian's church is full of his family. His witnessing has borne fruit. That's how the gospel spreads.

We find many such stories in churches that are active in outreach to non-believers. It is even more apparent in countries and societies with strong family bonds. Bryan Green is right in saying that evangelism finds its best agent in a Christian home.¹¹ And John E. Apeh, a specialist on mission among the Igala tribes in central Nigeria, says it is the family structure which sets the context for evangelism. To reach the tribe with the gospel means to understand the social dynamics within the target families.¹²

Thus, examples everywhere show that families are important agents – if not the most important – for evangelism and mission in our world. Those searching for right strategies and better methods of evangelizing should engage with the institution of the family.

---

9. Ralph Weimann, "Die Familie als Keimzelle der Erneuerung des Glaubens," in *Ehe und Familie: Wege zum Gelingen aus katholischer Perspektive*, ed. George Augustin and Ingo Proft (Freiburg: Herder, 2016), 474.

10. Walter Kasper, *Das Evangelium von der Familie* (Freiburg: Herder, 2014), 9.

11. Bryan Green, *The Praxis of Evangelism*, 4th ed. (London: Hodder & Stoughton, 1958), 181.

12. John E. Apeh, *Social Structure and Church Planting* (Shippensburg, PA: Companion Press, 1989), 13.

In What Context Do People Lose Their Faith?

We have pondered how faith grows in society, but let's ask the same question the other way round: In what context are people most likely to lose their faith? The fact is that hundreds of thousands of Christians in the so-called Christian (Western) world have left their churches over the past decades. Many among them have turned their backs on the Christian faith altogether. Why is faith disappearing in the West?

Eddie Gibbs, British missiologist who has studied nominal Christianity in the Western world, says that the lack of efficient small groups in churches is the main factor in nominal Christianity. He states that it is within a cell group, within a family, that Christians find positive and stable spiritual role models. Wherever there is no such stable structure, church mechanisms for preserving faith will fail.[13] According to Gibbs, we find nominal belief already among the Jews in the Old Testament whenever the people of Israel failed to pass on their faith to the next generation.[14] The same trend can also be found in the New Testament.

Unfortunately, Eddie Gibbs doesn't refer explicitly to the topic of family in his book, yet in Scripture, as we will see, it is first and foremost the family that is responsible for the religious instruction of the next generation. We could therefore complete Gibbs's argument by stating that when families are incapable of living out their faith in God positively at home, the result will be a lack of faith in the next generation.

Alarming proof of this argument is found in the USA where many young people are leaving their churches. The spiritual example set by their parents seems to be too poor for them to follow. Reggie McNeal, expert on mission and leadership, says that studies in 2003 already showed that 90 percent of church youth were leaving the church after finishing school.[15] I suppose figures in Germany would not be very different.

It therefore seems obvious that family plays a key role in mission, having a special responsibility for preserving and passing on faith. We will probe into this in the following chapters.

---

13. Eddie Gibbs, *Winning Them Back: Tackling the Problem of Nominal Christianity* (Tunbridge Wells: Monarch, 1993), 75.

14. Gibbs, *Winning Them Back*, 37–38.

15. Reggie McNeal, *The Present Future: Six Tough Questions for the Church* (San Francisco: Jossey-Bass, 2003), 4.

Responsible Evangelism

Simply put, evangelism means to pass on the good news of Jesus Christ, who brought us life eternal – and even life in abundance (John 1:12). Christians are people who have heard the good news and experienced this life. That's why they go to church: they go to worship God together and celebrate this life and his presence in their midst. They share experiences and prayer, which enable and lead them to carry the good news into all the world, to all people and all nations, in word and deed. That is God's will – it is what Jesus, our risen Lord, commanded us to do (Matt 28:19–20). We are salt and light for the world (Matt 5:13–15). When people see our works they will praise God in heaven. Hence, evangelism is a universal, holistic process.[16]

Such a process can hardly be tackled responsibly when done only casually. It is of little value to start random outreaches simply motivated by realizing, "It's been a long time since we did any evangelism. Why don't we . . . ?" If we are to deal with the most important concern of our God (his core request), the church has to come back to *responsible evangelism*, as Christopher Walker rightfully demands[17] – that is, evangelism carried out with a responsible attitude and in sensitive action. According to Walker, such evangelism requires (1) a biblical approach; (2) adequate teaching of God's character, intention and manifestation in Jesus Christ, the world's redeemer; (3) interdependence of the individual person and the collective, as intended in God's divine salvation plan; and (4) proclaiming a life abundant in faith, hope and love.[18]

These parameters set by Walker help us find the place and role family should have in the church's evangelism, which we will explore in this book. We will seek to understand God's intention for families and how he planned them to be life-giving, both literally and when it comes to his Great Commission. We will find answers to questions like: How does Jesus view family? What role did he intend the family to play when sending us out to make disciples? We will focus on the correlation between individuals as children of God and their collectives, especially whole families or the kinships these individuals belong to, and are affected by, in every aspect of their lives. All this will bring

---

16. Christopher C. Walker, *Connecting with the Spirit of Christ: Evangelism for a Secular Age* (Nashville: Discipleship Resources, 1988), 1–2.

17. Walker, *Connecting with the Spirit*, 88–90. David Evans talks of "Evangelism with theological credibility" (David Evans, "Evangelism with Theological Credibility," in *One Gospel, Many Clothes*, 29–33). Elmer Thiessen describes "Evangelism along with ethical responsibility" (Elmer Thiessen, *The Ethic of Evangelism* [London: Paternoster, 2011]).

18. Walker, *Connecting with the Spirit*, 88–107. In contrast, David Evans puts the emphasis on "Evangelism and authority, mission, culture and Christ" (Evans, "Evangelism," 29–30).

us to the ultimate question: Is it only by chance that we hear that families are effective in evangelism, or is this a mandate that has been given by God? And if the latter, how should the church be structured to fulfil God's intentions? How does a church that focuses on families accomplish outreach? These are some of the questions we will probe in the following chapters.

Missing the Family in Mission Theory

Although, as we have seen, most people come to know Christ through the testimony of close relatives, and findings around the world show that the family is essential in mission and evangelism, the startling reality is that teaching on mission and evangelistic communication hardly ever refers to the institution of the family.

In specialized literature and academic discussion, the silence regarding the role of family in mission is deafening. Even South African missiologist and brilliant theologian David J. Bosch remains silent on the significance of the family in mission, though offering sophisticated definitions of mission and appropriate communication of Christ's gospel.[19] The family does occur as a topic in publications on the mission of early Christianity,[20] but academic discussion on the role of the family in proclaiming the gospel is missing in modern missiology.[21] It is only on rare occasions that we find someone like Anneke Stasson talking about the "missiology of the Christian home."[22] While Stasson claims this is an important category in Protestant mission theory,[23]

---

19. David J. Bosch, *Transforming Mission: Paradigm Shifts in Theology of Mission* (Maryknoll, NY: Orbis, 1991), 368–370.

20. Michael Green, *Evangelisation zur Zeit der ersten Christen: Motivation, Methodik und Strategie* (Neuhausen-Stuttgart: Hänssler, 1970), 239–241; Eckhard J. Schnabel, *Urchristliche Mission* (Wuppertal: R. Brockhaus TVG, 2002), 1243–1244.

21. Peter Beyerhaus, *Er sandte sein Wort: Theologie der Christlichen Mission, Vol. 1: Die Bibel in der Mission* (Wuppertal: R. Brockhaus TVG, 1996); D. Dorr, *Mission in Today's World* (Maryknoll, NY: Orbis, 2002); A. Scott Moreau, Gary R. Corwin and Gary B. McGee, *Introducing World Mission: A Biblical, Historical and Practical Survey* (Grand Rapids, MI: Baker, 2004); Christopher Wright, *The Mission of God: Unlocking the Bible's Grand Narrative* (Downers Grove, IL: InterVarsity Press, 2006); Craig Ott, Stephen J. Strauss and Timothy Tennent, *Encountering Theology of Mission: Biblical Foundations, Historical Developments and Contemporary Issues* (Grand Rapids, MI: Baker Academic, 2010). Even in Asia, with its strong family-related culture, academic reflection on family in mission is missing. See Roger E. Hedlund and Paul Joshua Bhakiaraj, *Missiology for the 21st Century: South Asian Perspectives* (Delhi: ISPCK/MIIS, 2004).

22. Anneke Stasson, "Walter and Ingrid Trobisch and a Missiology of 'Couple Power,'" in *The Missionary Family: Witness, Concerns, Care*, ed. Dwight P. Baker and Robert J. Priest (Pasadena, CA: William Carey Library, 2014), 5.

23. Stasson, "Walter and Ingrid Trobisch."

there are hardly any Protestant publications about it. The fact that such reflection on family in mission is missing among Christians who think that their understanding of mission is closest to God's intentions for his creation order, and in denominations that see mission as *notae ecclesiae* (marks of a true church) – like the Baptist church with its battle cry, "Every Baptist is a missionary"[24] – is even more bewildering.[25]

We come across a similar lack of reflection when it comes to scholarly publishing on evangelism.[26] The family seems to be a dispensable factor in evangelistic strategies and masterplans on how to reach people for Christ.[27] It is simply missing in theological literature on evangelism[28] as well as in practical handbooks.[29] Dozens of evangelistic methods are described, but not one mentions family in mission.[30] If mentioned at all, the family is defined as a target group for evangelism and mission.[31]

In the festschrift in honour of the acknowledged German evangelist Gerhard Bergmann, the authors creatively pondered the best possible methods of evangelism. They covered everything, such as media, arts, science, even PR – but they didn't mention the family once.[32] More recent publishing on evangelism has also kept silent on the topic. German theologian Martin Werth laments that the family has failed to pass on the faith even though it played such

---

24. Kim Strübind, "Missionstheologie und missionarische Praxis der Baptisten im ökumenischen Kontext," *Zeitschrift für Theologie und Gemeinde* 12 (2007): 287.

25. See, for instance, Christopher Wright, *The Mission of God's People: A Biblical Theology of the Church's Mission* (Grand Rapids, MI: Zondervan, 2010), 25.

26. Michael Green, *Evangelism through the Local Church* (London: Hodder & Stoughton, 1990); Walter Klaiber, *Ruf und Antwort: Biblische Grundlagen einer Theologie der Evangelisation* (Stuttgart: Christliches Verlagshaus, 1990); Martin Werth, "Theologie der Evangelisation," (Neukirchen-Vluyn: Neukirchener Verlag, 2004).

27. Typical in this regard are the writings of the US author on evangelism Robert Coleman. One finds no mention of family-related evangelism in his books *The Master Plan of Evangelism* (Grand Rapids, MI: Revell, 2006) and *The Master's Way of Personal Evangelism* (Wheaton, IL: Crossway, 1997).

28. William Abraham, *The Logic of Evangelism* (Grand Rapids, MI: Eerdmans, 1989).

29. See, for instance, Ross Pilkinton, *Evangelistischer Lebensstil* (Marienheide: Bibellesebund, 1979); Anton Schulte, *Evangelisation – praktisch: Mit Anmerkungen zu einer deutschen Theologie der Evangelisation* (Moers: Brendow, 1979).

30. See, for instance, Michael Marshall, *The Gospel Connection: A Study in Evangelism for the Nineties* (London: Darton, Longman & Todd, 1991).

31. Scott Dawson, ed., *The Complete Evangelism Guidebook: Expert Advice on Reaching Others for Christ* (Grand Rapids, MI: Baker, 2006), 114–115.

32. Wilfried Reuter, . . . *Und bis ans Ende der Welt: Beiträge zur Evangelisation; Eine Festschrift zum 60. Geburtstag von Gerhard Bergmann* (Neuhausen-Stuttgart: Hänssler, 1974).

an important role in the past,[33] yet he offers neither theory on, nor possible solutions for, this problem. The role of family in mission is not even an issue for experts who – like the evangelist John Finney[34] – have understood that in the twenty-first century evangelism needs to happen in communities and include people groups.[35] The same holds true for John Wimber's well-received book on "power evangelism."[36] And to complete this picture, the family is not featured in publications on church growth or church development either. Hence, there's an urgent need to rediscover the family as God's prime agent of mission.

But why do experts on mission and evangelism avoid this issue? Why is there so little reflection and academic discussion about it? Why can't we acknowledge the role God has given to family in his divine plan? Is it because we take family in mission for granted? But if so, why is there very little practical instruction material? Why would we invest enormous amounts of money in different sectors of evangelism ministries, yet overlook the obvious? Let's find answers to these questions.

What We Learn from Church History

Dana Robert, a historian on mission, claims that the Christian family was the linchpin – the "cornerstone of mission work" – in the history of Anglo-American theory and practice of mission.[37] According to Robert, Protestant ministries put the emphasis on the moral example missionary families would set for the people around them, who could observe Christian values and would thus be drawn towards Christianity. In 1836, the General Secretary of the American Board of Mission (ABM), Rufus Anderson, told his missionaries that non-Christians ought to have the opportunity to witness the life of a Christian family.[38] Having discovered the potential of the family as mission agents, Protestant missions preferred to send out couples into the mission

---

33. Werth, *Theologie der Evangelisation*, 378.

34. John Finney, *Wie Gemeinde über sich hinauswächst: Zukunftsfähig evangelisieren im 21. Jahrhundert* (Neukirchen-Vluyn: Aussaat, 2007), 123–147.

35. See John Drane, *Evangelism for a New Age: Creating Churches for the Next Century* (London: Marshall Pickering, 1994).

36. John R. Wimber and Kevin Springer, *Power Evangelism* (San Francisco: Harper & Row, 1996).

37. Dana L. Robert, "The 'Christian Home' as a Cornerstone of Anglo-American Mission Thought and Practice," in *Converting Colonialism: Visions and Realities in Mission History, 1706–1914*, ed. Dana Robert (Grand Rapids, MI: Eerdmans, 2008), 134–165.

38. Cited in Stasson, "Walter and Ingrid Trobisch," 7.

fields. Yet how were these couples prepared for their role as whole-family missionaries? Usually they weren't, which often led to frustration, especially among women missionaries.[39]

Yet positive examples can be found. Anneke Stasson has written about the missionary couple Walter and Ingrid Trobisch in Africa.[40] This couple believed there was a God-given power within and through marriage. Ingrid Trobisch referred to God creating us as men and women to reflect his image in the world together.[41] The couple were convinced that God intended marriage not only to create families but also to promote spirituality, thus with a higher purpose than simply pursuing biological fruitfulness. They saw their marriage as a blessing for others,[42] the best way to proclaim the gospel.[43]

It was this example of a successful missionary couple which led Stasson to conclude that Protestant mission that focused on Christian homes had enormous potential in mission.[44] According to Stasson, the Trobisches were a typical example in Protestant history. She even sees the Christian home as inherent in Protestant missiology. Wives *and marriage itself* used to be essential to mission. Evangelism was perceived as a holistic process that used family life to exemplify values and good lifestyles, which became central aspects of preaching the gospel.[45] Other church historians share this interpretation. Dana Robert observes that it was the typical strategy of the wives of missionaries to turn their everyday lives into teaching lessons.[46]

How difficult it was to live out this ideal in practice can be seen in Mary C. Cloutier's reports on the strains a missionary's family were exposed to in childbirth and raising children.[47] Childbirth in primitive conditions like those in Equatorial Africa often proved fatal for both mother and child and the mortality rate was high among the indigenous people. Missionary families were

---

39. See the studies on missionary wives by Patricia Grimshaw (*Paths of Duty: American Missionary Wives in Nineteenth-Century Hawaii* [Honolulu: University of Hawaii Press, 1989]) and Jane Hunter (*The Gospel of Gentility: American Women Missionaries in Turn-of-the-Century China* [New Haven: Yale University Press, 1984]).

40. Stasson, "Walter and Ingrid Trobisch," 5–20.

41. Stasson, 13.

42. Stasson, 14.

43. Stasson, 10.

44. Stasson, 14.

45. Stasson, 13.

46. Dana L. Robert, *American Women in Mission: A Social History of Their Thought and Practice* (Macon, GA: Mercer University Press, 1997), 65.

47. Mary Carol Cloutier, "'Family Problem': Challenges in Balancing Maternity and Mission in Nineteenth-Century Equatorial Africa," in *Missionary Family*, 79–97.

therefore tempted to send pregnant women back home to deliver their children, which would simply confirm their privileged position and consequently harm their testimony.

In this context, William Carey (1761–1834), founder of family mission, shaped a great vision and lived out his ideas in practice.[48] Carey and his family experienced the difficulties typical to adapting to a foreign culture and these drove them to the brink of despair, ruining the mental health of his wife Dorothy. Carey found no way to support his family financially, nor were they able to proclaim the gospel together as a family. To solve this, he founded a *collective community* where missionaries could share their lives, running everything together. Within this "missionary family" Carey hoped to secure spiritual, social and financial support for both the missionaries and their families. He felt that this provided an alternative kind of community life and had enormous potential in sharing the gospel.[49] And he could rightly claim that his idea worked. Both the Baptist Missionary Society (BMS) to which he belonged and his own heavily afflicted family received real benefit from the collective community.[50] Carey's "family mission" would later inspire Sadhu Sundar Singh (1889–1929), a well-known evangelist in India, in his attempts to build community-relevant churches,[51] the so-called *Ashrams*.[52]

Rediscovering Family for Mission

As we have seen, people often come to faith in Jesus Christ through their family members. They know their testimonies and their stories; they are even part of those stories, part of their shared family history. They need not change their culture or adopt a new language. They see and observe Christian lives right in front of their eyes as they share life together. In this way, the family is a strong testimony.

This was also true for past generations. The importance of the family for evangelism is a *leitmotif* running throughout the centuries of church and mission history. It starts with the apostle Paul's approval of his assistant's

---

48. For further information see, for example, Andrew D. McFarland, "William Carey's Vision for Missionary Families," in *Missionary Family*, 98–115.
49. McFarland, "William Carey's Vision," 101.
50. McFarland, 109.
51. Mentioned in Michael Nazir-Ali, *From Everywhere to Everywhere: A World View of Christian Mission* (London: Collins, 1990), 155.
52. *Ashram* means a community where a group of people would share life as within a family, led by a household's "guru," called Sadhu.

relatives, Timothy's grandmother and mother, who had instructed him in the faith (2 Tim 1:3–5). St Augustine, the great church father, owed his faith to his mother Monica.[53]

Charles Spurgeon, the famous British preacher and revivalist, was convinced that family was intrinsic to the church and mission of Christ. He therefore complained about the slackness of Christians when it came to spiritually parenting their children. In his view, a family raised in the fear of the Lord and living a holy life would protect society against becoming godless and heretical.[54] This great man of God lamented the lack of family devotions and lack of nurture by the church. On the other hand, the Communists in Russia, enemies of the gospel, complained about families playing a key role in Christian socializing of the precious youth. Vladimir Lenin and his militant atheists even sought to abolish the family as an institution of society, which in the 1920s then left an army of "orphans" who became a heavy burden on the young Communist state. In the end, Stalin's Soviet Union had to return to supporting the family as the basis of society – even though they knew the risk of religious ideas being nurtured there. And although Christian churches had been almost eradicated from the Soviet map by the 1940s, church life reblossomed instantly when Christianity became legal again during the Second World War.[55]

So both friends and foes confirm the prominent role of the Christian family in mission and church development. David Watson states that the private home is the most important and most strategic place where the good news of Jesus Christ is shared.[56] And Bryan Green praises the family as a unique agent of evangelism because only the family ideally presents a place of deep unity in love, a place where hospitality is a natural element of existence. Nowhere else is the gospel as present in real-life situations and human relationships as here,

---

53. For more information and discussion, see, for example, the lectures of Larissa Carina Seelbach, "Das weibliche Geschlecht ist ja kein Gebrechen, sondern Natur: Augustins Wertschätzung der Frau" ("The Female Sex Is No Illness but Nature: St Augustine's Appreciation of Women") at the Augustine Study Day in Würzburg, Germany, 2004, https://www.augustinus.de/einfuehrung/texte-ueber-augustinus/zeitungsartikel-vortraege/199-das-weibliche-geschlecht-ist-kein-gebrechen, accessed 21 January 2020.

54. Charles Spurgeon, Sermon no. 1, 336, https://www.spurgeon.org/resource-library/sermons/a-family-sermon#flipbook/, accessed 21 January 2020.

55. Stalin loosened the strict regulations on religion in 1943 because he hoped the church would then side with him in fighting against Germany.

56. David Watson, *I Believe in Evangelism* (London: Hodder & Stoughton, 1976), 147.

provided the family lives under the lordship of Christ. Green patiently pleads that we rediscover the missionary and evangelistic power of the family.[57]

This book is a response to Green's plea. Klaus Schäfer hits the nail on the head by saying, "What you are unable to talk about you cannot really grasp, hence, it won't take place in the end."[58] I have therefore sought to address the subject of family in mission in order to find the words that will enable us to talk about this topic in theory (theology) and practice, and to inspire the church as a whole. I have also sought to listen to all Christian traditions and denominations. For throughout the world people have learned that the classical Western style of evangelism, the practice of mission one-on-one, while being a blessing, has also led to various problems, including the loss of family relationships, social belonging and so on. Thus, Asian theologians and missiologists are demanding a radical change in mission strategies towards family-focused mission.[59] The Roman Catholic Church has been examining the role family ought to and will play in church and mission since the Second Vatican Council (1962–1965). Pope John Paul II even called for a radical reorganization of the Roman Catholic Church into one based on the family.[60] It was clear to him that "as soon as family collapses, the world will vanish," and therefore "the future of our church . . . depends on family."[61]

Even evangelicals are starting to realize how important it is to integrate family into mission. For instance, a range of Baptist churches in the USA joined together to form a movement called Family Integrated Church (FIC), with the goal of explicitly integrating families into their church life and mission.[62] Thus in FIC churches, whole families attend Sunday services together. Scott T. Brown, Director of the National Center for Family Integrated Churches (NCFIC), calls it a substantial breach of clear biblical guidelines concerning church life to separate families during Sunday services.[63]

---

57. Bryan Green, *Praxis of Evangelism*, 181.

58. Klaus Schäfer, "Lernort Gemeinde," *Zeitschrift für theologische Praxis* 2 (2003): 18.

59. Paul H. De Neui, ed., *Family and Faith in Asia: The Missional Impact of Social Networks* (Pasadena, CA: William Carey Library, 2010).

60. FC 70; Gerald Foley, *Family-Centred Church: A New Parish Model* (Kansas City, MO: Sheed & Ward, 1995), 5, 19.

61. FC 3.75.

62. National Center for Family Integrated Churches (NCFIC), "A Declaration on the Complementary Roles of Church and Family," 21 October 2014, https://ncfic.org/resources/view/ncfic_declaration.

63. Scott Brown, "Children in the Meeting of the Ephesian Church," 1 July 2004, https://ncfic.org/resources/217.

Occasionally in Protestant and evangelical churches, you come across evangelistic outreaches aimed directly at families.[64] Theologian Andreas Köstenberger and David W. Jones have written a biblical theology on the family – a book well worth reading – in which they state that "families are the backbone of any healthy church."[65] Köstenberger calls for theological discussion about the role of family in God's mission, yet he is wary of the potential danger of families replacing or competing with church, which he suspects may happen in movements like FIC.[66]

In this book I seek to heed such wisdom in the search for a guiding principle concerning family in mission which is based upon good theology. My strategy is therefore as follows:

First, I will address family in the light of God's Word. Hence, I will scrutinize Scripture to understand family as God meant it to be. Our God is three in one. Essentially, his Trinity sets the framework for studying the role of family in God's mission on earth. Here we will seek to comprehend why and for what purpose God, our heavenly Father, created families, and what role he intended them to play in society and in religious settings. What does Scripture say regarding how we should teach about life and how to nurture faith within the family? Who was responsible for this in biblical times: the father, the mother or the whole people of Israel? Is there a biblical model of instruction within the family? Can we even expect a kind of precept, and, if so, what are the main aspects? Is this what mission means?

Equally important is the role that Jesus our Redeemer ascribes to family. Does he see the family as an agent of mission and evangelism? How did Christ treat families he came into contact with? Can we take Jesus's life and words as an example providing us with a theology of family? If so, what does that mean?

We will also explore the New Testament to study the practical methods of mission and evangelism among the early Christians. We will see that it was primarily the Holy Spirit who initiated and led mission. What role did the family play? Where and in what contexts do the authors of the New Testament mention families? What role did families play in proclaiming the gospel?

In this way we can reach a firm theology of family mission, including practical steps for churches to follow. In the remaining chapters, we will focus

---

64. Scripture Union approached this topic in 2000 in John Hattam, *Families Finding Faith: Reaching Today's Families with the Gospel* (Milton Keynes: Scripture Union, 2000). However, there has been no real change since then.

65. Andreas J. Köstenberger and David W. Jones, *God, Marriage, and Family: Rebuilding the Biblical Foundation*, 2nd rev. ed. (Wheaton, IL: Crossway, 2010), 261.

66. Köstenberger and Jones, *God, Marriage, and Family*, 253–254.

on the correlation of family to church in order to develop an action plan for family-based mission and evangelism. What needs to be considered here? How can families become active agents in the mission ministries of their churches? Do models of this already exist, and if so, what can we learn from them?

Finally, the book will end with a chapter on the special situation of families involved in world mission.

Family – the Future of the Church?

Western democracies have experienced great societal transformation over the last decades, including a profound change in how the family is defined and what it is expected to look like. Today our ideal of a family is an individualistic small unit, usually consisting of father and mother, plus one or two children. This family usually lives isolated in a home and focused on itself, and thus is very busy trying to survive. Christians lament these changes but have done little to find out what they really mean for us, for family life and for church life too. Full-time ministers do not currently get special training in pastoral care or family ministry, to the detriment of church and mission. Hardly anything is done to support families – except for making pleas and political statements which only look good on paper. The Christian family is still "idealized" today, even though for a long time such families have ceased to function well and fall short of meeting these high expectations. Thorough studies need to be carried out in this area. Wilhelm Faix has already done much work, offering important insights.[67]

The church must wake up. If Pope John Paul II is right that the future of the church depends on the future of the family, we had better invest all our resources in this unit of love and life, this "profound school of becoming human," as Vatican II put it.[68] This book can help on that journey.

Whenever I talk about "family" in this book, I do not mean the modern ideal of a small family of only three or four members. Family, as I want to draw out, is a real cluster, a whole collective of blood-related people, meaning

---

67. See, for example, the following by Wilhelm Faix, "Die individualisierte Familie: Familie mit Zukunft? Eine Lebensform im Umbruch," *JETh* 27 (2013): 187–215; "Familie heute: Zwischen Anspruch und Wirklichkeit," *JETh* 9 (1995): 116–145; "Familie im Wandel: Gesellschaftliche Bedingungen heutigen Familienlebens als Herausforderung für die christliche Familie," in *Theologische Wahrheit und die Postmoderne*, ed. H. H. Klement (Wuppertal: SCM Brockhaus, 2002), 378–411.

68. Foley, *Family-Centred Church*, 17.

a whole group of relatives (a kinship) of different generations. Note that this family cluster is only as strong as its members' relationships.

So a small modern family will be overburdened by what I lay out in this book: it will be nearly impossible for a small family to embrace all that is outlined here. Yet I do not want to burden anyone – the *nuclear family* is already under great attack as never before! We can only demand of the family what God requires of it. So let's see family with his eyes and help families be transformed into his image. What I want is to know how God views family, and to ask him to show us the ways and means in which families can become again what he intended them to be from the beginning.

Books have the potential to inspire us or even to ignite a movement. While reading we can get so excited that we immediately leap into action. I don't yet know whether this book has such potential, but I hope and pray that we realize the urgency of this issue and that we get ready for action. Please be inspired! At the end of each chapter you will find a list of questions to deepen your reflection on its content. It might help to find others – cell groups, families, study groups – with whom you can work through and discuss these questions. Read together, share, ponder. Please protest when you disagree! For only then will family again become the main agenda in churches and societies! Know that you are important: your opinion is important and it does count!

Questions for Reflection

1. What are your thoughts on the role of family in mission?
2. Do you know whole families committed to mission? If so, how do you perceive them?
3. Is there a special family ministry offered in your church? If so, what does it look like? On what theological grounds is the family ministry based upon?
4. What role does family play in your local outreach?
5. Why is family valued so highly in theory while usually playing a lower role in church life?

2

Family and Mission: Laying a Biblical Foundation

God, Family and Mission
Mission Is God's Idea!

Mission is, above all, God's idea. It "flows from the very heart of God," as Gisbertus Voetus phrased it in the sixteenth century.[1] Mission is God's initiative on behalf of creation.[2] Whoever takes part in this mission will be part of "God's manifestation in this World."[3] And God revealed himself as a Trinity: God the Father, Son and Holy Spirit. He is Creator of all, our Redeemer and the Source of all life. Whoever gets close to him must face him as the Three-in-one. In the same way, we need to comprehend mission as a three-fold process.[4]

Mission is God's work. Timothy C. Tennent, a US missiologist, says that mission reveals a lot more about God, and who he is, than it does about us and what we can do.[5] Whoever studies God's mission, the *missio Dei*, must ponder it as that of the Creator, Redeemer and source of life. Only a Trinitarian approach to mission can communicate God's character. Any compromise or reduction will result in a lopsided image of God and a narrow picture of his mission. We cannot and should not separate the three persons of God when we talk about

---

1. In David J. Bosch, *Transforming Mission: Paradigm Shifts in Theology of Mission* (Maryknoll, NY: Orbis, 1991), 257.

2. Timothy C. Tennent, *Invitation to World Mission: A Trinitarian Theology for the Twenty-First Century* (Grand Rapids, MI: Kregel, 2010), 54.

3. Paul Schütz, *Zwischen Nil und Kaukasus* (Munich: Kaiser, 1930), 245. See also John Piper, *Let the Nations Be Glad: The Supremacy of God in Missions* (Grand Rapids, MI: Baker, 2004).

4. Lesslie Newbigin, *The Open Secret: An Introduction to the Theology of Mission* (Grand Rapids, MI: Eerdmans, 1995), 29; Tennent, *Invitation*, 74.

5. Tennent, 55.

either his character or his mission. American theologian Dr Miroslav Volf, who observes classical church tradition, refers to God's Trinity as his "reciprocal nature" (complementary identity).[6] Every person of God indwells the other persons. You cannot think of one without the others. You cannot understand how the Father is acting without paying attention to how the Son and his Spirit work, and vice versa.[7] When asked to show them the Father, Jesus answered his disciples: "Don't you know me . . ., even after I have been among you such a long time? Anyone who has seen me has seen the Father" (John 14:9).

God reveals his will for mission in his Word, the Bible. Roland Hardmeier rightly states: "An integral approach to mission is based upon the conviction that Scripture is the authority for church and our mission. It is the gospel of the Old and New Testaments which defines our mission and how church is to fashion life and fulfill God's mission."[8] Therefore, if we are to find out what the family means in relationship to mission, we must turn to Scripture. In the books of the Old and New Testaments, God unfolds his thoughts on family and mission. And mission in the name of the Three-in-One includes creating, redeeming and giving life here on earth. So we need to ask three questions: What is the mandate of the family according to the mission of God, the Creator and Father? What role does the family play according to the Son, our Redeemer? And what place does the family take in the mission of the Holy Spirit, as the one giving and preserving life?

The Family Derives Its Name from God

Just like mission, the family was God's idea and design. He wanted families, he created them and he has been shaping them. When we think about the family we must turn to him, for, as Richard Howel says, the institution of the family has its roots in the nature of God's Trinity and it reflects his nature (Gen 1:27–28).[9]

If we want to comprehend the family's mission in this world, we must learn about God's character. As three in one, he is always in relationship, and this

---

6. For more on this, see Johannes Reimer, *Die Welt umarmen: Theologie des gesellschaftsrelevanten Gemeindebaus*, Transformationsstudien 1, 2nd ed. (Marburg: Francke Verlag, 2013), 150–160.

7. Reimer, *Die Welt umarmen*, 150–160.

8. Roland Hardmeier, *Kirche ist Mission: Auf dem Weg zu einem ganzheitlichen Missionsverständnis*, IGW 2 (Schwarzenfeld: Neufeld Verlag, 2009), 299.

9. Richard Howel, *Transformation in Action: A Case Study of India* (Thailand: Forum for World Evangelization, 2004), 7.

is perfectly reflected in the family. One of the pietist fathers of the eighteenth century, Count Nicholas Ludwig von Zinzendorf (1700–1760), spoke of the Trinity as "the Family of God."[10] And the apostle Paul writes to the church in Ephesus:

> For this reason I kneel before the Father, from whom every family in heaven and on earth derives its name. I pray that out of his glorious riches he may strengthen you with power through his Spirit in your inner being, so that Christ may dwell in your hearts through faith. And I pray that you, being rooted and established in love, may have power, together with all the Lord's holy people, to grasp how wide and long and high and deep is the love of Christ, and to know this love that surpasses knowledge – that you may be filled to the measure of all the fullness of God. (Eph 3:14–19)

The apostle kneels before God the Trinity as he seeks to gain all of God's fullness. His praise has three stages.

First, Paul kneels before the Father who has created the whole family. The apostle accepts creation as it is meant to be. Anything that was created by God needs no correction, because anything from the Creator's hand is wholly good. Wherever amendments were needed, for instance in creating the woman, the Adama for Adam, God himself made them. Therefore, when we tackle the topic of family in mission we need to know how God created the family in the first place, and we should accept his creation. Below we will focus on the family as the creation of God the Father.

Next, Paul kneels before God's Holy Spirit, because the Spirit wants to transform our inner being according to the riches of his glory. That's how faith and love – the very ingredients that have held families together since the beginning of this world – will grow. The family is the place where people trust one another and entrust themselves to one another, where they promise to stay loyal, and husbands and wives become one flesh out of mutual love and dedication (Gen 2:24). Trust and love are fragile vessels which are easy to break, but family life depends crucially on these two variables. Where people stop trusting each other, wherever there is no love left, relationships will turn cold and ultimately disintegrate. Paul therefore says that God's Spirit wants to transform us, and he will start this process in our innermost being. The Holy Spirit himself will change each member of a family, as well as the whole family,

---

10. In Wilhelm Faix, *Zinzendorf: Glaube und Identität eines Querdenkers* (Marburg: Francke Verlag, 2012), 48.

from the inside out. Therefore, we need to carefully study the work of God's Holy Spirit in transforming the family.

Finally, the apostle kneels before Jesus, longing to grasp Christ's love which is greater than any knowledge and reflects the fullness of God's character. For God is love, and the one who loves has been born of God, knows God and does his will (1 John 4:7). That's how Christ's mission turns into the mission of his disciples. The family therefore has to grasp Christ's love to be able to know and carry out his mission on earth.

Different, But Still One

As the family derives its name from God and reflects God's Trinity, we must deal with the family on the same terms as we deal with God's nature. First, God is one, yet three. The Father is not the Son, the Son is not the Spirit and the Spirit is not the Father. Yet, at the same time, the three are perfectly united and in perfect harmony! There is no greater variety, diversity and range than there is within God, yet there is no greater unity than God, who went so far as to become man in Jesus – true man without losing his divine nature. This tension between his true humanity and his divine nature was taken to the extreme when the immortal God, the Author of life itself, died on a piece of wood created by himself, without losing his divinity. God never changes; his unity and trinity can and will never be changed by history.

As the family is created in God's triune image, we find the same unity and also the same diverse range of functions. The family should be as God created, designed and wanted it to be.[11] Family is where there is a father, a mother and children. God created them wonderfully as individuals and yet, at the same time, wonderfully made for each other – he created a unique interrelationship. The father is not the mother, the mother will never be the father, and neither will have the status of children within their own family, but it is only when individual members of the family rebel against the "we-feeling" that this unity will be in trouble. In contrast, God will never rebel against himself; he will always stay three-in-one in perfect unity, while families have been rebellious from the beginning of humankind. The family as a social unit and its unique bonding have been attacked and endangered ever since. Men rule over women,

---

11. For further discussion on the difference between man and woman and also in relation to God's Trinity see, for example, Michelle M. Schumacher, *A Trinitarian Anthropology: Adrienne von Speyer and Hans Urs von Balthasar in Dialogue with Thomas Aquinas* (Washington, DC: Catholic University of America Press, 2014), 246–391.

women emancipate themselves *against* men and children *cultivate* rebellion against their parents. In this way, family unity is broken and harmony is lost. Yet the social system of the family cannot be replaced because it is unique, just as God is unique. It is important that we comprehend the family as a holistic system, and that we fathom and accept the mandates of individuals according to God's creative plan.

God's Trinity lives in intentional communication as God is the very embodiment of social life. The Spirit exists because Jesus is alive, and the Father lives because of the Son and the Spirit's existence. You cannot think of one without the others. All three are mutually dependent on each other 100 percent – in their nature and in their mission. They are related to each other reciprocally. We talk about only *one* God and *one* creative mind flowing into the Father's creation, the Son's redemption and the work of the Holy Spirit, which we can only grasp when we comprehend this mutual dependence. Whenever we separate God the Father from God the Spirit and God the Son, we narrow our view and have a very reduced concept of him. We end up with contradictory concepts such as those developed by religions like Islam or sects like the Jehovah's Witnesses. While we may easily *think* of God as small and even follow this reduced-concept God (some do so fanatically), we will not have a *personal relationship* with him. No other religion knows personal communion between human beings and God such as Christians have with their Trinitarian God. Why is this? Simply because God's Trinity *is* communion in itself. Fellowship is his very nature. And that allows us to have communion with him too. Also, God has always been communicating because his very being lives on communication. Fellowship was established by God.[12]

The same principle holds true for the family. When we accept the triune God as the Creator of the family, we cannot separate the family's *mission* from the family's *life*. Furthermore, the biblical family can only be perceived as the deep mutual dependency of a father, a mother and children. Whenever this unity is separated and gets broken, the family becomes a reduced construct, prone to difficulty. We may come across single-parent families and childless couples, but they do not reflect the ideal, for it is diversity that provides unity. And parallel to God's Trinity, we have to bear in mind that the family's unity refers to their oneness in nature, in mission *and* in everyday life. The family only stays a family when family *life* displays its *mission* and when the *mission* is reflected in the family's *nature* – both for the family as a unit and for its

---

12. Paul S. Fiddes, *Participating in God: A Pastoral Doctrine of the Trinity* (London: Darton, Longman & Todd, 2000), 11–15.

individual members. Whenever fathers don't take their commission seriously, when they don't follow God's plan for them, whenever their lifestyles fall short of their characters, they will endanger their families' unity and health. The same holds true for mothers and children. Therefore it makes sense to find positive examples of family social systems in Scripture.

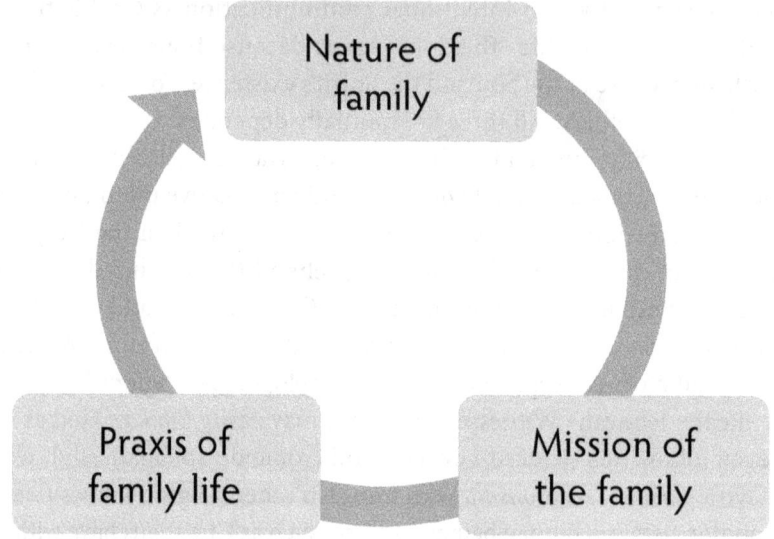

Figure 2.1: Cycle of the Missionary Identity of the Family

God revealed his Trinity to us through the process of salvation. It is true that God has always been and will always be the same, but he reveals himself in different faces. The early disciples desired to see their heavenly Father. Philip even asked Jesus at one point to show him the Father (John 14:8). As quoted earlier in this chapter, Jesus simply replied that whoever saw him was seeing the Father. Later they would witness Christ's resurrection and Christ commanded them to wait for the Holy Spirit. The apostles were to start mission around the world only after having received the Spirit (Acts 1:8). So God didn't reveal all his Trinitarian dimensions at once; Jesus came to earth only when "the set time had fully come" (Gal 4:4; cf. Heb 1:1–2), and the Holy Spirit was given only when Jesus had returned to his Father in heaven. In other words, God has been revealing himself to humankind step by step.

It seems reasonable to conclude that a family after God's heart needs a process for development. Those who have studied the family agree that reaching maturity in families is a lifelong process.[13] There are seasons within the family's everyday life as well as within its missionary way of life, seasons that run parallel to natural life cycles, as we'll discover in more detail in later chapters. But with regard to our theological approach to developing missionary families in practice, we need to take God's three dimensions as reference points: (1) unity in diversity; (2) character (nature) and commission; and (3) space for development and processes.

A Good Family Doctrine as a Commission for the Church

The apostle Paul was never prone to illusion when he wrote his letters. When teaching the Ephesians, he was well aware of the great dimension of God's mission for us: no person could ever comprehend, let alone comprise, God's fullness. One family alone will never know God in his fullness, let alone reflect him fully. So how can we fathom the meaning of Paul's words in Ephesians 3:15 that the family "derives its name" from God? Again, it is the apostle who shows us the way while kneeling before his God: we shall "have power, together with all the Lord's holy people, to grasp [it]" (Eph 3:18). Think of it: it is all these saints together who build the body of Christ, his whole body being "the fullness of him who fills everything in every way" (1:23). Hence, it is the church that is the place where God's mysteries can be discerned and will be unveiled again and again, including those mysteries inherent in the nature of each kingdom family.

This has led me to give up an exclusively European or even German approach to studying God's will for the family and instead to seek the counsel of saints worldwide on what they think and experience. Only by leaving behind exclusive perspectives can we reach true *catholicity* of all denominational beliefs. Theology always depends on context, so it is helpful to extend our journey to seeking God's truth beyond the garden fence of our own history and culture. That's why in this book many voices from different cultural and national backgrounds get a chance to speak. We will hear stories from Europe as well as from North and South America, examples from Africa as well as from Asia, and the opinions of black people and white people. Due to limitations of space and time, the studies offered here necessarily represent only a preliminary

---

13. Gerald Foley, *Family-Centred Church: A New Parish Model* (Kansas City, MO: Sheed & Ward, 1995), 42.

version, so I hope not only to inspire new ways of thinking but also to stimulate more research in this area.

Christ Sends Us – As Families?

As Christians we perceive our mission to be a logical progression of Christ's mission. He taught his disciples: "As the Father has sent me, I am sending you" (John 20:21). The apostle Paul confirms that those who follow Jesus are "Christ's ambassadors" (2 Cor 5:20). Swiss missiologist Dr Roland Hardmeier says: "Jesus is the reference point for our Christian lifestyle, for church life and for our mission throughout the world revealed in every aspect of his life and ministry."[14]

Yet what role does Jesus attribute to the family when it comes to evangelism and mission ministries? And does this role restrain God's divine plan of creation for the family? Does the Holy Spirit have a place for the family in his work?

In order to find some answers, let's look in detail at Scripture references to the family. What does the Bible say a family is? For what purpose did God create the family? How did Jesus see the family and what role did he attribute to it? And what was the family's special commission after the Spirit was given to the church?

The Family Created by God – the Mission of the Father
The Divine Plan of Creation

We can get closer to the correlation of family to mission by first studying the Father's mission – the *missio patri*.[15] First and foremost, mission is the mission of God the Creator. God created *everything* on earth for a good purpose. This holds true for the family as well. When we seek to understand the family we need to understand God's creative intentions. How did God think of the family and what did he design the family for in the first place? What is the family all about? What role does the family play in God's divine purpose for this world?

When God created the earth out of nothing, he started with a couple to whom he gave two commissions: they were to multiply and they were to subdue the earth:

---

14. Hardmeier, *Kirche ist Mission*, 294.
15. For more detail, see Reimer, *Die Welt umarmen*, 161–173.

> Then God said, "Let us make mankind in our image, in our likeness, so that they may rule over the fish in the sea and the birds in the sky, over the livestock and all the wild animals, and over all the creatures that move along the ground."
>
> So God created mankind in his own image,
> > in the image of God he created them;
> > male and female he created them.
>
> God blessed them and said to them, "Be fruitful and increase in number; fill the earth and subdue it. Rule over the fish in the sea and the birds in the sky and over every living creature that moves on the ground." (Gen 1:26–28)

Here we see how human life, the inhabited earth, culture, civilization – our society – started with God founding a family. And family started when God saw that his creation was very good; yet, realizing that it was not good for the man to be alone, God created Eve. And these two were the foundation of (family) life. It was both the man and the woman who were made in God's likeness. And God commanded them to be fruitful, to multiply, to fill the earth and to subdue it. Ever since, men and women have been attracted to each other and have become one. They have conceived children who themselves, in turn, become new families.

But what is a family for? Studying Genesis, we come to know the family as a strong unit of male and female assuming together their responsibility for the whole world. They conceive and nurture children and are to raise them for the glory of God. The family is to subdue, to manage and to shape the earth wisely. This unit reflects God himself; the family is created in his image. Therefore the invisible God can be seen and touched through the family. Also, the family is to promote his will and mission throughout his world.

God Desires Family

So the family exists only because God wanted it to be. Without the very first family, human life would soon have ceased to exist, and culture and civilization would have become extinct. Without culture and civilization, though, any kind of mission in this world would be senseless. The American Mennonite Dr George W. Peters says: "Man needs culture as much as he needs the gospel. There is a strong need for both. For without culture man would not be able to live life nor promote the gospel, and soon he would perish."[16] Peters and other theologians speak of the first of God's commissions as the "cultural mandate."[17] This commission was given to the first family and consequently to *all* families throughout space and time.

The history of humankind is directly tied to the history of the family. Indeed, God's history with his people, his history with all of us, truly and perhaps primarily is a history of families, as we see in Scripture. First, we encounter the family of Adam and Eve with their two sons, Cain and Abel, who add pain and suffering, tears and murder to humankind's history (Gen 4). Then there's the story of Noah and his children (from Gen 6), of Abram and his wives and two sons (from Gen 11). We read about God calling this very family of Abram to become a large people and to become a blessing to *all* families throughout the world.[18] We come across Moses (Exod 3), Joshua (Josh 1), David (1 and 2 Sam) and many other families. For example, we read about Joshua deciding, "as for me and my household, we will serve the LORD" (Josh 24:15). It is fascinating to read Scripture solely as a family history.

In the New Testament, Matthew gets to the heart of humankind's history as a family chronicle when presenting Christ's genealogy (Matt 1:1–17). And throughout the Bible God is often referred to as "the God of Abraham, the God of Isaac and the God of Jacob" – our God is a God of family (Exod 3:6; Mark 12:26)!

No wonder that the report of Christ's birth begins with a family story (Luke 2). In a touching way, Luke reports the story of a couple – Joseph and Mary – and their newborn baby son, who happens to be the promised Messiah of the Jews. This Son of Man would later speak about his mission to "proclaim the year of the Lord's favour" (Luke 4:19). This referred to a special time within Israel's history when God required his people to ransom *family* members from captivity or slavery and to restore *family* possessions back to their original owners. In this way, the whole people of Israel received a restart, redemption and release (Lev 25:8). Healthy families are the pillar of any healthy society. This was not only a key revelation within the history of the people of Israel,

---

16. George W. Peters, *Missionarisches Handeln und biblischer Auftrag: Eine Theologie der Mission* (Bad Liebenzell: VLM, 1977), 191.

17. Peters, *Missionarisches Handeln*, 182.

18. It is significant that God started his divine plan of salvation for the whole world with Abraham and his *family* (see Christopher J. H. Wright, *The Mission of God: Unlocking the Bible's Grand Narrative* [Downers Grove, IL: InterVarsity Press, 2006], 66). For further discussion, see the definitions of "people" and "family" in Piper, *Let the Nations*, 167.

but it seemed equally important to Jesus when he announced God's kingdom as the mission of the year of the Lord's favour.

God's ideal world is a world of perfect families. God's redemption plan for the world is all about redeemed families. God wants families! But let's delve deeper into this. Why is the family so important to God? What happens within the family? Are social and cultural agents able to exist without the family? Do we find mechanisms of faith that depend directly on whether the family succeeds in the world or not?

Family as the Nucleus of Culture

As noted above, God's first commission to the family was the Cultural Mandate, meaning that the family was called to create cultural life on earth. Indeed, life and the destiny of the planet still depend on humankind managing that task (Gen 1:28). So it is no surprise that you won't come across a culture that doesn't have some kind of family life. Humankind doesn't exist without families, though they may differ in style and appearance. The family is universal to human existence,[19] a global phenomenon. There is no civilization, no society, no tribe without family. But why is the family indispensable for any human culture? What does Scripture say?

First, the family is essential because humankind's survival depends on it biologically. Without any offspring, humankind will be extinct in the next generation – hence God's commission to be fruitful, to multiply and to fill the earth. Human beings are created and designed to procreate. People have been living out that calling within families ever since, and this was God's invention and intention!

Second, human beings were not supposed to randomly fill the earth but to manage and maintain God's creation. Fruitfulness was just *the first* part of God's Cultural Mandate. Human beings were to subdue and cultivate the world and thus create an appropriate environment to live in, which we call "culture."[20] German anthropologist Lothar Käser says: "Cultures are strategies to enable and shape human existence,"[21] and it is men and women who invent and execute such strategies. This is humankind cultivating and shaping the environment

---

19. Paul G. Hiebert, *Cultural Anthropology* (Grand Rapids, MI: Baker, 1983).

20. For a definition of culture see Eugene Nida, *Message and Mission: Communication of Christian Faith* (New York: Joanna Cotler Books, 1960), 28–29; Lothar Käser, *Fremde Kulturen: Eine Einführung in die Ethnologie* (Nuremberg: VTR, 2014).

21. Käser, *Fremde Kulturen*, 37. (Author's translation from the original German text here and elsewhere, if not specified otherwise.)

they live in. Yet they will only maintain this culture and environment if they pass it on from generation to generation. Hence, the family is important for nurturing; it is central to cultural influence and key in the passing on of social skills.[22] It is within our families that we become who we are, or at least who we are expected to be within a certain culture and society. It is in the family that we learn the appropriate standards and forms of social behaviour. It is here that we first experience what life is all about. It is the family that teaches us how to live our lives and how to discern good from evil, right from wrong. It is within the family that we first learn how to overcome conflict and how to foster healthy relationships in general – though we might not always learn the best methods for doing that. It is here that we develop fears and acquire courage. Some cultures raise, socialize and enculturate their children by means of pressure and punishment, while others do so through incentives, praise and reward. When these children have grown up, their approach to life will reflect this accordingly – and their culture, too. As a German, I would say that German culture tends to be anxious, averse to risk but quick to lament and complain. North Americans seem to be much bolder, more optimistic and better at taking risks than us. Some cultures hesitate and plan everything down to the smallest detail, while others venture into new territories without always thinking of the worst-case scenario. Our particular approach to life – and to everything else – is first learned through our families. The family is thus the nucleus and hothouse of culture and society. If the family is discarded as superfluous for social life and dismissed as a construct, the culture is doomed to decay sooner or later.

The Bible tells of humankind's colourful history, with all our ups and downs, and again and again this involves stories about families! They either obey God's intentions for their lives or they rebel against him. Their rebellion usually ends not only in the devastation of their own environments, but also in plunging many other people into disaster – see, for example, Adam and Eve's failure and its consequences (Gen 3–6) or the loss of unity and communication among the people at Babel (Gen 11). These stories always start with rebellion against God, which stems from dysfunctional families, and they lead to the decline of their whole culture. Societies crucially depend on their families.

The Family Life Cycle – God's Principle for Our Lives

Biblical history can be read as the history of families. Scripture is full of reports of how people were born into specific families, how they were raised and grew

---

22. Käser, 114–115.

up, and how they then started their own families. They conceived children and raised them, until those children also started their own families, and so on. Parents became grandparents. Some people even lived to see a third generation, but finally life reached its end and they passed away – maybe, like the patriarch Jacob, "old and full of years" (Gen 35:29).[23] For all of us, our lives pass from birth through childhood, becoming adults, getting married, becoming parents, raising our children, to finally entering old age. This is often called the family "life cycle" or "life spiral."[24]

No matter what our background or to which culture or religion we belong, everyone goes through this process. What is happening in our lives depends to a large extent on the period we are passing through within this cycle. Its different stages set the parameters for our existence in this world and the nature of the culture and society we live in. Scripture is consistent with modern anthropological findings that confirm the family to be the key variable in any culture.

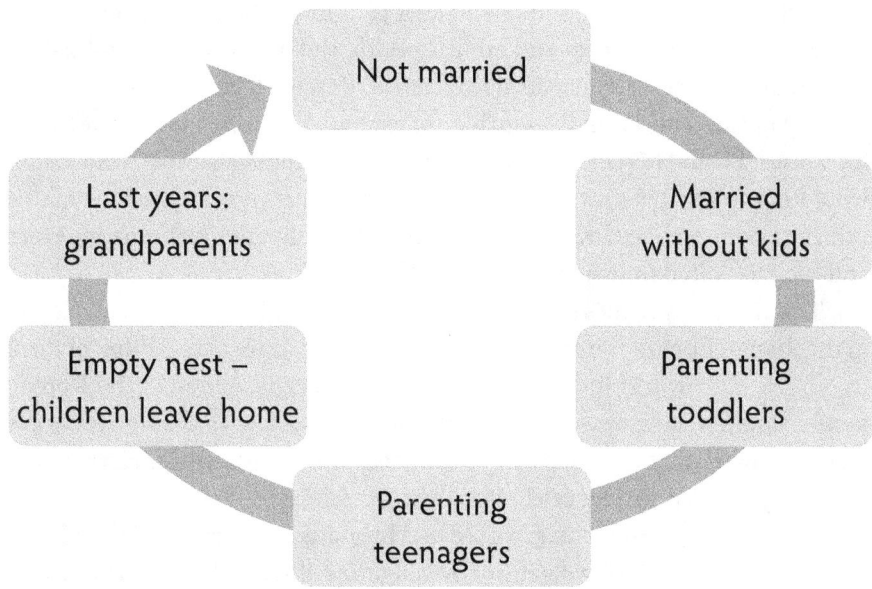

Figure 2.2: The Family Life Cycle

---

23. There are many passages in the Old Testament where history is presented as a chronology of generations and of periods in life, e.g. in 1–2 Chronicles.

24. For more details about this concept and critical exploration, see Sue Walrond-Skinner, *The Fulcrum and the Fire: Wrestling with Family Life* (London: Darton, Longman & Todd, 1993), 118.

Thus, it is the family that shapes culture and crucially moulds society, and it is the family's everyday life that forces certain schedules on all of us, whether we like it or not.

The Family and Social Interaction

The family manages and shapes our way of living. It is in our families that we learn to love or hate, to care for and step in for each other or to overlook and neglect one another. The family is the primary school when it comes to our social interaction, hence, family life is preparation for the social order we live in.[25] If the family is malfunctioning, our society will not function well either. When the family becomes corrupt, soon culture will get sick and become corrupt. And the opposite is also true: the family depends on society's development, too, and is shaped by society; as German sociologist Luhmann puts it, "Family executes society."[26]

Scripture confirms this, as we see in the examples of the ruling families of Israel. Whenever a judge, and later a king, followed God's instructions and his family displayed moral and ethical health, the whole society and nation thrived. But whenever rulers deviated from God's law, all Israel became corrupt and evil invaded the land. We see this, for example, in stories such as of Israel's high priest Eli and his corrupt sons (1 Sam 2), the prophet Samuel, whose sons would not follow his example as a just judge but perverted justice by taking bribes (1 Sam 8:3), and King Ahab, who wrongfully took Naboth's vineyard and then tolerated injustice throughout the land.

That the family shapes society was also true in New Testament times. Homes in the Roman Empire were not as private and closed as we like to think of them in our Western world today, as Rodney Clapp has described.[27] The Roman family would decide how to behave in society. And it was there that people would show loyalty or rebellion towards the ruling authorities. Here within the family, Roman society celebrated their victories and mourned their losses.

The family is the place where we humans are first socialized and enculturated. It is here we get our social and cultural identity. The saying "like father, like son" can be meant either positively or negatively, but as Robert

---

25. Louis J. Luzbetak, *The Church and Cultures: New Perspectives in Missiological Anthropology* (Maryknoll, NY: Orbis, 1988), 199.

26. Nicklas Luhmann, *Soziale Systeme: Grundriß einer allgemeinen Theorie* (Berlin: Suhrkamp, 1987), 76.

27. Rodney Clapp, *Families at the Crossroads: Beyond Traditional and Modern Options* (Downers Grove, IL: InterVarsity Press, 1993), 154.

Coleman points out, it demonstrates that the family lays the foundation for all our learning.[28]

Thus the family sets and influences all basic forms of human identity. However, in the Western world, which consists of individualistic societies, we have to acknowledge that it is not only our families which shape our identity; there is a set of institutions which also moulds us. Yet even here, our family still plays a key role in shaping us, influencing all aspects of our lives, including religious socialization.

The family provides a natural learning space to develop our identity because it is here we automatically find people who naturally nurture us, invest in us and teach us. This makes the family a unique educational institution. Hence, the family is the "school of deeper humanity."[29] We know that healthy families raise healthy adults! Unfortunately, the opposite is also true.

Even today, the family is still the primary place and natural environment for most people to grow up in.[30] It is the place we are born into. It is here that we first experience love and care or rejection and neglect. In the family, we first hear what's right and wrong, what's allowed and what's forbidden. Here we train our senses and learn to discern good from bad, what to enjoy and like, and what to dislike and disapprove of. Here we learn to use our feet, our hands, our eyes and even our teeth. Only in the family context do we learn such basic things in such a natural way. The family is the school we *live* in; all other institutions are ones we only visit for a few hours a day, while we will spend many years at home – although actually, we will never really become free of our family. It is in the family context that we learn to live real life. And nothing escapes the family.

In this natural environment of the family we learn about life through our relationships to people – through our parents and siblings. They will teach us, name the things around us, set the rules of behaviour and other norms, give us orders and, eventually, encourage us or forbid certain things. They will also set us an example with their very lives. They are our role models. It is our family members who show us how to live our lives, and children learn above all by observing their surroundings. Words might be important, but deeds are decisive. How parents behave manifests real life beyond the terminology and

---

28. Robert E. Coleman, "The Lifestyle of the Great Commission," in *Telling the Truth: Evangelizing Postmoderns*, ed. D. A. Carson (Grand Rapids, MI: Zondervan, 2000), 259.

29. *GS* 52.

30. Church of England Board for Social Responsibility, *Something to Celebrate: Valuing Families in Church and Society* (London: Church House, 1995), 70.

stories we hear. How they live provides guidelines for interpreting our own feelings and experiences. And these guidelines and codes will accompany us all our lives. For example, we learn what love and marriage are all about by the example our parents set us when we were little and not by books and teachings we encounter later on. What we learn about hate we understand by the way our parents fight with each other. What we understand about care we learn by experiencing the care our parents have for each other and for us. What we learn about faith is from closely observing the Christian lives of our family members. And how do we find out about mistrust, lack of love, irresponsibility and unbelief? It is through our experiences in close family.

But not only do children learn from their parents, parents learn from their children as well – especially as parents get older. No one knows their children better than their parents do. Whenever children are changed by their new faith, parents will be the first to notice.

A friend of mine, whom we will call Sina, told me her story:

> I haven't raised my son Dennis well. My husband left us when our boy was just eight years old. I had to work hard and had no time for him. It was far too late when I realized about the bad company Dennis kept, the drugs, the robberies and all the rest of it. There was no point trying to talk to him; he would just yell at me. My little boy was turning into a criminal. Until, one day, he came home telling me he had become a Christian. I thought it was a joke. Nobody in my family had ever seen the inside of a church, and now Dennis had become religious? But he was changing so much that, after two months, I decided to visit the church that he talked about so often. His example has made me believe.

Here, the son's testimony had such a strong influence because the mother knew her son well, so she instantly saw the big change in him. And as this change continued, she sought the same experience.

In Ephesians 6:4 the apostle Paul teaches, "Fathers, do not exasperate your children; instead, bring them up in the training and instruction of the Lord." The family is the natural place for training and instruction, which is a great opportunity yet also a big challenge. Fathers have the potential to either exasperate their children, causing them to become bitter and to rebel against any authority, even God, or to raise them up to become people who live holy lives pleasing to God. Parents set an example, whether for good or for bad.

I remember how, when we were children, my cousin complained about his father. My uncle was an alcoholic and would cause his family great trouble whenever he slipped back into his addictive habits. "I'll never drink alcohol," my cousin promised to himself. Unfortunately, though, that's exactly what he ended up doing. He had observed his father's behaviour and fell into the same trap in the end. When my uncle was drunk he felt he was "master of everything," but when he was sober he felt pressure quickly and failed to manage even the smallest tasks. Later, when his son faced challenges, he too turned to the bottle. Sadly, there was no other example for him to follow.

Thus parents are role models who condition their children whether positively or negatively. This is mainly a matter of trust or confidence. Confidence is the most important individual social ability and quality we have to learn. It is trust that affects our self-confidence and our capacity to trust others as well as God. And when we are self-confident, we don't suffer from inferiority complexes and we can prove ourselves in society. When we have learned to trust we are capable of building healthy relationships easily.

Any social environment which nurtures a culture of confidence and is a space of trust for us is the place we call our "home": it is here that we feel at home, that we literally have our home, where we know the ropes and feel safe. It is here that our friends live. Here we understand the language – and our environment understands us. Home is where we naturally feel safe. We all need such a home to live secure and content lives.

Why do we feel at home where we are? Is it because we were born here? Is "home" the country we were raised in? Maybe. However, I cannot identify a specific town or nation as my home. I was three years old when my parents moved from Siberia to South Kazakhstan, I was twelve when we moved from Kazakhstan to Estonia and twenty-two when we all moved to Germany. I have studied and lived in the USA, Canada, South Africa and Belgium. I would call none of these countries my home today. However, I know how it feels to be at home. I know the habits and customs of those nations. I even have a certain Russian and German accent, which proves that I am a "man who belongs." Yet I couldn't choose a "home country" from among all those nations where I spent my childhood and youth. Rather, my home is where my family is. It is the family that makes home a home! And this holds true for any human being. The family conveys a sense of belonging, of "home." And the more our family is rooted in a certain community and society, the more we will feel we belong there, too.

A healthy family nurtures a culture of trust, which enables us to have faith in ourselves, to trust our neighbours and to believe in God. It is here that we are recognized and understood. Our parents have seen our needs from day one, and they have sought to meet them ever since. Of course, this doesn't mean that everything has always been wonderful for us (for example, not every wish of ours was granted) and, yes, we will have had to find our place in our family. Yet the family is still the most natural home and the most familiar place for us on earth. Nowhere else are we involved so much, nowhere else integrated in such close relationships.

All family members are integral parts of an established system. This means the family is about obedience, submission and how we adapt – or about resistance, rebellion and how we fight for our self-assertion. No family is free from these dynamics. Think of puberty. Teenagers have to go through a certain period of rebellion against the rules and norms established by their parents. In this way, they find their own identity. Of course, we are disciplined and have to face consequences when we misbehave. Yet, in contrast to all other social institutions, in most cases our families will stay our families despite all our failures and mistakes. Most families, especially healthy families, will forgive our wrongdoings, particularly when we repent. For example, a mother who once bitterly complained about her son to me finally said, "My son has been a failure, doing wrong all his life, yet he is still my son, and he will stay my son for ever. How could I ever abandon him?"

Conflict and troubles belong to normal family life, yet such problems do not threaten these relationships and bonding as much as they would in any other social institution. For those who are related to us and close to us, we will always grant a second and a third chance. Even though we might not always agree with a certain family member's behaviour, we will not automatically end contact.

Some people argue, though, that there is a difference between cultures that are "shame-oriented" and those that are "guilt-oriented," as well as between individualistic and collectivist societies. It is true that shame cultures and collectivist societies tend to have closer family ties – their members seem to have less leeway to express their individuality. Still, the family remains the family anywhere!

A young Kurdish friend of mine, Oktai, told me how his decision to follow Christ led to anger and rage within his family. His relatives accused him of having brought shame upon the whole family. His father even threatened to kill him. However, after the first intense reactions, Oktai's family turned to reconciliation. After several years of being rejected by his family he was allowed to come back, and today, his relationship with his family is closer than ever.

Through its ties of trust, the family is a safe place for us to experiment with alternative ideas. For even if we leave our traditional lifestyles and belief systems, the chances are high that our family ties will not be torn apart, even if the culture and society to which our family belongs will not tolerate such changes. For example, Khalil, an only son of an official in Azerbaijan, came to faith in Jesus. All his relatives, who were Shiite Muslims, urged his father to bring him back to his senses or settle the disgrace by any means necessary. However, the father helped his son to emigrate to Australia instead. Years later, I met Khalil's father and he told me, "How on earth could I have killed my only son? Sure, I disagreed with his decision. To be honest, I was really angry at him. But should religion have the victory over my father heart? *No*. And today, I've got really close to Khalil's faith. Maybe my son is even right in his commitment to Christianity."

The family therefore fosters the natural processes of change. For example, among our family members we can say things that elsewhere would end a relationship instantly. Of course, we might face tensions and friction as a result, but most of the time we are given room to speak up.

Liberal societies in the Western world tend to be individualistic. When they talk about family, they generally mean the nuclear family. Western culture has largely given up the biblical example of kinship – the extended tribal form of family. In the small families of the West, whether we learn to feel secure or not depends to a great extent on the family's specific circumstances. In any case, the individual family members have more autonomy and greater freedom to experiment, though the family might still offer correction.[31]

Add up all these factors and we understand why the family is such a good place to talk about God. Where else do we find such perfect examples and role models of those who have changed their worldview and accepted Jesus as their Lord and Saviour?

Family and Religious Instruction

It is also within the family that we learn the doctrines and lifestyles of our belief systems. Our families influence us as to whether we believe in one God or many and in how we approach the transcendent and supernatural world.

It is fascinating to see the role the Bible attributes to the family in passing on religion to the next generation. You cannot instruct a child to believe in God as faith is always a gift that is granted to us. Yet the way we are raised can pave the way to faith later on. We see this in the order given to parents by Moses (Deut 6:4–7) – and here parents in the Hebrew text always means both

---

31. See, for instance, Wilhelm Faix, "Die individualisierte Familie: Familie mit Zukunft? Eine Lebensform im Umbruch," *JETh* 27 (2013): 187–215.

father and mother (Deut 6:11 and Eccl 1:7). It was clear to the people of Israel that they were to keep God's commands and they were to teach their children to do the same. And they should do so at home and in everyday life. Thus, the family was meant to be the primary place of religious instruction – both in teaching the law and in showing how to live it out in real life. Also, Israel didn't believe in a God who dealt with only one generation, but in the "God of Abraham, Isaac and Jacob." Therefore we read in Psalm 78:3–4:

> ... things we have heard and known,
>> things our ancestors have told us.
> We will not hide them from their descendants;
>> we will tell the next generation
> the praiseworthy deeds of the LORD,
>> his power, and the wonders he has done.

The New Testament does not repeal this calling to teach our children. The apostle Paul urges the Ephesians: "Children, obey your parents in the Lord, for this is right. 'Honour your father and mother' – which is the first commandment with a promise – 'so that it may go well with you and that you may enjoy long life on the earth.' Fathers, do not exasperate your children; instead, bring them up in the training and instruction of the Lord" (Eph 6:1–4).

The best New Testament example of such religious upbringing is Timothy, one of Paul's most important assistants. The apostle writes to him, "I am reminded of your sincere faith, which first lived in your grandmother Lois and in your mother Eunice and, I am persuaded, now lives in you also" (2 Tim 1:5). It was Lois and Eunice, a grandmother and a mother, who raised Timothy in the faith and led him to believe in Christ. They were such impressive role models that Paul mentions their strong example and reminds Timothy to learn from them.

This intrinsic role of the family to convey religious convictions is even confirmed by cultural anthropology today, which concludes that religious socialization first and foremost takes place within the family.[32] So it is the family that lays the foundations for the basic forms of our beliefs; the family has an influence on our openness to any kind of religion. Here within our families, we learn the language that gives us words for transcendent realities and enables us to comprehend transcendent correlations. Thus, our families shape us either to be open for realities beyond what we see or to have a dismissive attitude

---

32. Peter Hammond, *Cultural and Social Anthropology: Selected Readings* (New York: Macmillan, 1964), 145–146.

towards spiritual things. The family's classroom on religion opens a window for us to find categories for the inexplicable with the help of other family members. According to Robert E. Coleman, we learn in the most natural way within the harmonious setting of our families.[33]

I was raised in a family with little connection to God. Soviet society rejected Christianity as a naive and non-scientific mindset (*Weltanschauung*). Whoever believed in a God would have less chance of a successful career. And yet my parents knew of God and taught us to say grace for our food and to celebrate Christmas and Easter. This little impulse was enough for me as a child to ask whether God existed. Neither atheistic culture nor schooling would keep me from believing. The tiny seed of faith would grow in me.

This is even more so for families who are active in their faith and talk about it with their children – these children will count on God's existence quite naturally even later in their lives. This childhood belief might not be a conscious decision for him, yet it will pave the way for a personal relationship with him later. And the more we can trust our parents (as we can in a godly family, where they prove to be trustworthy), the better we will be able to confide in God.

As we saw above, trust is a basic factor for any social interaction. It is trust that builds our character and, above all, shapes our religious identity. Whenever we believe in something we will invest trust. In the letter to the Hebrews we read that "faith is confidence in what we hope for and assurance about what we do not see. This is what the ancients were commended for. By faith we understand that the universe was formed at God's command, so that what is seen was not made out of what was visible" (Heb 11:1–3). The New Testament Greek word *pistis* (here translated as "faith") can be translated into both meanings: faith and trust. Anyone who believes basically confides in God, without necessarily looking for a rational justification. While we might say we believe somebody – which means we *think* that person is right – when we say we believe *in* somebody it speaks of a personal intimate *relationship* beyond just the rational. Faith and trust are interconnected: our self-*confidence* will manifest itself in our *believing in* our own chances; when we *trust* our neighbours we will have *faith* that our society has great potential; and *confiding* in God will manifest itself in *living out* our faith.

It is our parents who lay the foundation for our ability to trust – they nurture our self-confidence, foster our trust in others and influence our faith in God. A negative example of this is Wassili, who has struggled to trust in

---

33. Coleman, "Lifestyle of the Great Commission," 260.

God the Father ever since his conversion. Why? Because his earthly father didn't nurture trust in him at all. Wassili told me:

> My father would drink day and night. I remember him as a bitter man who would take offence at the whole world. Even from afar anyone could recognize he was drunk. Dad would never keep his promises, would never show me affection and would never make me feel secure. I soon learned to stay out of his way and keep everything to myself. "Father" was synonymous with distrust and was an embodiment of suspicion. Still today I find it difficult to trust men, who could be my father. And whenever Christians tell me about God being their Father, my stomach turns.

Wassili's heart is slowly healing. He believes in God, but his faith lacks power as he is not able to trust God. He lacks the basic confidence in life to build upon. It takes time to regain what his parents failed to nurture in him. Yet he is getting stronger.

So family builds the fundamentals of our spiritual identity. Our parents nourish basic convictions in us even when they don't believe in God themselves. It is easier for children raised in love to have healthy relationships later on – living in harmony with themselves and with others – and therefore it is easier for them to enjoy a personal relationship with God, too. Only a culture of trust fosters healthy identities.

The Family and the People of God

Families in the Bible are always an integral part of a larger community. Nations and people – humanity itself – started with a family: Adam and Eve founded the first family, then Noah's family marked a new beginning, and later Abram received the promise that his little family would grow into a large people and become a blessing to all nations (Gen 12:1–3). God started society with individual families. Thus, the family serves a purpose beyond its own borders. Conversely, any tribe or nation is built upon its families; and the community may function as a safety net whenever family members fall into poverty and their relatives cannot support them alone. In the Old Testament we often find the following hierarchy: single families belong to larger kinships, which themselves are part of a tribe, which belongs to a people or nation, which is a part of God's creation of all humankind. Any family in the Bible is part of the collective of families worldwide that owe their existence to God, who is the "Father from whom every family in heaven and on earth derives its name" (Eph 3:14–15).

Parallel to Old Testament times God gathered one big family in Christ (Eph 2:19). Here, all human social status is set aside (see Gal 3:28). The body of Christ, his church, is like one big family, as is evident in the many verses instructing the church about care and social provision. The following is a short list of commands given by God to all members within Christian churches:

- Love one another (John 13:34–35; Rom 12:10; 1 Thess 4:9; 1 Pet 1:22; 1 John 3:11; 4:7, 11, 21);
- Honour one another (Rom 12:10);
- Live in harmony with one another (Rom 12:16; 15:5);
- Accept one another (Rom 15:7);
- Build each other up (1 Thess 5:11);
- Greet one another with a holy kiss (Rom 16:16; 2 Cor 13:12);
- Serve one another humbly in love (Gal 5:13);
- Carry each other's burdens (Gal 6:2);
- Be kind and compassionate to one another (Eph 4:32);
- Be patient and gentle, bearing one another in love (Eph 4:2);
- Submit to one another (Eph 5:21);
- Forgive one another (Col 3:13);
- Confess your sins to each other (Jas 5:16);
- Encourage one another daily (Heb 3:13); and
- Offer hospitality to one another (1 Pet 4:9).

Christians are not only to encourage one another, but also to challenge, assess and reprove one another. This is because we are God's family. For in one Spirit we are all baptized into one body (1 Cor 12:13). We belong to Christ and we are a new creation in him. This means that we are only able to live his mission in this world collectively. Jesus's commands leave us in no doubt: we are not on a mission on our own but we are called on a mission together! Several verses underline that collective mandate, such as:

- We are the salt of the earth (Matt 5:13–15);
- We are ambassadors for Christ (2 Cor 5:18–20);
- We are the righteousness of God (2 Cor 5:21); and
- We are to be hospitable towards anyone (Heb 13:2; Rom 12:13).

Christians – and this includes Christian families – exist only as a fellowship, which means together with other Christians (families) within the one family of God. The Lausanne Committee for World Evangelization states, "Families and households do not dissolve within God's family. But they keep their identities as small units where people will be nurtured and healed, where they mature and learn, where you find hospitality and good neighborhood in practice and teaching."[34] What is described here will only be found within healthy and godly families. Families need to have spiritual maturity and that is the task of the churches to which they belong. The Lausanne Committee says that "Church plays the key role to teach families how to live their faith in this world – a world that keeps turning farther away from God each day."[35]

Family, Sin and Salvation

There is no perfect family. All human beings are sinners, all of us die in Adam, no one is righteous, not even one, and everyone falls short of the glory of God (Rom 3:10, 23). This holds true for any institution, culture or society in this world. And it is true for the family as well. Without holding back the ugly details, the Bible is full of reports of sin and the fall of families. Cain, Adam's eldest, kills his brother and becomes a murderer (Gen 4:1–16). Abram is such a coward that he almost loses his wife Sarai to Pharaoh's harem (Gen 12:15–18) and his son Isaac even follows that example (Gen 26:7–10). Jacob betrays his brother to get Isaac's blessing and has to flee far from home to escape his brother's revenge (Gen 25–27). Jacob's sons sell their brother into slavery (Gen 37:12–27). There's nothing that could happen in a family that we don't find in Scripture already. When we take a closer look, even the great men and women in the Bible turn out to be easily seduced. Think of King David and his beautiful neighbour Bathsheba, the wife of his captain Uriah (2 Sam 11:1–17). David's army has just left town and is out of sight when the king gives in to lust and commits adultery. In order to cover his tracks, David then arranges for the killing of the loyal Uriah. God's chosen king and the man after his own heart was a murderer and adulterer. Later, David's weakness would lead to many tears and the spilling of blood among his own family. And King David is by no means the only example.

It is our sinful nature, and this very incapacity to live in peace and harmony, that called for God's divine plan of salvation. Nowhere more than in families are we confronted with sin's misery. When we look at our world through God's eyes we see that our families are broken. We see broken homes, divorce, tears and

---

34. Lausanne Committee for World Evangelization, "Non-Traditional Families: Reaching Families with the Good News," Lausanne Occasional Paper (LOP) 36, in *A New Vision, a New Heart, a Renewed New Call: Lausanne Occasional Papers*, ed. David Claydon (Pasadena, CA: William Carey Library, 2005), 450.

35. LOP 36, 460.

much distress. If you want to assess the real condition of any society, just look at the lives of its families. The condition of the family indicates how healthy a society really is. And the opposite is true: no other social institution shows when people are restored and renewed better than the family. Whenever Jesus heals and restores people, God's peace and restoration is first shown within their families.

Summary

1. The family is God's invention and gift to this world. Families are made in his image, thus reflecting him. The family was created to administer our earth.
2. The family is God's cornerstone of culture and society and his main resource for all human life.
3. A biblical family consists of a man (the father), a woman (the mother) and their children. That's the only way the family is made to be within the social system.
4. The family is the most natural place to teach and learn.
5. The family provides the space for religion; it shapes the modes and conventions of faith lived out in practice.
6. Any family is part of a collective of families such as an ethnic group, tribe or nation, and ideally families are part of God's people, the *familia Dei*.
7. Since the fall of humanity the family has been in great danger and as a consequence, society has been in trouble.

The Family Renewed by Christ the Saviour
God Our Saviour – the Son's Mission

Humanity has been in trouble ever since the fall; it was our hopeless case which called God into action. God's love for his creation made him take care of and change our destiny. In John 3:16 we read, "For God so loved the world that he gave his one and only Son, that whoever believes in him shall not perish but have eternal life." God's plan of salvation started with him sending the second manifestation of his Trinity – Jesus, who himself is the good news, the gospel for all people. He is fundamental for evangelism and the only good news we proclaim. Only through Jesus Christ can God's ultimate goal to renew us all be reached. Our Lord himself passed on this mandate by sending his disciples "as the Father has sent me" (John 20:21). "As Jesus Christ is head of the church, the mission of church is to participate in the mission of Jesus Christ . . . equally the church is called to be light in the world."[36]

Evangelism has its roots in Jesus alone. Christ is "God's best missionary."[37] When we look for strategies and methods of evangelism we need first to study Jesus and his ministry. He is the perfect example for us. Christ's mission, the *missio Christi*, must be the template for all our action.[38]

Therefore, it is logical to look in Scripture to study Christ's relationship to family. What role did the family play in his mission strategy? Do we find proof in his teachings and ministry that the family plays a key role in his mandate? Given that we have already seen that the family is central within the Father's creation story, we ought to find the same to be true in the Son's salvation story too.

His Mission Starts in the Family

When Jesus was born, it was God himself entering our world. Christ came to reconcile humanity to God (John 3:16; 2 Cor 5:18). As seeing Jesus meant seeing the Father (e.g. John 14:9), Christ, so the Scriptures tell us, though being in very nature God, didn't count equality with God as something to be used to his own advantage (Phil 2:6). Also, in the beginning, Jesus was with God and was God: the first chapter of John's gospel says, "In the beginning was the Word, and the Word was with God, and the Word was God. He was with God in the beginning. . . . The Word became flesh and made his dwelling among us. We have seen his glory" (John 1:1–2, 14).

Think of it: the God of all the universe decided to become flesh – and he started this undertaking by being born into a human *family*! How amazing that the Creator of all the earth would become like his creatures in order to save his whole creation! God started his mission, his ultimate evangelism ministry, by his incarnation. This was the very first act of Jesus's ministry and salvation – that he was born as a child – and crucially it is related to family!

---

36. Charles Van Engen, *Mission on the Way: Issues in Mission Theology* (Grand Rapids, MI: Baker, 1996), 186.

37. Samuel Escobar, *A Time for Mission: The Challenge for Global Christianity* (Leicester: Inter-Varsity Press, 2003), 97.

38. For more discussion of this, see Reimer, *Die Welt umarmen*, 172–184.

Salvation to humankind started with God becoming a baby – to be exact, a member of a Jewish family and culture. Jesus was ethically different – in the letter to the Hebrews we read that Christ, being human like us, was tempted in every respect as we are, yet was without sin (Heb 4:15) – but he was not ethnically different. Children mattered little in the Jewish society of the first century AD.[39] We can see this in the comment Matthew makes in his report on the feeding of the multitude: "The number of those who ate was about five thousand men, *besides* women and children" (Matt 14:21).[40] No one counted the children. They were neither valued nor listened to. Yet our Saviour was born as a child. He could have come to earth as an adult, but he preferred to become a baby in a Jewish family. What a statement! How this shows that God identifies with us, and with family as the basis of human society, including children too!

The world's redeemer was born into and socialized in a carpenter's family that was obviously very pious. It is no wonder, therefore, that his divinity was first recognized by a relative – his cousin, the son of Zechariah and Elizabeth, who saw in him the "Lamb of God, who takes away the sin of the world" (John 1:29). I can't get rid of the impression that God wanted to reveal himself not only within his people, but more precisely within one of their families.

The family remained Christ's focus, too. He lived only for and within his family in Nazareth during the many years before he was baptized with the Holy Spirit and started his ministry. We know little about his childhood, teenage years and early adult life – only that his mother Mary treasured up all the precious things concerning her son's life, pondering them in her heart. And later we see not only Mary being among his disciples, but also his brothers; for example, James, the "Lord's brother," led the church of Jerusalem (Gal 1:19; cf. Mark 6:3) and Jude later wrote the Epistle of Jude (Jude 1; cf. Mark 6:3).

The Family Is Jesus's Concern and Mission Field

Jesus understood his mission as a legacy of the "year of the Lord's favour" as it had been revealed by the prophet Isaiah (Isa 61:1–2). In Luke 4:16–22 we read,

> He went to Nazareth, where he had been brought up, and on the Sabbath day he went into the synagogue, as was his custom. He stood up to read, and the scroll of the prophet Isaiah was handed to him. Unrolling it, he found the place where it is written:

---

39. See W. A. Strange, *Children in the Early Church: Children in the Ancient World, the New Testament and the Early Church* (London: Paternoster, 1996), 1–37.

40. All emphasis in Scripture quotes throughout the book has been added.

> "The Spirit of the Lord is on me,
>   because he has anointed me
>   to proclaim good news to the poor.
> He has sent me to proclaim freedom for the prisoners
>   and recovery of sight for the blind,
> to set the oppressed free,
>   to proclaim the year of the Lord's favour."
>
> Then he rolled up the scroll, gave it back to the attendant and sat down. The eyes of everyone in the synagogue were fastened on him. He began by saying to them, "Today this scripture is fulfilled in your hearing."
>
> All spoke well of him and were amazed at the gracious words that came from his lips. "Isn't this Joseph's son?" they asked.

The "year of the Lord's favour" had finally come since Jesus brought it near – something that was highly regarded and yet had never been kept in Israel's history. Right at the beginning of his ministry Christ quotes these prophetic words of Isaiah and identifies himself with them. When we watch him closely on his mission and in his ministry we see this indeed to be the essence of Jesus's mandate. The year of the Lord's favour was meant not only for renewing the relationship with God but as a deep transformation of the Jewish *Lebensraum*. It would be a time when God restored the family as the social core within the whole people of Israel (Lev 25; Isa 65:19). After seven times seven years, Israel was to release and renew all families. People were to ransom their relatives. Land that had been lost due to mismanagement was given back to the families who were the original proprietors. So, when we take a closer look, the year of the Lord's favour was really a year of families! And this is what Jesus announced right at the start of his ministry. Through his coming, Israel had been granted this, the Lord's favour. The gospel which Jesus proclaimed about the coming kingdom was a gospel of family restoration.

No wonder we read about families in many reports of his life. The first disciples Jesus calls belong to the same family: Andrew, after meeting Jesus, runs home to find his brother Simon and brings him to Jesus (John 1:40–42); then, when Jesus visits Simon's home, he heals Simon's mother-in-law (Mark 1:29–31). One person had turned to him, and the whole family received salvation. News of the miracle spread like wildfire and the crowds gathered before Simon's house (1:32–33). Jesus served them all: "Jesus healed many who had various diseases. He also drove out many demons, but he would not let the demons speak because they knew who he was" (1:34). Thus it was at the threshold of the home of a family that had experienced God's grace that people saw signs and wonders of God's presence.

Again and again we find Jesus ministering in public – not only in the market place but in the homes of families. His very first miracle took place at a wedding – in Cana of Galilee – where he turned water into wine. John comments, "What Jesus did here in Cana of Galilee was the first of the signs through which he revealed his glory; and his disciples believed in him" (John 2:11). Jesus first revealed his glory at a family celebration – a wedding.

Then we follow him entering a home in Capernaum – probably the house of Andrew and Simon Peter – where he heals a lame man (Mark 2:1–12). It is here that Jesus mentions his authority to forgive sins (2:5–11). He visits the home of Jairus, a synagogue leader, and raises his daughter from the dead (Matt 9:18–20). On one occasion, he invites himself into the home of a tax collector, Zacchaeus, a visit which culminates in Jesus declaring, "Today salvation has come to this house" (Luke 19:9). In other words, the Messiah brings healing into the homes of his people.

Again and again Jesus enters homes which are said to be lost and beyond redemption. He sits and eats in the homes of sinners, bringing salvation and healing. More than once this is used in accusations against him, as is evident when he repeats what is said about him: "The Son of Man came eating and drinking wine, and you say, 'Here is a glutton and a drunkard, a friend of tax collectors and sinners'" (Luke 7:34). Yet he regarded his ministry to be that of a doctor who served the sick and not the healthy (Matt 9:9–13). He sat and ate with sinners and served the weak and the poor in their homes and from within their families. Ajith Fernando, Christian writer and director of Youth for Christ, Sri Lanka, summarizes Jesus's ministry by stating that a private home was an important place for Jesus to serve people.[41]

Of course, Christ stayed single and never married. Yet he was never critical of the family or hostile towards it. On the contrary, he taught about the precious role of the family for human existence in this world (Matt 19:1–9). He condemned adultery and divorce as sin (Matt 5:27–31). And he clearly loved being around the families of his friends. He touched on issues of family life, he healed family members and he brought peace to homes. Nowhere do we find him speaking out against the conventional ways of family life. At the same time, he dealt with family situations as he found them; for example,

---

41. Ajith Fernando, *Checkliste Glaube: Dienen wie Jesus* (Marburg: Francke Verlag, 2011), 274.

we might understand Jairus to have been a single parent, and the woman of Samaria probably wasn't married to the man she lived with. Jesus healed people right where they were. And after he had cast the demons out of the man in the Gerasenes, he sent him back to his family (Luke 8:39). He always told people to tell their families what he had done for them.

God's Kingdom First

While the family is, therefore, important to Jesus, for him, family is not the ultimate goal in life; in his eyes God's kingdom is far more important. The earthly family will come to an end, but the family of God will last for eternity (Mark 3:31–35; 10:29–30). And as he focused totally on God's kingdom, he surrendered founding a family of his own. The families of his disciples also had to face some sacrifices. Yet they were promised a special reward for this (Mark 10:28–31). However, he rebuked the Pharisees for trying to pit their religious lives against family duties (Mark 7:9–13).

The story of the twelve-year-old Jesus staying behind in the temple is well known. His parents lost sight of him, unaware that he had remained behind in Jerusalem. When after three days they finally found him, Mary told him off, but Jesus rejected the reproach publicly: "'Why were you searching for me?' he asked. 'Didn't you know I had to be in my Father's house?'" (Luke 2:49). It was there the teenage boy made his family relations clear to everybody: his father wasn't Joseph but God himself. His earthly family would not have the final say on his life; God would.

In Mark 3:31–36 we read of his family sending for him, but again, his reaction is direct: "Then Jesus' mother and brothers arrived. Standing outside, they sent someone in to call him. A crowd was sitting around him, and they told him, 'Your mother and brothers are outside looking for you.' 'Who are my mother and my brothers?' he asked. Then he looked at those seated in a circle around him and said, 'Here are my mother and my brothers! Whoever does God's will is my brother and sister and mother.'" Christ leaves no doubt about his priorities: his life is not focused on his family but on God's kingdom; it's not about his relatives or their family honour, but God's glory.

Many disciples are reported to have put God's kingdom before their families as well – men and women alike. We read about Joanna, the wife of Chuza, Herod's steward, Susanna, and Mary, called Magdalene, all serving him (Luke 8:1–3). We know of Peter, Andrew, Matthew, John and James, among others, who left behind their families to follow him (Luke 9:1–6). And Jesus appointed and sent seventy-two disciples ahead of him all over Israel to proclaim that God's kingdom had come near (Luke 10:1–12). They seem to have left their families too. Jesus's calling was radical and exclusive. We notice this especially when he confronted people who wanted to follow him yet still gave their families priority. In Luke 9:57–62 we read,

> As they were walking along the road, a man said to him, "I will follow you wherever you go."
>
> Jesus replied, "Foxes have dens and birds have nests, but the Son of Man has nowhere to lay his head."
>
> He said to another, "Follow me."
>
> But he replied, "Lord, first let me go and bury my father."
>
> Jesus said to him, "Let the dead bury their own dead, but you go and proclaim the kingdom of God."
>
> Still another said, "I will follow you, Lord; but first let me go back and say goodbye to my family."
>
> Jesus replied, "No one who puts a hand to the plough and looks back is fit for service in the kingdom of God."

And Christ is even clearer when stating that he has come to bring division rather than peace to families: "Do you think I came to bring peace on earth? No, I tell you, but division. From now on there will be five in one family divided against each other, three against two and two against three. They will be divided, father against son and son against father, mother against daughter and daughter against mother, mother-in-law against daughter-in-law and daughter-in-law against mother-in-law" (Luke 12:51–53).

These verses illustrate that for Jesus, God's kingdom has priority over the family. Thus, whoever follows him must put God before family: "If anyone comes to me and does not hate father and mother, wife and children, brothers and sisters – yes, even their own life – such a person cannot be my disciple. And whoever does not carry their cross and follow me cannot be my disciple" (Luke 14:26–27). In other words, to follow Christ means to submit our family to him. Yet the measure of our reward will correspond to the measure of the sacrifice. Peter asked Jesus about this reward:

> Peter answered him, "We have left everything to follow you! What then will there be for us?"
>
> Jesus said to them, "Truly I tell you, at the renewal of all things, when the Son of Man sits on his glorious throne, you who have followed me will also sit on twelve thrones, judging the twelve tribes of Israel. And everyone who has left houses or brothers or sisters or father or mother or wife or children or fields for my

sake will receive a hundred times as much and will inherit eternal life." (Matt 19:27–29)

Jesus promised special blessings for those who seek his kingdom first. Does that mean he devalued the family? Does he approve of husbands and wives neglecting their partners for the sake of God's kingdom – or even divorcing them? Does he approve of parents neglecting their children for his sake – or even abandoning them? Of course not. Why else would he show such affection and responsibility towards children – even calling them to come to him? "People were also bringing babies to Jesus for him to place his hands on them. When the disciples saw this, they rebuked them. But Jesus called the children to him and said, 'Let the little children come to me, and do not hinder them, for the kingdom of God belongs to such as these. Truly I tell you, anyone who will not receive the kingdom of God like a little child will never enter it'" (Luke 18:15–17). Children are important to Jesus. They are not to be neglected. Whenever Jesus calls us to leave everything behind for his sake, he never means we should leave our children to their fate. On the contrary, God will take special care of them! Jesus promised a hundred-fold blessing on those who invest themselves fully in his kingdom – and this blessing is promised for their families, too!

It would be false to pit our commitment to God's kingdom against our responsibility to our families. Jesus doesn't do that. Whenever he allowed trials to continue in a family it was for their good – to build up their faith. For example, in the account of the raising of Lazarus from the dead (John 11) we see Christ's close relationship with the family of Martha, Mary and Lazarus; verse 5 states that Jesus loved them dearly. And yet he delayed his coming and the sick brother died. What negligence, we might think. Is this true love for close friends? We can hear this very reproach in the words of Lazarus's sisters. However, when Jesus loves us, he doesn't want us simply to feel good, but to grow in our faith! That is why Lazarus had to die: in order to glorify God and to enlarge the faith of his whole family.

We don't find Jesus devaluing the family on any occasion. On the contrary, he confirmed the status of the family and he called family into mission.

As for Him, So for Us

The life of Christ shows that the institution of the family was directly connected to his ministry and outreach. Therefore, if we want our theologies of mission to be Christ-centred, we need to take the family into account; otherwise we are neglecting a core factor of Jesus-like evangelism. His mission was and is to restore families, which is crucial for the transformation of society. The people of Israel knew that the "year of the Lord's favour" was all about their families, and the Messiah himself proclaimed the dawning of this year with his coming. The time had come. God had turned towards his people, that is, towards their oppressed families in need of salvation.

Christ's followers have the same mandate as their master. The risen Lord himself made that clear. When he suddenly appeared among the frightened disciples, he greeted them with the blessing, "Peace be with you! As the Father has sent me, I am sending you" (John 20:21). Their mission, therefore, was to follow Christ's example – not only in talking about his teachings, but also in the practical ways demonstrated by his life.

Does this mean that his followers need to start with the family when it comes to mission and evangelism? If we take Christ's example seriously, our answer must be "Yes." His will was seen when he sent his disciples to "the lost sheep of Israel." He sent them to stay in the houses in the villages and towns of Israel:

> These twelve Jesus sent out with the following instructions: "Do not go among the Gentiles or enter any town of the Samaritans. Go rather to the lost sheep of Israel. As you go, proclaim this message: 'The kingdom of heaven has come near.' Heal those who are ill, raise the dead, cleanse those who have leprosy, drive out demons. Freely you have received; freely give.
>
> "Do not get any gold or silver or copper to take with you in your belts – no bag for the journey or extra shirt or sandals or a staff, for the worker is worth his keep. Whatever town or village you enter, search there for some worthy person and stay at their house until you leave. As you enter the home, give it your greeting. If the home is deserving, let your peace rest on it; if it is not, let your peace return to you. If anyone will not welcome you or listen to your words, leave that home or town and shake the dust off your feet. Truly I tell you, it will be more bearable for Sodom and Gomorrah on the day of judgment than for that town." (Matt 10:5–15)

Thus, evangelism starts in the houses of a particular area. So, to reach a village or town with the gospel of Christ, we should begin by proclaiming God's kingdom in the home of a family. It is here we will find the "worthy person" who will be the key to reach the whole town.

Summary

1. The family is the very place where Jesus started his mission of salvation.
2. The gospel of Jesus aims at restoring families. The renewal and salvation of the family brings healing to the whole people.
3. On no occasion did Christ alter the role or function of the family; on the contrary, he confirmed God's creation order. The family saved by Jesus plays a key role in this world.
4. When reaching out to people Jesus mainly focused on families. He started proclaiming God's kingdom in private homes which were centres of his evangelism.
5. Christ was clear in proclaiming God as the author of life and family. That's why God the Father has a higher priority than the family (the family comes second). Whenever Jesus was confronted by his family demanding more of him, he would repudiate these claims.
6. Christ's disciples were on the same mission as their Lord. They carried the same responsibility towards their families that Jesus did. And Jesus sent them out to stay at the homes of the lost sheep of Israel as he did.

The Holy Spirit and His Worldwide Mission
The Mission Started at Pentecost

The mission of the church started at Pentecost. The risen Lord commanded his disciples to wait in Jerusalem for the Holy Spirit to come, promising that they would "receive power when the Holy Spirit comes on you; and you will be my witnesses in Jerusalem, and in all Judea and Samaria, and to the ends of the earth" (Acts 1:8). Receiving Christ's Spirit mobilized the disciples on their mission. It is the Spirit who grows faith (1 Cor 12:3), who equips Christ's disciples with the gifts they need to reach the world (12:4) and who gives them their place in the church (12:13) and in mission (12:5). Jesus promised that the Holy Spirit would lead us into truth (John 16:13) and will carry out his mission in and through us (16:14). We are unable to live out the Great Commission in practice without Christ's Helper; mission really is the Spirit's mission, the *missio Spiritus*.[42] We see this in the practice of the first Christians and within

---

42. For more on this, see Reimer, *Die Welt umarmen*, 185–190.

the ministries of the missionaries of the first century. Paul, for example, is called to mission by the Holy Spirit himself (Acts 13:1-3), and it is God's Spirit who guides the apostles in where to go and what to do. When Paul started out on his second missionary journey, the Holy Spirit closed the door until Paul listened again to God's voice calling him to Macedonia (Acts 15:36 – 16:9). And throughout church history we see Christ's Spirit present and active in and through the lives of the great men and women of God.

It is therefore important to seek the guidance of the Spirit when exploring the role of the family within mission and society. The apostle Paul, for instance, was *not* married. He even made a stand for celibacy (1 Cor 7:1), though also saying that we ought to live according to the way God has gifted us. And just as the Holy Spirit gives spiritual gifts (1 Cor 12:4), so marriage and celibacy are his work and gifting too.

Does that mean that marriage and family are constrained by Christ's Spirit? Hardly. On the contrary, the family is raised to a higher level as marriage is now recognized as a spiritual gift and no longer merely the outcome of human desire. God's Spirit did not suspend the family in any way. In fact, private homes and the family became strategic bases in the mission he began.

They Would Meet in Their Homes

The evangelist Luke reports in Acts 2 the events of the mighty outpouring of the Spirit on the day of Pentecost. Tongues of fire appeared on each disciple, and when they began speaking, everybody listening miraculously understood them in their own language and dialect. This astonishing event demanded an explanation, resulting in the first evangelistic preaching by the followers of Christ. Peter stood up to address the crowd, and after his passionate preaching three thousand people followed his call to repent. If you seek a role model for mass church planting, look no further than here. It is simply amazing how the church was birthed in Jerusalem.

Having planted churches myself, I can imagine the number of challenges the young leadership of this Jesus movement had to face after such an awakening. They had to find practical solutions to questions like: Which venue should they use for services? Where would they spiritually disciple and train all these people? Only a few days later five thousand more were added to the church. Again, we hear Peter preach at the temple after healing the lame man at the temple gate called Beautiful (Acts 3:1). Soon they found that there were many among their new converts who were missing the basic necessities of life. They needed to act quickly. And don't forget how young the apostles were! Also, they were countrymen from backwards Galilee, simple fishermen. Not one of them had been trained in church leadership, never mind the job of leading a megachurch! During the three years of sharing their lives with Jesus they had not experienced such massive fellowship – the rabbi's regular circle of followers was much smaller. Now they needed help! Where better to get that support than from the Helper and Advocate himself? And the Holy Spirit did act after Peter and John had been threatened by the high priest and the elders:

> On their release, Peter and John went back to their own people and reported all that the chief priests and the elders had said to them. When they heard this, they raised their voices together in prayer to God. "Sovereign Lord," they said, "you made the heavens and the earth and the sea, and everything in them. You spoke by the Holy Spirit through the mouth of your servant, our father David:
> 'Why do the nations rage
>   and the peoples plot in vain?
> The kings of the earth rise up
>   and the rulers band together
> against the Lord
>   and against his anointed one.'
> Indeed Herod and Pontius Pilate met together with the Gentiles and the people of Israel in this city to conspire against your holy servant Jesus, whom you anointed. They did what your power and will had decided beforehand should happen. Now, Lord, consider their threats and enable your servants to speak your word with great boldness. Stretch out your hand to heal and perform signs and wonders through the name of your holy servant Jesus."
> After they prayed, the place where they were meeting was shaken. And they were all filled with the Holy Spirit and spoke the word of God boldly. (Acts 4:23–31)

The apostles cried out for God's help and intervention. They did not have the resources nor the means to lead such a movement by themselves; they needed God to guide them. As a result, the place where they were gathered together was shaken and they were all filled with the Holy Spirit again. God's Spirit then brought order and structure into his new church movement: he unmasked hypocrites (Acts 5), he filled deacons with wisdom so that they could organize the fair provision of food for all (6:1–6) and he gave power and authority to the apostles to preach the good news of Jesus Christ. Through this, people found faith in the Lord daily. And these masses met together in private homes:

> They devoted themselves to the apostles' teaching and to fellowship, to the breaking of bread and to prayer. Everyone was filled with awe at the many wonders and signs performed by the apostles. All the believers were together and had everything in common. They sold property and possessions to give to anyone who had need. Every day they continued to meet together in the temple courts. They broke bread in their homes and ate together with glad and sincere hearts, praising God and enjoying the favour of all the people. And the Lord added to their number daily those who were being saved. (Acts 2:42–47)

Hence, it was private homes that were the places of spiritual edification and fellowship for believers. We don't know how the apostles got the idea. Maybe they simply followed their master's example or they copied the Jewish system of small synagogues. In any case, it seems obvious they were guided by the Spirit here as well; Luke's report is so imbued with the presence of the Holy Spirit in every detail of the lives of the early Christians that we cannot imagine them having acted alone in this respect, simply following logical reasoning, so we can safely claim that the four walls of private homes were exactly where God's Spirit wanted to found his church. And it was from there that the first church tackled the task of reaching the whole world for Christ. As Jesus had started his mission on earth in the home of Joseph and Mary, now his church started world mission in private homes.

What about the Gentiles?

Jesus promised his disciples that as soon as the Spirit came upon them they would be his witnesses in Jerusalem, in all Judea and Samaria, and to the ends of the earth (Acts 1:8). Yet how did this mission actually develop in the early church? Outside Jerusalem, were homes and families still the best way to win people for Christ? Or was this focus on homes just a short-lived phenomenon only for Jerusalem in those early days?

Again, reading Luke's account in Acts, we see that it was Peter who was chosen by God's Spirit to take the gospel beyond the Jewish culture to the Gentiles. In Acts 10:1 – 11:18 we read the breathtaking story of how the

Spirit moved Peter to enter the home of a Roman centurion, Cornelius, who had gathered devout and God-fearing people who prayed together and gave generously to those in need. Peter preached the gospel to them, and while doing so the Holy Spirit fell on Cornelius and his household. They all began to speak in tongues and praise God. This was the proof that God really had given grace to the Gentiles and wanted to reach them as well – and it all happened in a private home! In Acts, we find even more examples of whole families coming to faith: the households of Lydia (16:15), of the jailer in Philippi (16:25–34), and of Crispus the synagogue leader (18:8), to name just a few.

All these reports of early mission leave but one conclusion: "The standard in evangelism of the Early Church is Oikos-Evangelism."[43] *Oikos* is the Greek word for "household" and can also be translated as "family." *Oikos* evangelism is confirmed by Michael Green who carried out in-depth studies on the evangelism of the early Christians. Based on examples from Scripture and additional historical documents, Green concluded, "It's no surprise that home churches were the key factor in spreading Christianity."[44] Evangelism by the early church was primarily carried out in private homes, reaching out to families. Whenever a person got saved, other family members soon followed. Whole households were baptized.

When we read the apostle Paul describing the blessings we have when family members believe in Christ, we see how important the family was for early church mission. Paul tells the Corinthians that unsaved people are sanctified by their believing partners – and their children are made holy too (1 Cor 7:14; see also 1 Pet 3:1–4). That's why, for Paul, divorce is not worth considering as long as the unbelieving partner is willing to remain married. Swiss theologian Jörg Frey confirms that the contacts within the family were essential for early church mission.[45] Early Christians who were active in outreach would always include their families, and this "inclusion of the family" was critical.[46] In this way whole households came to follow Christ, and the new

---

43. On "oikos evangelism," see Dr Thomas Wolf, "Oikos Evangelism: The Biblical Pattern," https://www.apostolic.edu/oikos-evangelism-the-biblical-pattern/, accessed 21 January 2020.

44. Michael Green, *Evangelisation zur Zeit der ersten Christen: Motivation, Methodik und Strategie* (Neuhausen-Stuttgart: Hänssler, 1970), 240.

45. Jörg Frey, "Die Ausbreitung des frühen Christentums: Perspektiven für die gegenwärtige Praxis der Kirche," in *Kirche zwischen postmoderner Kultur und Evangelium*, ed. Martin Reppenhagen, Beiträge zu Evangelisation und Gemeindeentwicklung 15 (Neukirchen-Vluyn: Neukirchner Verlag, 2010), 109.

46. Frey, "Die Ausbreitung," 105.

converts would devote their homes to the "service of the Lord's people," as is written of Stephanas (1 Cor 16:15). We may presume that his home was the meeting place for a house church, as were other homes in the Roman Empire at the time (e.g. Rom 16:14–15).

Early church mission, therefore, was primarily family evangelism. When somebody was saved, like the jailer in Philippi, the apostles focused on the family members as well, and they baptized whole families on those occasions (Acts 16:31–34). And these families would pass on the gospel. It is not difficult to recognize the Spirit's strategy in this kind of approach: he restored whole families, gathering them into his church, and on that basis the gospel was carried throughout the nations.

Homes and False Teachers

As the private home was the central location for mission, and families were key to mission in the strategy of the Holy Spirit, both were targeted by the enemy from the very beginning of the church. We see Ananias and Sapphira seduced, keeping back part of the proceeds of the property they sold while pretending to have given all (Acts 5). The Holy Spirit exposed their lie and the couple were dramatically removed from the church.

In the letters of the apostles we read of the increasing number of false teachings that were spreading through the Roman Empire. The false prophets and teachers also met in private homes, demanding hospitality as they travelled around preaching. The reaction of the apostle John is very strong:

> I say this because many deceivers, who do not acknowledge Jesus Christ as coming in the flesh, have gone out into the world. Any such person is the deceiver and the antichrist. Watch out that you do not lose what we have worked for, but that you may be rewarded fully. Anyone who runs ahead and does not continue in the teaching of Christ does not have God; whoever continues in the teaching has both the Father and the Son. If anyone comes to you and does not bring this teaching, do not take them into your house or welcome them. Anyone who welcomes them shares in their wicked work. (2 John 7–11)

It is important for John that the Christian home isn't abused as a stage for false teaching but is devoted to God and his good work. When homes are opened up for false prophets, he says that they share their wicked work.

Summary

1. The Holy Spirit initiates mission and evangelism in and through the church of Christ. He is the founder of local churches, which in the early church met in the family atmosphere of private homes.
2. From day one, family evangelism has been a key element of any mission under the guidance of the Holy Spirit.
3. The private home of a family is the perfect base for strategic mission – for outreach both to Jews as well as to Gentiles.
4. Above all, it was families who provided spiritual nurture and teaching plus practical provision for those who sought the Lord.
5. The Christian home has been attacked ever since the beginning of the church and it has the potential either to build the church or to be a place of division and backsliding.

The Trinity Is the Author of the Family's Mission

Through our exploration of Scripture concerning God's plan for the family we've seen that God invented the family, creating it in his image to carry out his divine plan on earth. Consequently, we find that the Trinity is present in the nature, mission and daily life of the family. This is the genius of our Creator who designed the nature of the family; and when families seek to manifest their godly nature in real life they will fulfil their destiny, satisfy their needs and live up to God's intentions. A family is only truly happy and fulfilled when it is living according to the Creator's purposes and intentions. Whenever families are not in line with God's purposes we see dark clouds on the horizon, and ultimately such families will fail and disintegrate. Broken families, in turn, cause society to collapse. To think that the family has become superfluous in today's society is to help dig the pit where dreams of happiness will get buried sooner or later. If we try to shape our world by removing the ultimate creative power – the family – we will face stagnation and ultimately the collapse of our culture.

This is why the restoration of the family is key to the redemption of our whole world, and also why Christ's mission is based on the family. If families are restored, the gospel will influence whole societies. God builds his kingdom "home by home." Reaching one's own people is primarily based on reaching their families. Any Christian church trying just to reach individuals for Christ will soon realize that its efforts are wasted. Evangelizing families, however, will lead to growth in faith and numbers.

Why? Because God intended it that way, and this is how the Holy Spirit has been working ever since. Christ's Spirit is Lord of any mission (2 Cor 3:17) and it's the Spirit's strategy that counts in our mission. Whenever we neglect his directives, we get into trouble.

Family and mission are rooted in the Trinity. In the next chapter we will look at the family as the primary agent of mission.

Questions for Reflection

1. This chapter showed that the family is Trinitarian. Do you have any questions about this idea?
2. How does knowing that the family reflects God's Trinity help us to understand the unity, fellowship and ability to complement each other in our families?
3. The family is called to create and be fruitful. What does that mean for your daily life in your family?
4. God has structured and designed the family in a specific way. What are the practical consequences of this in light of today's discussions about and new definitions of the family?
5. In the New Testament, evangelism primarily took place in the homes of expanded families. Is this important for today? Why?
6. If mission in the early church originated in homes (i.e. in the family), what does that mean for our churches and families today?

3

Families in Mission

The Family and Mission: How Do They Relate to Each Other?

When it comes to academic discussion regarding mission and evangelism, the family is not included at all. As mentioned in chapter 1, there is to my knowledge no published doctrine of family in mission as yet, nor is there much to read in the relevant manuals. The following example is symptomatic. Elmer Towns is the editor of *Evangelism and Church Growth*, a helpful and globally unique encyclopaedia containing a list of all the different approaches to evangelism. But even though Towns mentions "*oikos* evangelism," he defines it as, and confines it to, evangelism carried out within the walls of our private homes, rather than exploring mission through families in general.[1] There is nothing about the family being important as a unit for active outreach and discipleship[2] in church. Yet, as we have seen, statistics have proved empirically that most people come to faith through their families. Thus, if we take those figures seriously we can't but conclude that the family is a key agent of mission (providing that the husband and wife have realized their calling). Some studies have specifically explored the effectiveness of families on the mission field. They show that such families are most effective when both husband and wife focus on their family life *and* their mission together – especially when also getting their children involved.[3] Why shouldn't this hold true for all Christian families, given that – as we saw in chapter 2 – every family reflects the Trinity and is part of God's divine mission plan?

---

1. Elmer L. Towns, ed., *Evangelism and Church Growth: A Practical Encyclopedia* (Ventura, CA: Regal, 1995), 219.

2. Towns, *Evangelism and Church Growth*, 140–180.

3. Jerry Rankin, "The Family and Mission: Reflections from the Life of a US Missionary," in *The Missionary Family: Witness, Concerns, Care*, ed. Dwight P. Baker and Robert J. Priest (Pasadena, CA: William Carey Library, 2014), 51.

We need to talk about the family if we want to address God's mission in this world, and we need to talk about God's mission in this world if we want to address the family, because we've seen that the family is an intrinsic part of God's plan for his creation; it is at the heart of his purposes. It is no coincidence that the Catholic Church regards the family as the future both of the church and of our existence.[4] George W. Peters is right in saying, "When we take into account that worldwide, the family is not only a social institution but really created and intended by God as a unique social unit, then we must focus on family evangelism as a biblical priority and biblical standard."[5]

It is difficult to keep quiet about the family when talking about God's redemption plan for the world. As we have seen, no institution plays such an essential part in sustaining human life as the family. Just think of the biological aspect: we only secure our very existence when there are families and family-like structures. That's how God created life, and hence our lives; this was his intention for the family whose name is derived from him (Eph 3:14–15). And to reach our full potential as true human beings we have to bow the knee before him. The apostle Paul even talks of *theosis* – we are like God (Eph 3:19). Having been made in God's image, we are to create like him, and this is best reflected in marriage and family (Gen 1:27–28).

As the family also offers us a place of confidence, and since true trust is a prerequisite for any positive change – for a change of opinions as well as change in general – the family is also the starting point for any cultural and social transformation. Certainly it is not without tension and resistance; but friction is not dangerous but creative within the safe space of a family. As love drives out all fear (1 John 4:18), the family is not a threat to us but enables development through benevolent eyes. The family coaches and accompanies us critically, and evaluates according to traditional and proven values.

And finally, family and mission belong to each other. As we have seen, for Jesus, the first and primary missionary on earth, the family was highly important. Later, the Holy Spirit chose the family and homes as the main base for the triumphant advance of the gospel. The early church followed this approach. Indeed, when we explore Scripture and church history we can speak of a close relationship between family and mission.

Nevertheless, nobody has so far succeeded in drafting a theology of family in mission. This is a problem for missionaries who take their families

---

4. *FC* 75.

5. George W. Peters, *Evangelisation: Total, durchdringend, umfassend* (Bad Liebenzell: VLM, 1977), 64.

to dangerous places to preach the gospel. More than anyone else, it is these men and women on the front line who lament and suffer from the lack of sound theology, as demonstrated in a study by Donald and Margaret Grigorenko, missionaries in Nepal for many years.[6] They have demanded a theology of family in mission which deals with the opportunities and risks for families committed to mission.[7]

But we must go further: such a theology is important not only for world mission and for the families of pastors and missionaries, but for the whole church of Christ – for all of us within God's mission plan for this world. Any church which is engaged in mission and reaching out to its community ought to engage in family mission and family ministry. There's no way round it if we want to be successful and fruitful in what we do; as we saw in chapter 1, most people come to faith through their families. And there are several reasons for this.

The Family as a Living Testimony

Our mission for Christ means fundamentally that we are his witnesses. After his resurrection Jesus told his disciples, "you will receive power when the Holy Spirit comes upon you; and you will be my witnesses in Jerusalem, and in all Judea and Samaria, and to the ends of the earth" (Acts 1:8). The apostle Paul called Christians to be a letter for all to read (2 Cor 3:2–9). The world will recognize Christ by the love and unity that Christians have for and with each other (John 13:35). For the people of the first century AD, such love was experienced mainly within the setting of a household. Was this the reason why homes and families were central to the mission of the early church? Probably it was. But has anything changed today? Why not open up our homes and families again? Practising hospitality towards strangers will open their hearts to receive our testimony and give us opportunities to proclaim the gospel of Christ (Heb 13:2). It is within the family that people who don't yet know Jesus may observe his life most closely. They may watch, study and even imitate this life that he grants his followers.

Michael Nazir-Ali, an Anglican bishop, observes that the Christian family is the most effective testimony to Muslims; for example, Muslim women cannot

---

6. Donald and Margaret Grigorenko, "Experiencing Risk: Missionary Families in Dangerous Places," in Baker and Priest, *Missionary Family*, 25–43.

7. Grigorenko, "Experiencing Risk," 34–37.

be sure of the lifelong care, love and faithfulness of their husbands.[8] When they witness the lives of their Christian neighbours manifesting what they are sorely missing in their own families, it can make them think about Christianity. Hence, it makes sense to commit ourselves to both supportive and releasing family structures among us, and especially among missionaries abroad.[9] Jerry Rankin, a missionary who lives with his family in a Muslim country, agrees:

> The family has great potential for the mission's mandate. Not only because our children will observe our outreach model and learn how to hand out tracts, but because we live as a family in a cross cultural context, we will be a living testimony. For example, when in contrast to the host culture, our wives are cherished and respected in a loving marriage, it becomes very clear that Christ makes the difference in our lives. Or, when people see our children disciplined and respectful, nice and kind to each other and the world around them, it's "passive" testimony, but nonetheless it will leave quite an impression. God calls families into mission to testify to Christ's love that will be seen in our everyday family life.[10]

Alfred Yeo confirms that when it comes to effective evangelism in Singapore too, open families play a significant role in reaching their relatives, colleagues and friends,[11] because it is easy to see how faith is changing a person's everyday (and real) life. Within the natural environment of friends and family we don't need to search for new contacts artificially as we already have them. And we don't need to formulate our testimonies because our lives display our faith for all to see. The gospel will attract most attention when it is real and authentic and can be experienced in everyday life.

Yet it is not only abroad but also in the context of church and neighbourhood mission that successful family life can be a wonderful testimony. The Becker family is an outstanding example of this. This family brings along non-church folk to our Sunday services on a regular basis. One day I asked some of these folk why they came when invited. The answers were not surprising: "We often go to the Beckers's house and we feel at home there. We wanted to find out what's special about them and where they go to church, as we saw that their

---

8. Michael Nazir-Ali, *From Everywhere to Everywhere: A World View of Christian Mission* (London: Collins, 1990), 142.

9. Nazir-Ali, *From Everywhere*, 79.

10. Rankin, "Family and Mission," 53.

11. Alfred Yeo, "The Local Church Reaches Its Neighbourhood," in *The Church: God's Agent for Change*, ed. Bruce J. Nicolls (Exeter: Paternoster, 1986), 142–145.

faith is so important to them." These people came to church with the Beckers on their own initiative because the Beckers's family life was so interesting, exciting, open and authentic – not because the Beckers had had to persuade them to come. Any family that is open to the world around it is a living testimony and will attract non-believers, paving the way to faith for them.

Unfortunately, many Christian families stay removed from their environments and neighbourhoods, especially those with young children as they fear the potential bad influence on their children. If we think we've got to keep our distance, we will live in opposition to God's mission call; and people around us will sense this distance and feel rejected.

Mission Lives by Trust

Mission is based on trust: it is most effective when people can trust each other. US missiologist Marvin Mayers refers to this factor as the "question of prior trust" (QPT),[12] claiming that an atmosphere of confidence is a priority for any mission strategy. The idea is simple: we will only risk a life-changing action or decision when we can trust the person who suggests it. That's why it is so important today to find trustworthy people and connect them with those who are seeking God.[13] Yet we are only able to trust somebody when we've been on a journey together, when we've shared our lives and experiences – in short, when we have a personal relationship with that person. We will not be filled with confidence out of the blue, nor will we be persuaded to trust somebody because he or she inundates us with well-meant words, even if these words tell us the truth. Confidence is not built through nice words, flyers or tracts, but through shared experiences.

And where better do we find a place to share life than in the family? Here we know each other, we share a common history and common experiences; here love and trust are natural! A healthy family offers a safe place where people may reclaim their identity, dignity and self-respect in an atmosphere of protection. People in the Western world today need such safe places more than ever before because they are lost in individualism and confusion.[14] Whenever outsiders enter the protected space of a family and become witnesses of all the

---

12. Marvin K. Mayers, *Christianity Confronts Culture* (Grand Rapids, MI: Zondervan, 1981), 32.

13. George G. Hunter III, *How to Reach Secular People* (Nashville: Abingdon Press, 1992), 59.

14. For more on this, see Hunter, *How to Reach*, 55–72.

love and its potential, they become curious and interested, and even hungry to experience the same.

Therefore, it makes great sense to choose families and homes as central places for mission and evangelism. Whenever we succeed in reaching families for the gospel we will see them in turn reaching out effectively to their family members. In the previous chapter we saw the example of Andrew, one of the first disciples of Jesus, who, having realized that Jesus was the Messiah, went to find his brother Simon and led him to the Lord (John 1:40–42). In other words, having found faith in Christ, Andrew immediately shared this exciting revelation with the person he knew understood him best – his brother. He could share openly with Simon without fear of being laughed at. In addition, Simon Peter was the more active of the two, therefore Andrew expected his brother to know what to do next. Simon was also older and already a married man. We can imagine the family dynamic vividly when reading these few verses. It is natural for us to want to share important news we receive with the people we love, and it is within the family that we find the natural space to trust; that's why it's the best place to pass on the best of all news within the family.

Of course, there are broken homes too. Trust has been nipped in the bud, relationships have been disturbed and there may be almost nothing left of the kind of family life described above. Even so, family is and remains family – hence the saying, "Blood is thicker than water." Blood relations stay unique. If anywhere, it is within the family that we are able to rebuild damaged relationships and learn to grow in confidence again.

Whenever a family is lacking trust, it is right there that people miss it most, and most desire to regain it. People with broken family backgrounds often tell me, "I only wish I could have a good relationship with my family again, I only wish we could trust each other again." We should use this healthy desire as a stepping stone to share the good news of peace and reconciliation. Jesus has the power to reconcile people, making them one (Eph 2:14–19). He is the Prince of Peace who is able to turn the hearts of fathers to their children and the hearts of children to their fathers (Mal 4:6). When we proclaim this gospel, preaching this peace to people who long for reconciliation, we will surely get their attention. And when they accept this message, their testimony will be all the stronger.

A young man, whom we will call Sergei, was the son of very influential government officials in Moscow. Sergei had made a successful career as a boxer. One day in Tallinn, Estonia, he happened to visit our church, the *Olai* Baptist Church, when we were in the midst of a revival. Sergei's life at that point was a shambles and his relationship with his family had hit rock-bottom. When he told me that his mother had never kissed him in his life I was aghast. "We are not physical in our family, we don't know how to hug and embrace," he told me. "All our lives have been about career and success." He didn't want to see his parents ever again. Yet, when Sergei gave his life to Jesus, he wrote to his parents that same day, telling them about his decision. His parents, being atheists, were shocked. They were worried about his sports career and instantly flew to Tallinn. They all met at the church. When Sergei saw his mother, he ran over to her and kissed her. His desire to be reconciled with her was so great that he didn't hesitate to hug and kiss her as little children do. That was heartbreaking for her. And instead of giving him a lecture, both his parents stayed for the service. For the first time in their atheistic lives they attended church, sitting and listening to a sermon. And they returned, again and again. It wasn't long before both of them accepted Jesus as their Lord. These parents had been overwhelmed by their son's love – love that he owed to our Lord Jesus Christ.

Mission Takes Place within Relationships

Building on the previous point, it is relationships that open the door to trust. Louis J. Lutzbetak did some profound research on how much missionaries approached those they are trying to reach and he found that the following three factors are most important for the success of any missionary's preaching:

1. Their empathy – their ability to connect with the emotions of the people they address;
2. Their willingness to preach the good news in line with local and cultural methods of communication – when in line with Christian ethics and theology;
3. Their adaptation to local culture.[15]

If we want to reach people with the gospel, we will only be successful when we seek to understand them and feel with them, and when we find the way to preach Christ's message in their language, as if we were "one of them." South African missiologist S. Gourdet says, "we can only identify with people when we share lives – that means when we work together with them."[16]

When we apply this to evangelism, it means that missionaries will only be able to reach people's hearts effectively when they really engage with them and

---

15. In S. Gourdet, "Identification in Intercultural Communication," *Missionalia* 24, no. 3 (1996): 399.

16. Gourdet, "Identification," 470.

their lives[17] by learning with and from them. We will never be able to identify without this willingness to learn.[18] For any outreach it is necessary to create an open space so that everyone can participate. Evangelism thrives in a "welcome culture" which gives us space to share the world – a culture which does not exclude anyone.[19] Evangelistic communication needs an atmosphere in which people can trust each other because they allow each other to speak and they listen to each other. Such an atmosphere is free from fear, and, though possibly critical, is based on common ground. Here, people speak the same language and use the same metaphors, thus creating an atmosphere of trust. In such a safe space we know, "This is where I'm understood by other people, and this is where I understand everyone else, too." We need empathy and sensitivity to reach such a level of communication.

Again, it is the family that is an ideal basis for this effective natural communication. It is here we know each other best, we learn to have empathy and we become the people we really are. We feel at home within our families. Relationships are natural, allowing us to talk freely – even about the gospel of Christ. Nowhere else in the world will we find such freedom to talk as within the family. Past frictions have taught us to understand each other's way of expressing ourselves: our family members will not turn away from us because of one careless statement or because of our way of talking. Certainly, family life also knows anger and frustration. So it is here we sharpen each other; we learn to deal with the mistakes of others and at times we have to swallow some bitter pills. Within the family, we will have had to learn to forgive each other at some point, and also to receive forgiveness. It is here that we are allowed to provoke each other, ask difficult questions and find the courage to think outside the box. Thus it is within the family that it is easiest to share the gospel.

Yet mission is only that simple when our lives display authentic change. For it is also true that our families will unmask any artificial behaviour and superficial talk sooner or later; they will expose hypocrisy in an instant and reject religiosity. Felix once told me:

> When I first met Jesus I went to a charismatic church. It was so exciting how they would "pump" me up spiritually there. Yet, when

---

17. David Hesselgrave, *Communicating Christ Cross-Culturally: An Introduction to Missionary Communication* (Grand Rapids, MI: Zondervan, 1991), 46.

18. Jacob A. Loewen, *Culture and Human Values: Christian Intervention in Anthropological Perspective* (Pasadena, CA: William Carey Library, 1977), 36; also see: Gourdet, "Identification," 407.

19. For more on "welcome culture" and what it means for evangelism, see Johannes Reimer, *Hereinspaziert: Willkommenskultur und Evangelisation* (Schwarzenfeld: Neufeld Verlag, 2013), 140–141.

I was back home, I would bash my family's traditional faith. I kept telling them how wrong they were and if they didn't convert correctly they would all go to hell. Today, to be honest, I feel really ashamed of my words back then. I even told them that I was free from any sin because of having Jesus in my life. Only two days later my mum caught me red-handed when I was rolling a joint. You can imagine what my testimony was worth: it didn't inspire them – it made them laugh at me. It would have been better if I had shut up at the beginning and let my life speak on its own. . . . However, I did change. Day by day, I changed a little bit more – until one day, Mum came up to me saying she had started to take my words about Jesus more seriously.

Within our families, we are exposed for all to see. What a potential for true fellowship! What a chance to really support one another! What an opportunity to share our faith! Yet, at the same time, what a challenge to live our faith authentically, sharing the gospel wisely among our family members!

Even when we are strangers in another culture, our family life will have points of contact with the lives of families in that culture when it comes to everyday business and life. Raising children, for example, is such a universal issue, concerning all families alike, that we will always find common ground and mutual understanding. I often hear of young women who have met through toddlers' groups. They might have different national or ethnic backgrounds, but they are connected by their children's needs and by facing the same challenges in their daily lives. As families, we are united by sharing the same challenges, and this opens doors for friendship and for the gospel as well.

The Family Is the Foundation of Christian Mission

We have seen that God created the family and that he is God of all mankind. We have learned that God carries out his mission on earth mainly through the institution of the family. God has committed himself to the family, and healthy families are the foundation of his kingdom on earth. Both in the Old and New Testaments, God called the family to play a key role in his divine plan of salvation. Indeed, the family wouldn't exist if God hadn't given Adam and Eve the Cultural Mandate.[20] And we find the family as the foundation of the

---

20. For further information on the Cultural Mandate and its meaning for modern missiology and theology, see Craig Ott, Stephen J. Strauss and Timothy Tennent, *Encountering Theology of Mission: Biblical Foundations, Historical Developments and Contemporary Issues* (Grand Rapids, MI: Baker Academic, 2010), 149.

people of Israel throughout the Old Testament. Then, in Christ's ministry on earth, the restoration of the family, understood as the "year of the Lord's favour," was central to his mission (Luke 4:18; Lev 25). Later, the family turns into the essential nucleus of mission within the life of the early church as portrayed in the New Testament. Both family and church are God's ambassadors on earth to proclaim that he has reconciled humankind to himself through Christ the Lord (2 Cor 5:18–21).

Wherever the Master himself builds the house, the builders will be successful, but wherever he is missing "the builders labour in vain" (Ps 127:1). And when God himself is on a mission, above all it is through the family! The God of mission is the Father of every family (Eph 3:14–15) – *missio Dei* is also a *missio familiae*.

In addition, the family is the nucleus of human existence, of any culture and of our beliefs; it helps shape our environment, our own culture, as well as the culture of God's kingdom. It is in the family – and nowhere else – that we are enculturated; so to learn about culture outside the family will never be as complete an acculturation. Thus, the family will also be the nucleus of faith.[21] Jesus commanded us to make disciples of all nations (Matt 28:19–20) – and that must include families as they are the heart of any people on earth. It is families who mainly manifest God's kingdom values, and it is within families that people become part of his kingdom and that Christian social care can take place. Therefore, it is no coincidence that Scripture attaches such high value to religious socializing within the family. As we've seen, God commanded the families of Israel to raise their children in the faith and in the fear of the Lord. Where else can we influence people as effectively as within the family? Where else can we shape fellowship and life as well as within healthy families? This is especially true for families on the mission field, and it is an essential factor of growing in faith, too. Missionaries report how important it is for their spiritual lives to live as families "abroad" in a different culture.[22] Where else than within a family, serving God, do children get the opportunity to observe God at work in real life?

Gerald Foley writes, "Family is our first fellowship and family is the foundation of how God is uniting us, shaping us and operating through us

---

21. Ralph Weimann, "Die Familie als Keimzelle der Erneuerung des Glaubens," in *Ehe und Familie: Wege zum Gelingen aus katholischer Perspektive*, ed. George Augustin and Ingo Proft (Freiburg: Herder, 2016), 474–477.

22. Rankin, "Family and Mission," 54.

in this world."[23] Family is the base unit of society and the mission agent of God's church on earth.[24] In a nutshell, it is the family that guarantees human proliferation, social fellowship and the best opportunities to share the gospel.

Thus, family and mission belong together. The one cannot exist without the other. Families on earth can't help but be missional – by its very nature, the family cannot be non-missional. The only question is whether individual families still need specific callings into mission. Each Christian family consists of individual followers of Christ who are right in claiming to be "God's handiwork, created in Christ Jesus to do good works, which God *prepared in advance for us to do*" (Eph 2:10). This verse leaves no doubt that each one of us is called to specific works God has prepared for us individually. His universal mandate doesn't stay arbitrary; we are not to choose our home or profession at random if we want to follow Christ's mission.

What does that mean practically? As Christian families we ought first to explore the basics of God's mission and his Great Commission. In this way we will soon discover the following general guidelines which will help us:

1. God calls us to live our lives according to his will and intentions. We are to "become the righteousness of God" (2 Cor 5:21). In every aspect of our lives, we are to testify to and manifest his presence so that we "might be for the praise of his glory" (Eph 1:12). Therefore, any Christian family should focus on proclaiming and displaying God's good works in all their fullness (Eph 3:14–17).

2. God calls us to live our lives among his people. On the day we were born again, we were baptized into the body of Christ by his Holy Spirit (1 Cor 12:13). By definition, being a Christian means being part of a collective – we are automatically members of Christ's body, his worldwide church. Any Christian family is part of God's collective family, the *familia Dei*.

3. God calls us to live our lives in this world. We are to be the salt and light of this world (Matt 5:13–15). We are Christ's ambassadors to proclaim that he has reconciled the world to God (2 Cor 5:18–20). He called us out of the world *in order to* take responsibility for this

---

23. Gerald Foley, *Family-Centred Church: A New Parish Model* (Kansas City, MO: Sheed & Ward, 1995), 17.

24. Rodney Clapp, *Families at the Crossroads: Beyond Traditional and Modern Options* (Downers Grove, IL: InterVarsity Press, 1993), 155.

world. Thus, as families we are called to be seen in public; we are called to be role models. We don't live solely for ourselves.

4. God calls us to live specific callings in specific local places – the church is called to be a local player. We are called to take responsibility for specific people in a specific area.[25] Hence, also as families together, we are called to serve our neighbourhoods, taking responsibility for the people around us. It needs an explicit call of God if we are to move to do mission abroad instead of where we live, which is our first calling (see ch. 9).

5. God calls us to live our lives using the gifts he has given us. The parameters are clearly set; as we read in 1 Corinthians 12:4–6, it is the Spirit who distributes all kinds of gifts, it is the Lord who calls us to different kinds of service and it is God who works the power in us to do so. Every Christian is given gifts by the Spirit; each one of us is called by God; thus, we are all capable of bearing good fruit accordingly – provided we know what kind of gift we've got and which kind of service we are actually called to. Therefore, any Christian family has to discern the gifts, skills and competences of each of its members in order to serve and to fulfil its common mission effectively.

Indeed, we see that families are called specifically to find "their places in God's plan for this world."[26] Whenever families are at a loss and unsure about their specific callings, the church leadership ought to equip these saints for the work of service, as Paul recommends in Ephesians 4:11–12.

What does this look like in practice? How does the family's mission function in practical terms? We will try to find answers in later chapters through exploring the role of the family in mission, social care, evangelism and discipleship training.

---

25. For more on this, see Johannes Reimer, *Die Welt umarmen: Theologie des gesellschaftsrelevanten Gemeindebaus*, Transformationsstudien 1, 2nd ed. (Marburg: Francke Verlag, 2013), 42–48.

26. David Sills, *The Missionary Call: Find Your Place in God's Plan for the World* (Chicago: Moody, 2008).

Missional Families – Theory and Practice

Any church which is reaching out to its community and has set its focus on mission is called "missional" in today's literature.[27] Applying this to the Christian family, we could, or perhaps must, speak of the "missional family" as the prominent agent in God's mission plan on earth. Lawrence O. Richards, professor of Christian education and youth ministry, confirms the unique role the "family dynamic" plays in church life.[28]

The word "missional" was originally used as a synonym for "missionary," as found in the Oxford English Dictionary of 1907.[29] Yet "missional" has a slightly different meaning today, one which goes back to discussions on the *missio Dei* at the missions conference in Willingen, Germany, in 1952. On that occasion, experts for the first time recognized that churches are missionary by nature.[30] After the 1970s we find this term "missional" coming up again and again, always indicating that the church is missionary by nature. But it wasn't until 1998, when Darrell Guder published his book *Missional Church: A Vision for the Sending of the Church in North America*, that this term had a breakthrough.[31] The book, published in the USA by the Gospel and Our Culture Network (GOCN), soon stirred up great interest worldwide.

Today, when people use the term "missional" they mostly mean "missionary by nature,"[32] as opposed to the term "missionary" which means "missionary by action/in action." *Missionary* churches *do* mission; they undertake outreaches and see evangelism as one task among others. In contrast, *missional* churches *are* God's mission – it is their very essence and character, their very nature, their DNA, to reach out to the world around them. If we apply this to the family, missional families are designed for mission by nature; this means that they don't *go on* mission but they *are* God's mission to the world. Missional families serve to manifest God's kingdom on earth as do missional churches.[33]

---

27. David Barrett, "Defining Missional Church," in *Evangelical, Ecumenical and Anabaptist Missiology in Conversation: Essays in Honor of Wilbert Shenk*, ed. James Krabill, Walter Sawatsky and Charles E. Van Engen (Maryknoll, NY: Orbis, 2006), 177–183.

28. Lawrence Richards, *Christian Education: Seeking to Become Like Jesus Christ* (Grand Rapids, MI: Zondervan, 1975), 40.

29. Barrett, "Defining Missional Church," 177.

30. Barrett, 178.

31. Darrell Guder, *Missional Church: A Vision for the Sending of the Church in North America* (Grand Rapids, MI: Eerdmans, 1998).

32. Barrett, "Defining Missional Church," 179.

33. Reggie McNeal, *Missional Renaissance: Changing the Scorecard for the Church* (San Francisco: Jossey-Bass, 2009), 24.

Reggie McNeal has found the following three characteristics[34] to be inherent to missional churches, and they can equally be applied to the missional family:

1. A missional church is God's agent in mission, perceiving God's calling to be the only reason for its existence. Everything in this church is focused on God's mission – nothing happens outside this ultimate goal to be God's mission agent on earth and to reach the world for Christ.

2. Such missional churches derive their *raison d'être* from both their relationship with God (*coram Deo*) and their relationship with the world (*coram mundo*). This holds true for missional families too, because the family is named by God (Eph 3:14–15) and the family guarantees life on earth. A church (or family) can only be considered missional when it has these two factors: connected to God and reaching out to the world.

3. Missional church is holistic: evangelism is not a one-sided activity. Such churches (and families) reach out to the world with their very being – with their hearts, minds, souls and bodies, their actions and their words.

The family is the very space where life is conceived, where life is fostered and where life (culture) is shaped. Swiss missionary Edith Schaeffer, author and co-founder of L'Abri Ministries and an expert in Christian social work, even defined "social environment" as equal to "the *Lebensraum* of the family."[35] She argued that the family is the centre of communication where we all learn about social and cultural standards, and that we become social beings and members of society only within the family. Within the family, life and faith are passed on. And the family offers the best place for people to just be, do things and talk – all three aspects being essential keys in evangelism as well. Therefore, Christian families can – or even must – be considered as missional in the very sense of this term.

---

34. McNeal, *Missional Renaissance*, 180–183.
35. Edith Schaeffer, *Lebensraum Familie* (Kassel: Oncken Verlag, 1976).

Questions for Reflection

1. Mission is the family's nature. Why is the family God's number one mission agent?
2. Why are relationships and friendships so important for evangelism?
3. "We cannot reach out to the world around us if people are not able to trust us." Is this sentence true? If so, why? Is evangelism only about proclaiming the Word?
4. What are the characteristics of a missional church? Is it right to talk about the missional family? Why or why not?
5. Would you call your church and your family "missional"? Why or why not?
6. What does a missional family look like?
7. What might be typical problems or challenges that arise for missional families?
8. What needs to be changed in your church in order to equip families to be missional families?

4

Family and Church

A Missional Church Is Focused on the Family

Families belong to a larger community together with other families, in accordance with God's plan. And as we see in the Old and New Testaments, the family also belongs to the people of God as a whole, the *familia Dei*. As pastor Joan King, of Mission Ministries SEND, Maine, says: "Any local church represents a 'family' gathering, families manifesting God's Kingdom on earth."[1] Thus, Christian families ought to be involved in local churches. But what role does church play in mission, and what role does the family play in that whole dynamic?

Exploring the New Testament on church, we see[2] that church at first meant local churches, equipped for God's mission in their local neighbourhoods and communities, responsible for the people living there. Churches take shape on the ground locally. We are his witnesses right where we are in our neighbourhoods, within our specific local communities – "the setting and place that meets our basic needs and . . . where we turn for help in the ups and downs of our lives."[3] So when we talk about local community, we are talking about neighbourhood assistance, our social networks and our social life within a certain area. This is the setting which is the framework for all our basic relationships and our fundamental trust, which, as we have seen, is a prerequisite for any human communication and transformation.

---

1. Joan King, "Families: Something to Celebrate," *Ministry Today* 8 (Oct 1996): 52.
2. For more on this, see Johannes Reimer, *Die Welt umarmen: Theologie des gesellschaftsrelevanten Gemeindebaus*, Transformationsstudien 1, 2nd ed. (Marburg: Francke Verlag, 2013), 33–107.
3. Herbert Lindner, *Kirche am Ort: Gemeindetheorie*, Praktische Theologie heute 16 (Stuttgart: Kohlhammer, 1974), 132.

Any church that wants to influence people and their lives has to be a local player. A church belongs to a local community. Deprive any area of its church and you deprive the people there of God's presence manifested in the church. This is also true the other way round: take the local aspect from churches and they will lose their significance for the people they are sent to. Our message, the gospel, is no theory – it is all about everyday life. Therefore the church ought to deal with the real lives of real people, and it ought to confront their specific needs and share their particular challenges. Only when the church gets involved locally will people gain trust in the church and ultimately trust our message and our Lord. Even in these days of globalization and virtual reality, the words of Dr Herbert Lindner, German theologian and author on church growth, remain true: "Local residence still matters to all of us, our community still fulfils essential functions which are determining for our local churches as well. Any 'community church' has to live in – not against – its local setting and has to minister to – not beyond – its local needs in order to be truly relevant."[4]

This local character of the church becomes even more important whenever people realize the close interrelationship between family and church. For it is in the local environment and its social setting that families live and grow as basic building blocks of society. Therefore any church has to be alive right where these families are resident: where their kids go to school, where their teenagers and parents spend their leisure time, where they earn their money, and so on. Any church that takes the concerns and the people of its community seriously will be a family-related church as local missional churches are the sum total of all their missional families.

And any local church will be sensitive to its context and environment. Such a community church will care for the people living in its community in order to build God's kingdom right there. Such a church will adapt its structures to the local setting and its ministries to the local needs, focusing on the particular demands of its particular neighbourhood. And transforming the local environment will be the aim of all its programmes. The ultimate goal of such missional churches is to bring people closer to Jesus – that is, to manifest his redeeming presence by reaching local families in their relationships and their fellowships within their context. In other words, whenever a church is contextual, it will be a family-related and a family-friendly church.

Missional churches are very determined and focused, too. Therefore they will show the characteristics typical of their local environment rather than of their denomination. They will want to be seen in the market place rather than

---

4. Lindner, *Kirche am Ort*, 132.

be hidden behind walls. They will want to be active in their communities rather than in their church buildings. Their programmes will not just aim at inviting people into their buildings, but they will minister to their communities – and neighbours, friends and local officials will be an active part of these *church ministries*. Our Lord and Saviour commanded us to "Go!," not to "Invite!," and this principle of going and reaching out is the very essence, the DNA, of missional churches. And they will go and reach out to . . . families! For it is within this context that they will draw closest to people. Within the family setting missional churches will create new social structures and shape society. In this way they can disciple whole localities, societies, nations – *ethnos* – fulfilling our Lord's commission to go and make disciples of all *ethne* (Matt 28:18–20). And when mission aims at a particular *ethnos*, it will need to focus on the families first.

Such a missional church will therefore take the gospel into the real lives of real people in a particular local context, using their ways of communication and their language.

Focusing on People's Salvation

The local church is responsible for the full and comprehensive salvation of local people. Thus, church is God's "primary agent" to fulfil his mission on earth. Whenever churches stop evangelizing, they cease to be the church of Christ.[5] Mission is the church's primary task, and that means proclaiming the gospel in word and deeds, interacting with the people around us and celebrating our services in the sight of the world. All that we live and do is missionary. Hence, missional churches have finally overcome the distinction that used to be made between proclaiming the gospel (in words) and social ministries (proclaiming it in deeds). Yet this does not mean that preaching and social work have to automatically go hand in hand. The church, the *ekklesia*, which is responsible to reach the world, consists of different individuals with different giftings and callings. We are a team; nobody has to do everything, but we each have to do only the work that God has prepared for each one of us (Eph 2:10). At the same time, however, everyone works, serves and lives for the common good according to the manifestation of the Spirit (1 Cor 12:7); otherwise we will

---

5. Craig Ott, Stephen J. Strauss and Timothy Tennent, *Encountering Theology of Mission: Biblical Foundations, Historical Developments and Contemporary Issues* (Grand Rapids, MI: Baker Academic, 2010), 195.

not fulfil this huge task to transform a whole community, a whole society, a whole nation, a whole world.

So our churches need to become holistic (integrating team players) and missional, as well as collaborative and collective fellowships. In order to become a collective we need to be one: one people of God, one body of Christ, one fellowship in his Spirit. Only true unity makes us attractive to others and successful in our mission. Jesus got to the heart of this imperative by asking the Father "that all of them may be one . . . so that the world may believe that you have sent me" (John 17:21).

Family-centred churches will focus on a fellowship that is as broad as possible and on collaboration among families. For these families are the primary agents of God's mission. Therefore, missional churches will make it a priority to support and encourage families, discerning the gifts and equipping the callings of individual family members, which is a task for the whole church. Whenever families start to live according to their giftings and to act according to God's plan the whole church can grow in faith and mission – and evangelism will automatically take place.

Missional church planting is an integral, all-encompassing and holistic endeavour, so churches need to take their responsibility for their communities seriously. They may not pick out only particular tasks, social classes or target groups, excluding others. The bigger picture of this integral task cannot be compartmentalized, as some church-planting movements want us to believe. On the contrary, evangelism and church planting are easiest when we realize that the best target groups are our own social contacts and our own interest groups – that is, the world around us.[6]

Developing missional churches means taking God's message to our neighbourhoods, our local communities and our natural social groups, not just to certain categories of people or subcultures within our society. God's mission is about our families, friends and fellow human beings. It is about our neighbourhoods, communities and whole societies; these people will shape our churches socially and will determine their character and ministries. C. Wayne Zunkel talks about two sorts of blindness among Christians and in churches: the "peoples and kingdom blindness."[7] Missional church planting means overcoming such blindness, reaching everyone with the gospel of God's kingdom, which involves all areas of life. Therefore, families will naturally be

---

6. Peter Roenfeld, *Handbuch für Gemeindegründer* (Lüneburg: Advent Verlag, 2003), 6–10.

7. C. Wayne Zunkel, *Church Growth under Fire* (Scottdale, PA: Herald Press, 1987), 105–107.

a key focus as they influence their environments. Whenever we want to reach a community we need to reach its families. We need to bring their challenges into our focus: local shopping, childcare, the balance of family and work life, leisure programmes and facilities for kids and adults, and so on. A healthy social environment is required to grow healthy families. Whenever families are neglected in a community, this area will in time become a social flashpoint. Politicians and local authorities have forgotten this simple truth, but sadly churches, social institutions and training centres have forgotten it too. As Christ's church, we have responsibility for our society and to work for the transformation God has in mind for the family. This ministry will certainly include active outreach and evangelism. Only when people follow Christ will their lives improve. And families will be renewed when they believe in Jesus, and their renewal will lead to a permanent, positive change in society.

Missional Churches and Their Evangelistic Approach

When we think in missional terms and we plant missional churches, the mission and outreach of such churches will change accordingly. This new kind of missional evangelism, built upon solid biblical and theological foundations, is the cornerstone of the new paradigm in church planting which is spreading around the world. McNeal defines four dimensions of this paradigm shift:[8]

1. God's perspective: evangelism within missional church planting is all about building his kingdom.
2. Eyes open to the world: evangelism within missional church planting is always focused outside the church.
3. Eyes open to every person: evangelism within missional church planting never loses sight of people and their needs and lives.
4. Eyes open to the (local) church: evangelism within missional church planting means organic church planting.

Let's explore these dimensions in more detail.

---

8. Reggie McNeal, *Missional Renaissance: Changing the Scorecard for the Church* (San Francisco: Jossey-Bass, 2009), 42–66.

Evangelism Is God's Idea!

Within missional church planting, evangelism is seen as God's mandate and his initiative; it was his plan, his creation, from the beginning. So, in missional outreach, everything is about building his kingdom on earth. The key aspect of this kingdom is that God has always intended to reconcile human beings to himself through Christ (2 Cor 5:18) – this is the key message of the gospel. There is no place where this reconciliation manifests itself better than in the church, as it is there that God shows what he wants to offer us. Note that God is the most active preacher and evangelist himself, for by his Spirit he is at work in us and through us – we just get to join him in what he is already doing. The church simply needs to embrace the works he has prepared; to do otherwise, undertaking an independent mission alone, leads to disaster. Instead of this, missional churches seek to carry out outreach only in connection with God. They observe what is happening and recognize when God is at work, and they take the Spirit's invitation to join him and follow in his footsteps.

In the life of the average church, however, things often look different – at least in conventional congregations: the average church considers itself as a "lone wolf" and tries to fulfil God's mandate simply in its own power, using human effort. Randy Frazee, an author and teacher passionate about spiritual transformation and community, once described the church as the loneliest nation on earth.[9] However, this is not true at all! We are not orphans, and the church of Christ is never alone when reaching out to the world. We are guided by God's Holy Spirit, who is the Lord of mission himself (2 Cor 3:17). Hence, we may rely on heaven to be present in all our evangelistic efforts. Anyway, it is not about our success – or what seems to be successful to us; rather, it is all about God's presence in our everyday (church) lives. Also, God knows his world and his creation much better than we do. After all, he created us all, and Jesus gave his life for us all because he loves us so much, and it is the Holy Spirit who convicts the world, opening our eyes to see God. God is love, and because of his love he has always been reaching out to us. He is, therefore, much more interested in evangelism than we could ever be.

Jeff Van Vonderen, author, interventionist and former pastor, calls any family who has lost this love and compassion a sick family.[10] The opposite is also true: it is healthy families who give space to God's endless mercy and grace.[11] When churches lift their eyes to God, they will wait upon him, they will be in

---

9. Randy Frazee, *The Connecting Church* (Grand Rapids, MI: Zondervan, 2001), 23–24.
10. Jeff Van Vonderen, *Familien: Von Gott getragen* (Asslar: Projektion J, 1996), 7–8.
11. Van Vonderen, *Familien*, 137.

the places he expects them to be and they will support those institutions of human life he wants to strengthen. Such churches offer everything they have and are to God, above all when it comes to the family, as they want to meet him and join him by coming closer to his heart. And lifting our eyes to God means opening our eyes to his creation, especially to the world around us and to its families, as families reflect his image in this world.

Eyes Open to the World around Us

To fulfil God's commission according to a missional lifestyle and missional evangelism means we will need to learn to live our lives in alignment with the families around us. As the church, we owe our very existence to the world around us and it is here that we find our proper place to exist as well as all the resources we need.[12] It is the mandate of every church to live among people.[13] Just like the Lord, his church dwells among men and women here on earth to manifest his glory. In addition, the true church of Christ always remains human, just as the Word of God became flesh, manifesting himself to real people in the history of humankind and in our human culture. The gospel of Christ is not only a humane message but it is also a truly human one.

For the average church, however, it is their congregation and their members who are most important. Church culture is usually a membership culture. They focus on the sanctification of their members; how outsiders perceive the church is less important. And average churches support their own families only indirectly – as a kind of side benefit of their children's ministry, youth work, teenage ministry and family ministry. Their care and support is aimed at insiders only, encouraging Christians to grow and to be ready for when the Lord returns one day. Church programmes are mostly tailored to their own folk and not to the lost world around them.

Missional churches, however, focus on shaping a missional culture in line with the Great Commission (Matt 28:19–20). They also aim at the sanctification of the saints, but this is in order to help the world see the "Light of the world" and get a taste and understanding of the "Salt of the world." Growing in faith is primarily for the benefit of the people around them. When the families of such churches grow spiritually, the families outside these churches benefit too. Any member of a missional church will automatically be a missionary;

---

12. Frazee, *Connecting Church*, 8.
13. Frazee, 118.

consequently, any family that is part of such a church will be involved in active mission.

Conventional churches prepare their members for the second coming of Christ, while missional churches "equip [Christ's] people for works of service" (Eph 4:11–12) – the work they have been called to fulfil here on earth. Yes, missional Christians look forward to heaven and long for Christ's return too. Yet in the meantime, as long as we still live here on the earth, we want to commit ourselves to Christ's mandate to disciple and transform this earth, as well as to his goal to build his kingdom on earth "as it is in heaven" (Matt 6:5–13), which should be our daily prayer.

Evangelism Requires Talking and Listening

If we want to reach the world, we need to really *see* people. How we perceive people in general is therefore important: our idea of people and our worldview will determine the manner in which we reach out to them. For example, if we regard people outside the church as vicious and corrupt, it is unlikely that we will seek to contact them in the first place. And if we do so, our contact will consist of monologues and our evangelism will resemble a verbal fight rather than both talking and listening. However, when we expect God's image to be alive in our counterpart, as is true for all his creation (at least to a certain degree), we will be able to meet non-believers eye-to-eye and enter into a true dialogue with them. In this way, outreach will be a demonstration of God's presence and love rather than a confrontation. Most often we are told to simply *tell* people the truth about God; thus conventional churches focus on preaching and proclaiming the gospel, whereas missional churches seek to *demonstrate* the gospel and *manifest* God's truth to the world. Thus, conventional outreach is all about organizing programmes, whereas missional evangelism is all about being a living testimony. Missional outreach is therefore organic – all of our lives, words and deeds are missionary – so reaching out to people is equally organic in a missional church.

Conventional churches seek to reach people for Christ who will then become assimilated and integrated into their congregations; missional churches, on the other hand, seek to integrate people into God's kingdom and involve them in his work on earth. Such churches acknowledge their interdependence with the world.[14] Church is not built *for* but *with* people;

---

14. Frazee, 203.

and they are not *confronted* with God's truth but taken into a culture and environment which is *permeated* by the gospel.

Any church based on programmes will face various difficulties. According to McNeal's studies, there is a close connection between the rise of programme-oriented churches in the US and the American idea of *feasibility* as postulated by post-war capitalism.[15] Just think of all the refined teachings on church growth that have kept Christians in the Western world busy ever since 1955. Yet as the Western world faces crisis after crisis, and as more and more people are coming to doubt the feasibility of economic growth and social success, the more people are starting to question programme-oriented approaches to church growth.

Missional churches, in contrast, are about people, not church programmes; they "invest in a church culture supporting people,"[16] which shows in different emphases and targets. McNeal discerns the following seven characteristics that demonstrate the differences between these two approaches:[17]

1. *Customer Reference (Targets v. People)*. The average church seeks to apply standard teaching material and uniform spiritual training programmes, while missional churches seek to support individual people to discover their specific giftings, callings and ministries. As far as evangelism is concerned, traditional outreach follows a linear strategy in which we can tick off certain steps that are followed point by point. It seems that the same method and strategy is more than good enough as all people are the same: as sinners, they are all lost and need to be saved. In contrast, missional evangelism regards people as individuals with specific stories, needs and personal sins. Here, it is not about a three-step plan but introducing people to a kingdom environment full of God's grace and truth. This way, people experience the gospel with their bodies, souls and minds. This missional approach is organic and individual, and it may happen best when homes are open to others. Within the family, people share their lives and thus may experience the changes that the gospel has brought about in the lives of other family members.

2. *Manifestation of Life (Rules v. Life)*. Conventional churches put the emphasis on rules that need to be followed. We are good Christians

---

15. McNeal, *Missional Renaissance*, 92.
16. McNeal, 94.
17. McNeal, 95–110.

when we behave according to church doctrine. Christianity is measured by moral standards and our faith is judged by our behaviour. Everybody in church knows right from wrong and how to behave accordingly. Christians with such backgrounds who visit my church in search of a new fellowship might ask me, "What's allowed in your church? And what's forbidden?" In contrast, missional churches are all about manifesting Jesus in their lives – which touches ethical and moral questions too, but here the key focus is on our personal potential to become like Christ and not just on our moral behaviour. Each one of us is to mature and attain the full measure of the fullness of Christ (Eph 4:13–17). So the focus is not on our sin – our mistakes and misbehaviour – but on the positive possibilities, our potential life, according to the gospel. And the gospel is good news, not condemning news. Why not preach this gospel by reaching out to the world with our arms open wide, instead of wagging our fingers at people and pointing out their sins? This is not about hiding sin; but evangelism either will focus on God's law and judgment alone, relying on preaching and teaching lectures as the main tool and taking place in crusade tents and public halls; or it will mainly preach about God's mercy and grace, relying on testimonies and relationships in the context of our everyday lives – which again makes the family the best setting for missional outreach.

3. *How We Mature (Programmes v. Intimacy).* Conventional churches want their members to take part in the programmes they offer. The congregation receives lectures and teaching on how to live good lives as Christians – and it's hard work. If we want to belong to such a church, we need to prove ourselves first. And our spiritual maturity and growth will be measured by the degree to which we adapt ourselves to the lifestyle of the church. In contrast, missional churches want their members to grow in Christ and in their personal relationship with God. Here, Christians rely on the truth that an intimate relationship with Jesus will bring forth a fruitful life automatically and progressively. Spiritual maturity and growth will be measured by personal intimacy with God. Conventional churches focus on how to follow the rules of faith and behaviour – people talk a lot *about* God and *hear* a lot of Bible verses; while missional churches put the emphasis on a life guided individually by the Holy Spirit – people will talk *to* God and *listen* to his Spirit who teaches

them when and how to apply the Bible in their lives. Conventional outreach is a religious duty and a chore, while missional outreach is simply the expression of life.

4. *How We Act (Instruction v. Conviction).* Christians in conventional churches become active by following instructions – they take part in outreaches and programmes once in a while and then go back to life. Missional Christians, on the other hand, act intentionally out of inner conviction – they will naturally do what they are gifted for and live outreach as a daily way of life.

5. *Life Focus (Legality v. Relationship).* Conventional churches love catalogues of *the* truth, and life as a Christian is about fulfilling a spiritual curriculum. For missional churches, however, truth is based on a personal relationship with Jesus and is rooted in love, which makes a Christian's life grow both in truth and in love (1 John 1:1). Conventional evangelism will therefore emphasize the laws of a life with God, giving lectures about such life in big halls and special outreach venues. In contrast, missional churches put the emphasis on the love relationship between God and human beings, accompanying people in their daily lives, which makes evangelistic outreach something that happens in everyday life – that is, in the family.

6. *Ministry Focus (Ministries v. Learning by Doing).* Conventional churches train and prepare people for later ministry, hence we start to serve or do a particular ministry only when we have demonstrated enough academic knowledge, practical competence and moral or personal maturity. The focus is on our willingness to serve God and on fulfilling our duties. In contrast, missional Christians learn by doing; they grow and mature while serving others. Missional churches call people to serve God while reaching out to the world, just as the apostle Paul described the Christians of Thessalonica doing (1 Thess 1:9).

7. *Integration (Compartmentalization v. Integration).* Conventional churches tend to compartmentalize life: everyday business and church are two completely different spaces. As Martin Luther taught us five hundred years ago, we are subjects of the world order on the one hand, and members of the church on the other hand. Another example is the compartmentalization of church programmes into

different age groups. In contrast, missional churches have a holistic approach: all our life is an integral part of our mission; and all family members (may) get involved in Sunday services, projects and meetings. Therefore, conventional evangelism will rely on words (proclaiming the gospel verbally), while missional outreach includes all areas of life (relying on integration).

McNeal's characterization is helpful. Yet I want to complete this list with another important aspect – Sunday services. The church service is central to church life for most congregations, so it must be central for mission too. Evangelism, in turn, reflects the nature of a church. In the missional approach, any church member is a missionary and anything that happens in and through the church is evangelistic. In conventional churches, however, Sunday services are primarily conventions for all members in order to nurture believers. "Today we are going to have a guest preacher who will serve *us*," you might hear someone say. In contrast, missional services want to serve God and the people who don't yet know him. German pastor and author Bernd Schlottoff is right in demanding that missionary churches make their Sunday services inspiring for everyone.[18] Indeed, church services may play a central role for people who do not yet know Jesus. Any missional church should have services which aim to serve outsiders first, as German doctor of theology Christian Schwark says. This is how church will "[get] closer to missional church services (missional worship?)"[19] – in other words, closer to "celebrat[ing] service in the presence of the world."[20]

Of course, it is unfair to directly compare different systems like this because we overlook important details and nuances. Therefore, any average church reading this would be right to disagree with such a black-and-white, superficial judgment. I'm sure some "traditional" churches are far more missional than some "missional" churches. Yet this rough and even critical classification does allow us to see tendencies among churches. The point we want to make here is simply that the family is significant for any missional church life. Local churches that aspire to the missional outlook as characterized above need to organically create room for their families, as those families will become the

---

18. Bernd Schlottoff, *Ein Traum von der Gemeinde: Mut zum missionarischen Gemeindebau* (Wuppertal: SCM Brockhaus, 2011), 47.

19. Christian Schwark, *Gottesdienste für Kirchendistanzierte: Auf dem Weg zum missionalen Gottesdienst* (Schwarzenfeld: Neufeld Verlag, 2006).

20. I have written a whole book on this topic: Johannes Reimer, *Gott in der Welt feiern: Auf dem Weg zum missionalen Gottesdienst*, 2nd ed. (Schwarzenfeld: Neufeld Verlag, 2011).

most important agents in the missional ministries of their churches. Catholic author Mitch Finley quotes an American pastor who once told him, "Our church either is a family consisting of families or it is just a bunch of people showing their religious feelings (getting religious and emotional?) once a week."[21] Such a "bunch" is neither attractive nor influential in society.

The Family on the Mission of Christ's Church

While we have seen that the family should play a key role in missional churches, the reality looks quite different in many churches around the globe. Unfortunately, families have in some cases become a problem and even an obstacle to local evangelism and outreach. Experts who have been exploring mission ministries and church-planting projects note with great concern that when missionaries and pastors fail, it's mostly because of their family situations. Therefore they increasingly warn that prospective missionaries should not take their families out into the mission field without adequate preparation. Aubrey Malphurs, a US expert on church planting, states, "Whenever the family of a prospective church planter does not stand behind his vision, it might not be God's will for him to plant a church."[22] J. D. Payne, professor of Christian ministry at Samford University, underlines this argument, pointing to studies in the USA that show that pastors' families are the major cause of stress within their ministries of church planting.[23]

It leads to huge problems if families are not prepared for their specific mission and if they think that mission is just for some of their members and not for the rest. For then the family's great missional potential, as discussed so far, becomes the very problem – for the families themselves and for mission.

In contrast, it is a great source of blessing when families are prepared for their missional role, when they know their responsibility and when missionaries and couples understand that their families are an integral part of their mission and ministries.[24] Hence, Payne calls for family-related training for those who are called to mission or who are about to plant churches.[25]

---

21. Mitch Finley, "A Family Ecclesiology," *America* 149 (30 July 1983): 50.

22. Aubrey Malphurs, *Planting Churches for the 21st Century*, 3rd ed. (Grand Rapids, MI: Baker, 2004), 91.

23. J. D. Payne, *Discovering Church Planting: An Introduction to the Whats, Whys, and Hows of Global Church Planting* (Colorado Springs/Milton Keynes/Hyderabad: Paternoster, 2009), 297–298.

24. Payne, *Discovering Church Planting*, 103.

25. Payne, 302.

While family and mission belong to each other and the family is the key agent in God's mission, this mission doesn't happen automatically. Churches that want to have an active part in God's mission need to prepare their families accordingly. If they don't, those families will soon become an obstacle to missional church life. Statements like the following are familiar: "I'm sorry I can't be part of this because my family is so demanding at the moment." Pastors, missional teams and groups who are about to plant churches often desperately seek extra hands, but reconciling our family lives and ministries has become a problem today, especially in the Western world. Why is this? Don't we trust that if God is calling us, he will provide for us and bless us? Why then do we struggle to integrate our family lives into our calling and our reaching out to the world? Do we have wrong ideas about mission and outreach? Are we ill prepared as families? Or have we not understood the interrelationship of church mission and family ministry?

A Church of Families

Recognizing this close interrelationship of family and church, it became clear to Catholic priest Gerald Foley that any Christian church has to be thought of and built in relation to the family. Consequently, he changed his own church ministry radically so that he focused only on the family. This focus led to drastic changes in both church life and church growth. Foley even speaks of a paradigm shift in church growth whenever a local church decides to become family-based. He speaks of six key areas that need to be radically changed and transformed in the Catholic context.[26]

First, the *role of laymen* will have to change: believers may not be considered as passive recipients any longer but must be viewed as active participants in the mission of the church and the churches. To Foley, there is no alternative for dealing with the vast range of tasks within a church aligned to parish families and their needs. Thus, every church member is essential for the success of this family project – just as in a real family where each member counts and has a share in the family's success. All members are important: men and women, adults and children alike.

Second, the *role of the parish church* will have to be amended: the church itself no longer has the most importance, nor its building and ministries; rather, what matters is the families living there, and their growth and health. Hence the

---

26. Gerald Foley, *Family-Centred Church: A New Parish Model* (Kansas City, MO: Sheed & Ward, 1995), 7–8.

church loses its self-sufficiency; it is no longer an end in itself. Church is church because it has a calling, a task to fulfil: namely, to reach its community – the families living in the neighbourhood – the society and the world.

Third, Foley talks about *spirituality* that needs to change. Conventional churches focus on personal faith and individual spiritual growth, but when a church is based on family work the emphasis will be on relationships throughout different generations, which will affect the people's spirituality, becoming a common experience and thus gaining social depth. Transcendent faith aimed at eternity will become less prominent than the issues of our everyday lives. Families face challenges every day that need to be solved here and now. Life after death is also important, but it is not the central focus in a Christian family's life. If our goal is to grow healthy families we need a grounded spirituality and our faith has to be connected to our daily lives.

Fourth, it is about amending the *sacrament of matrimony*: this refers not just to the wedding ceremony but to married and family life throughout people's lives. The church ought not only to defend the canonical aspects of matrimony but also to care for marriages and shape healthy families. In this way, the church will grow closer to people and their needs and will become more Christlike – that is, an institution relevant to life.

Fifth, Foley underlines the *importance of sexuality* as an area that needs to be transformed: the focus should be not only on reproduction and sex but on a man and wife enjoying each other and taking responsibility for each other – caring for each other's well-being. Sexuality ought to become more relevant in social aspects, and we ought to emphasize responsible intercourse between men and women.

And lastly, Foley wants to see the *Sunday service* transformed: worship in a family-centred church is not, according to him, only about a weekly event with liturgies in a sacred building. A Sunday morning spent in a church building needs to be supplemented by worship within the four walls of our private homes; the latter might even be preferred to the former.

These and similar changes are inevitable if we take Foley's concept of FCC (family-centred church) seriously. In such a FCC we will test our programmes and ministries to see whether they serve the ultimate goal of growing healthy families.[27] It is no secret today that any church leadership invests most of its energy and time in administration and programmes. In contrast, members *and* leaders of any FCC will invest most of their time and energy in families while paying attention to individuals as significant parts of the family. Hence,

---

27. Foley, *Family-Centred Church*, 10.

individual needs and problems are dealt with, not in an isolated approach, but in the context of family relations. In this way, fellowship is nurtured, and people build bridges between the generations and take responsibility for each other. In other words, it is the central focus on the family that enables church planting, church growth and true fellowship.[28]

While Foley was referring to a parish church in a strong traditional denomination, when we probe into his arguments we see that much of what he says holds true for any other church as well. Even if our theologies, doctrines or focus might differ at times, we all have to acknowledge that most of our churches need to change their structures and settings. By exploring this interrelationship of family and mission we will come to the conclusion that "churches have to make every effort to strengthen marriages and families"[29] – in church and in society.

Questions for Reflection

1. What do you think about the interrelationship of family and church?
2. What is the church's responsibility towards the family?
3. What is the family's responsibility towards the church?
4. In what respect are family-centred churches (FCC) responsible for the world?
5. What needs to change if a church aspires to be missional?
6. What should the church setting and the interaction between churches and their families look like in order for them to become missional families?
7. How should preachers teach and preach so that people are inspired to become a missional church and missional families?

---

28. Foley, 28.
29. Andreas J. Köstenberger and David W. Jones, *God, Marriage, and Family: Rebuilding the Biblical Foundation*, 2nd rev. ed. (Wheaton, IL: Crossway, 2010), 257.

5

Growing Family-Centred Churches

Church, Evangelism and Family

> The church is nothing but an organ, it is the agent of proclaiming the good news of the kingdom of God. In other words, church is everything that serves this promulgation, for only then is church, church – its very existence is a *proclaiming existence*: it follows its historical role to preach the gospel, thus continuing God's revelations to the world. We have to bear in mind though that preaching the gospel does not mean verbal promulgation only. That's why I say "proclaiming *existence.*" Because it is not about uttering words to people but passing on the Life itself that God has given to us.[1]

Here we see clearly, in the words of Emil Brunner, that the church has no option other than to reach out to the world, to preach the gospel and to pass on the life we have received from God. Church is a "community of proclamation,"[2] the "translator and interpreter of the gospel"[3] and "God's agent of evangelism."[4] As Anglican vicar John Stott said, "We can easily recognize that evangelism through the local church is the simplest, the most authentic and the most

---

1. Emil Brunner, *Die Christliche Lehre von der Kirche, dem Glauben und der Vollendung* (Zurich: Zwingli, 1964), 17.

2. Michael Marshall, *The Gospel Connection: A Study in Evangelism for the Nineties* (London: Darton, Longman & Todd, 1991), 117.

3. Michael Herbst, *Deine Gemeinde komme: Wachstum und Gottes Verheißungen*, 2nd ed. (Holzgermingen: Hänssler, 2008), 53.

4. David Watson, *I Believe in Evangelism* (London: Hodder & Stoughton, 1976), 135.

effective method of spreading the gospel."[5] Everything in church should be submitted to God's Great Commission. Outreach is the DNA of all churches and therefore the DNA of their members. Hence, all families in a church contribute to God's mission for their church.

According to Roland Hardmeier, the church is the "laboratory for a new humanity."[6] Christ's church truly is the *familia Dei* – God's family – in the real sense of the word.[7] Jesus builds his family within, through and in his church, which does not abolish the biological and natural families we've been raised in. On the contrary, our families become basic units of the *familia Dei* manifest on earth. And the church starts with the family, which is God's ideal of life and his role model for the church. Indeed, every Christian family reflects the church in all aspects. It is the family that spreads the gospel and shines the light to all people.[8]

Therefore, it makes sense to reflect on evangelism from the family's perspective, for the family is the primary target and the primary agent of all evangelism. Whenever churches want to reach out to the world, they should first reach out to and through their church families.[9] And this will only be possible within a particular church culture.

The Culture of Relationships

If churches want to reach out to the world they need to know themselves and understand their own identity.[10] All churches live according to a particular culture, and it is this church culture that will determine why and how Christians do what they do and are who they are. Our culture sets the parameters for our actions and our mission. There is nothing more basic than the culture of

---

5. John R. W. Stott, "Evangelism through the Local Church," in *One Gospel, Many Clothes: Anglicans and the Decade of Evangelism*, ed. Chris Wright and Chris Sugden (London: Regnum, 1990), 14.

6. Roland Hardmeier, *Geliebte Welt: Auf dem Weg zu einem neuen missionarischen Paradigma* (Schwarzenfeld: Neufeld Verlag, 2012), 234.

7. Michael Nazir-Ali, *From Everywhere to Everywhere: A World View of Christian Mission* (London: Collins, 1990), 186.

8. *EN* 71.

9. For this consequence that the family is the first among many important target groups, see Scott Dawson, *The Complete Evangelism Guidebook: Expert Advice on Reaching Others for Christ* (Grand Rapids, MI: Baker, 2006), 113–117.

10. Stott, "Evangelism," 15. Stott recommends that churches carry out surveys to identify their image and current culture.

a church as it reflects its very essence and personality.[11] In fact, every social entity relies on having a particular identity. Thus, it is a serious error not to understand the specific identity of our own church, or even to neglect it. The culture of our church will show in the kind of leadership we have, in the part church members play in church life, in the songs and music styles we cultivate, in the manner we pray, and so on.

Of course, we are not always conscious of the specific culture within our congregations. Often, we only become aware of it when visitors are puzzled by particular aspects of it. Yet being unaware of our particular church culture can become a problem when we reach out to people, as our culture can at times be a major obstacle to mission and evangelism. This is especially the case when our church culture differs greatly from our home culture. This way we lose our authenticity – and our credibility as a consequence – for people will not believe our testimonies.

In contrast, family-centred missional churches will explicitly cultivate a culture of relationships. Well-known British evangelist David Watson once said simply about a gospel lifestyle: "The essence of evangelism is developing new relationships."[12] Thus, our church life and culture will have to rely on relationships, especially if the family, being a tapestry of relationships, is the primary agent of mission. So any family-centred church will primarily depend on its networks and relationships as it is home and family and supports anything to do with family life.

Of course, this culture of relationships must not be selfish and self-sufficient. Churches should not be nurturing good friendships and fellowships only among their members; we're talking about missional culture, which means a culture that is rooted in the mission of the church – the *missia ecclesiae* – that is, a "culture of outreach."[13] Such a culture is first committed to God's Great Commission, and it shapes and organizes church primarily as the agent of God's mission, reaching out to its surroundings in any form and through any means.[14] Church members of a missional culture regard themselves as missionaries – and indeed, each one is a missionary. Therefore, all families are missional, as we saw earlier: the world around them will always be the centre of their attention, and the focus will lie outside, not inside, the church. In other

---

11. Philip Jinadu and David Lawrence, *Winning Ways: Creating a Culture of Outreach in Your Church* (London: Authentic, 2007), 16.
12. Watson, *I Believe in Evangelism*, 137.
13. Jinadu and Lawrence, *Winning Ways*, 28.
14. Jinadu and Lawrence, 20–26.

words, the church is God's family for all of us, including everyone outside. Hence, every family within a local church is a role model and testimony to the people around. Every family is a manifestation of God's special offer to renew and heal the family.

Such missional churches will cultivate a "welcome culture,"[15] which means a culture where everyone receives a warm welcome and will be seen and heard. No one is left out, no one is alone. Everyone will get a helping hand when in need. And people will be supported to reclaim their dignity and respect as given by God, no matter what background they come from. Above all, it is families with open homes, true love and hospitality that create this culture and atmosphere within a church. In short, hospitality is the trademark of any welcome culture. This was seen in the early church: the first Christians would receive strangers in their homes, they would feed and support the poor and they would always have their tables filled with good food for everyone, especially the hungry and needy. It was this hospitality which was the key factor in spreading the gospel so successfully.[16]

Today is no different. I remember once, when invited to speak at a Bible week in an evangelical Lutheran church in central Germany, Sister Christa proudly told me: "When people visit us they always enjoy being here." Soon I found out this Sister was in charge of the church's kitchen. When she put a wonderful bowl of cheese soup in front of me, I answered her: "Sure, the food is delicious too!" Her reply hit the nail on the head: "That's how it's got to be, Mr Reimer. There's no way around good food, because the way to a man's heart is through his stomach. In that respect, all people are the same. No matter whether they believe in God or not, people will decide to come back again when they have been served good food. And I assure you, they come back again here!" And with a joyful giggle she returned to the kitchen. David Watson makes the same point, even going a step farther, when he claims, "I believe that evangelism will only develop from a healthy body."[17]

When we observe churches carrying out outreaches over a long period of time, we notice certain changes in their evangelistic practice: evangelism will change from being a single event to a process. Outreach is no longer about a programme or special event; instead, we come across small groups where

---

15. For more on this, see Johannes Reimer, *Hereinspaziert: Willkommenskultur und Evangelisation* (Schwarzenfeld: Neufeld Verlag, 2013).

16. Watson, *I Believe in Evangelism*, 138.

17. Watson, 137.

faith is discussed over a period of time.[18] The point to such small groups is not to preach and listen to monologues but to enter into dialogue with those who are seeking for relevant answers to questions that arise in daily life. The main focus will be on finding a new identity (in Christ) rather than in seeking the absolute truth.[19] Thus it seems that people gain access to faith not via the right doctrine but by experiencing spirituality,[20] which usually doesn't happen through discussion but by sharing our lives.[21]

Structures Are Important

Life looks different in different churches and is organized in different ways. Family-centred churches need structures that allow individual families to be hospitable and successful missional units within the community.[22] In such churches the life cycle of the family (see figure 2.2 in chapter 2) will determine the life and programmes of the church. Churches should at least "try to understand this life cycle and take that as a framework to plan their ministries through and for the family."[23] This cycle has the potential to become the main factor in shaping and structuring the mission work of a missional church as human existence is inextricably linked to it: the seasons of life are known universally. Who does not enjoy the festivity of a wedding when two people express their deep mutual love for each other? Who is not enchanted at the sight of a newborn baby? Who does not lament when hearing about a marriage breakdown, children losing their parents or a beloved family member passing away? Of course, different cultures have different rituals and expressions for celebrating and mourning, yet we are all familiar with this cycle of life. Hence, it makes sense to make this the basis for the structure of a family-centred missional church.

---

18. For examples of this, see Robert Warren, *Signs of Life: How Goes the Decade of Evangelism?* (London: Church House, 1996), 65–70. Warren explored half a decade of outreaches in Great Britain, observing that evangelism had changed from inviting people to single events to inviting them into small groups to discuss issues of faith.

19. Warren, *Signs of Life*, 73.

20. Warren, 69.

21. Warren, 75.

22. Nazir-Ali, *From Everywhere*, 187.

23. Lausanne Committee for World Evangelization, "Non-Traditional Families: Reaching Families with the Good News," Lausanne Occasional Paper (LOP) 36, in *A New Vision, a New Heart, a Renewed New Call: Lausanne Occasional Papers*, ed. David Claydon (Pasadena, CA: William Carey Library, 2005), 480.

The Family Is Mission's Core Concern

As the church, God's agent of evangelism, is his family for all to see and experience, the family is of great concern to God. So the family ought to be of the utmost concern for any Christian mission! As we have seen, whenever the early church proclaimed the gospel, whole families were led to Christ and became the starting point for spiritual awakening throughout the Roman Empire. This should be possible today too!

But like no other social institution, the family has entered a state of crisis. Reinhold Ruthe, a German therapist, speaks of "family chaos."[24] Many families have broken away from God's original plan for the family, which has brought them under the "curse of sin," and this curse is passed on from generation to generation.[25] Research in Germany shows that conflict within family life and broken homes have become the norm.[26] Many parents today feel insecure about their role and responsibility and unsure of the right way to raise their children.[27] If we want to reach this world with the good news we should focus on the family because the destruction of our homes causes the whole of society to collapse.

Therefore every local church has a responsibility to strengthen the family first. Some helpful programmes already exist: for example, Focus on the Family founded by James C. Dobson, US author, family therapist and psychologist, is a family ministry that helps and encourages families. It offers a programme called "Family Builders" which is based on Deuteronomy 6 and aims to strengthen families in line with biblical principles in order for them to live in fellowship and to raise their children in godly and healthy ways. This programme has been officially recommended by the Lausanne Consultation on Evangelism.[28] One of its great ideas is for a "family night," a special evening for families organized at local church venues.

Indeed, families learn best from and together with other families. Consequently, it's a good idea to build family "clusters" in our churches

---

24. Reinhold Ruthe, *Familie – Oase oder Chaos: Wege aus der Familienkrise* (Moers: Brendow Verlag, 1991).

25. Jeff Van Vonderen, *Familien: Von Gott getragen* (Asslar: Projektion J., 1996), 13–70.

26. Allensbach Institut, *Familienstudie 2013* (Wuppertal: Vorwerk, 2013), 36–44.

27. See the AOK study by the Sinus Institut Berlin: AOK, *Familienstudie 2014* (Berlin: AOK, 2014), 28–29.

28. LOP 36, 477.

consisting of different families who meet together on a regular basis for fellowship and friendship. Singles and single parents are also welcome to join.[29]

Any church – no matter which denomination or which local situation – would do well to more consistently include the family in its programmes and services, starting with an intentional warm welcome of families on Sunday mornings and continuing with family worship, special family afternoons or evenings, family retreats, and so on.

Susanne's story illustrates this concept. She came to seek my pastoral counsel as she wanted to leave her husband and father of their two children. Through tears she told me, "Things are really bad at home. We're in trouble. My husband keeps humiliating me and the kids have watched our terrible arguments far too often. How will they ever have good marriages themselves?" For a long time she had resisted even thinking of divorce, but now she knew they couldn't go on like this. I asked her why she had stayed with her husband for so long and was surprised by her answer: "I don't know. Maybe it's in our family. My granny got divorced, my mum divorced my dad, now it seems to be my turn. Isn't this normal?" But not at all! It is never "normal" when a marriage fails. Obviously, in this case there were powers at work that went far beyond the broken relationship between Susanne and her husband Peter. I asked Susanne whether she had ever heard about the possibility of a potential generational curse. I also met with Peter for talks, and we prayed a lot together. In the end, chains were broken and their family was healed. The couple joined a family cluster in church and got further coaching and counselling. Today, they are a happy family, committed to their local church.

The Family – Mission Agent Number One

The Christian family is one of the best instruments for mission and evangelism,[30] having potential in evangelism that other groups cannot even dream of.[31] Basically, to reach families is the heart of any church life. For both family life and church life are intended to engage in God's family and to manifest the good news of Christ – both are about showing and sharing love in everyday life, rough as it can be at times. Rightly, missiologists and theologians speak

---

29. For more on family clusters, see Barbara Vance, *Planning and Conducting Family Cluster: Education for Family Wellness* (Newbury Park, CA: Sage, 1989).

30. James Dobson, "Keys to a Family Friendly Church," *Leadership* 7, no. 1 (1986): 19.

31. A. Grace Wenger and Dave and Neta Jackson, *Witness: Empowering the Church through Worship, Community and Mission* (Scottdale, PA: Herald, 1989), 142.

of "household evangelism."³² "Household" in this context does not refer only to one family but to any community sharing life under one roof, which goes back to the biblical concept of *oikos*. Household evangelism follows in the footsteps of the early Christians who worshipped and preached the gospel in private homes.³³ They opened their homes for outreach, inviting outsiders and friends alike to come – and even to move in and share life. This soon led to the development of trustworthy homes and communities that became spaces where Christians would *share* and *be* a testimony for their Lord.

Mark R. Gornik, author and church founder, has probably invested more in missionary church planting in inner cities than anyone else. He speaks of three dimensions of church life: God's kingdom life, everyday life and testimonial life,³⁴ referring to all aspects of the lives of all church members. Each one among them is important for the testimony of the whole church they belong to. All Christians are able to share the gospel – some with their lives, some with their deeds, and some even with their refined words. That's how the church becomes an "informative community."³⁵ Only this way can the church be truly missional and a "church seen in the market place."³⁶

Arnell Motz, member of the Faculty of Bethel Seminary, studied the reasons for church growth in Canada. He found that the churches growing the fastest are those that have consciously chosen to "present and proclaim the gospel" as their main evangelistic methods.³⁷

Wise evangelists will approach people with caution and care and preach the gospel either directly or indirectly, depending on their readiness to receive the truth. If mission aims to really be relevant to society and effective in the market place it will follow what I call a "society-relevant cycle."³⁸ This cycle invites people to observe the lives of Christians before explaining Christianity

---

32. Robert D. Runyon, "Principles and Methods of Household Evangelism," in *Vital Missions Issues: Examining Challenges and Changes in World Evangelization*, ed. Roy B. Zuck (Grand Rapids, MI: Kregel, 1998), 218–227.

33. Michael Green, *Evangelism through the Local Church* (London: Hodder & Stoughton, 1990), 194–228; Runyon, "Principles and Methods," 219–220.

34. Mark Gornik, *To Live in Peace: Biblical Faith and the Changing Inner City* (Grand Rapids, MI: Eerdmans, 2002), 65–95.

35. Herbst, *Deine Gemeinde komme*, 71.

36. Herbst, 65.

37. Arnell Motz, "How Churches Are Doing Evangelism," in *Reclaiming a Nation: The Challenge of Evangelizing Canada in the Year 2000* (Richmond, BC: Church Leadership Library, 1990), 180.

38. For more on this, see Johannes Reimer, *Leben, Rufen, Verändern: Theologie der gesellschaftstransformierenden Evangelisation* (Marburg: Francke Verlag, 2013), 239–245.

to them. Author Jim Petersen confirms that "Conversion is a step-by-step process."[39] When we acknowledge evangelism and mission to be such a process, we recognize its cycles, ranging from presenting and manifesting the gospel only indirectly, through to more active approaches, depending on the situation, to direct and clear proclaiming and preaching. Belgian evangelist Johan Lukasse compares this process to the cultivation of an agricultural field. First you've got to plough the land, then you sow the right seeds, then you care for the plants while they grow; and it is only after all those months of work that you might reap a harvest.[40] Whenever you shortcut this process it will harm or even destroy the harvest. And if you reap too early, you will only get crude, unripe and sour fruit which nobody will be able to eat.

Growing Faith

Healthy families are the very place where our faith can grow because, as we saw in chapter 3, it is there where we live in close contact and relationships that we find innumerable opportunities for our faith to manifest itself in real life. Jeff Van Vonderen refers to this when talking about "the world of learning and working" and "the realm of education and social contact,"[41] distinguishing between different values and priorities for different families. Families that successfully reach their communities display spiritual health and possess specific qualities essential for their mission. US evangelist Scott Dawson speaks of love being the key prerequisite for evangelizing any community as love is the most important constant in human relationships.[42] Peter Cha, Professor of Pastoral Theology (Illinois), and Greg Jao, US author, President of InterVarsity Christian Fellowship, see the following three attributes as key to an effective evangelistic community: treating one another mercifully, always supporting one another to the best of one's ability and, above all, being rooted in God's Word.[43] Many biblical characteristics are vital to successful missional families, the following five probably being the most important:

---

39. Jim Petersen, *Living Proof: Sharing the Gospel Naturally* (Colorado Springs, CO: NavPress, 1989), 147.

40. Johann Lukasse and Ted Kamp, *Divide and Multiply* (Hasseln: European Church Planting Consultation, 2010), 89.

41. Van Vonderen, *Familien*, 106.

42. Dawson, *Evangelism Guidebook*, 114–116.

43. Peter Cha and Greg Jao, "Reaching out to Postmodern Asian Americans," in *Telling the Truth: Evangelizing Postmoderns*, ed. D. A. Carson (Grand Rapids, MI: Zondervan, 2000), 233–240.

- Love as the source of any relationship;
- Faith and trust as the motivation for any relationship;
- Hope and grace as the operating principles of any relationship;
- Fellowship and dialogue as the lifestyle of any relationship; and
- God's Word as the foundation of any relationship.

Love as the Source of Any Relationship

Actually, family only exists because there is love: where people love each other, when two hearts and lives connect, then there is family. And God intended the family to be full of love. It is this love within a family that shows God's character, for God is love (1 John 4:7).

When Christians are on mission they make God's love known to people. That's why Jesus became flesh: for God so *loved* the world (John 3:16). It is God's love that is the good news for the world and, consequently, it is his love that makes evangelism make sense. His love reaches out to people who do not know him, do not want him and do not love him – indeed, even hate him, like those who nailed him to the cross. "Greater love has no one than this: to lay down one's life for one's friends" (John 15:13). Love is the source of mission and love always wants the best for everybody. Such love will find ways to people's hearts, building friendship and trust. And such love opens ears to hear the truth and facilitates the willingness to obey. When we are loved it is easier for us to be open to correction, counsel and commendation, for love catches our attention and opens the door to change.

When families are full of love – full of God's love for the world around them – their homes become places where people encounter God's love. Certainly, it is not always easy to love one another and our neighbour. At times, it's hardest to love our family members. Parents sometimes have to decide to love their disobedient, rebellious children, and we all know stories of parents who fail to love their children, let alone their neighbours. This is where Christian families are better off. For our Father in heaven wants to give us the love we don't have, and he gives abundantly. Our God is able to overcome our hatred and heal our disappointed hearts. And true love that can be seen and touched is one of the greatest qualities of a family that belongs to God's kingdom. Where we meet real love, God is close. And where we find an atmosphere of love we see people motivated to serve and care for their neighbours in need. So any family ministry in church will put the emphasis on love as it is the source of missional families and the foundation for all Christian mission.

Faith and Trust as the Motivation for Any Relationship

Where people love each other, they also trust each other. The family is a well-defined social unit where people love, believe and trust each other. From the very first moment of our lives, we learn within our families how to live with other people, how to support and like each other, how to get along and how to love each other. The family is naturally about trust. Within families, even rejection and exclusion come to an end somehow. Certainly, we might struggle in the family – maybe *above all* in our families; we might rebel and protest against anything new or unknown. And non-conforming members of any social group, including families, may be punished or marginalized; this also holds true when family members give their lives to Jesus. Yet even the strangest religious family member remains part of his or her family! In the end, the blood bond will be stronger than any other. Our family is the natural setting to keep trusting more than anywhere else. Therefore it's in the family, unlike in any other social institution, that we keep seeking to understand each other and hesitate to jeopardize our relationships.

Mission and evangelism is only possible in an atmosphere of trust, where people allow us to tell them the good news. Any outreach will only be successful as long as people can trust us; it will fail when their trust is broken. Only when people are able to trust will they be open to the gospel. In his book *Permission Evangelism: When to Talk, When to Walk*,[44] US author Michael L. Simson says that evangelism is only possible when those we want to reach give us permission to do so.[45] And nowhere will we get this permission as easily as in our family, where we've been trusting each other from early childhood. And yet these natural patterns of confidence need to be stretched and strengthened. Just as children need to be stretched to trust beyond their family – trusting their close community, their society and even the "strangers out there" – so even Christian families need to be stretched in trusting. For churches as well as their families have lost trust in society, and society has lost trust in the church: for most people, churches are no longer trustworthy. The average Christian family will need training and spiritual edification to be able to win back people's trust. So a missionary church will put an emphasis on being trustworthy and on creating an atmosphere of trust in its family ministries.

---

44. Michael L. Simson, *Permission Evangelism: When to Talk, When to Walk* (Colorado Springs, CO: NexGen, 2003).

45. Simson, *Permission Evangelism*, 80.

Hope and Grace as the Operating Principles of Any Relationship

Even within Christian families, trust can sometimes be breached and broken. Even here, we might be betrayed or disappointed by our loved ones. However, these failures don't necessarily lead to discord and brokenness, as we know how to overcome conflict by applying God's grace. Hence, wherever we love, grace must also be found because love is selfless and seeks the best for everyone. We know that love always hopes, always perseveres, and so on (1 Cor 13). British author Michael Marshall describes an "environment of grace" as the natural setting for evangelism.[46] He finds such environments in local churches – without referring explicitly to the family, though. Yet any church is part of the *familia Dei* which in turn consists of families who have been transformed by Christ. So church is a fellowship of people who know God's grace as well as his mandate to love one another and to care for each other. Marshall speaks of an "obligation to counsel and care for our neighbor," and he finds this a necessary attribute of an evangelistic church.[47]

Especially within shame-oriented cultures, healthy and redeemed family structures will quickly and widely open the doors for the gospel. For within such cultures any fault or offence means losing one's honour – and this breach must be punished and settled to restore the honour of the family again. Therefore any family that has learned to speak about guilt and confront transgressions by *forgiving* has a powerful and attractive testimony, with great potential to reach people with the gospel.[48] In other words, we need to discern problems due to this shame orientation within our church families and we need to commit ourselves to implementing grace orientation instead. Equally, mission experts exploring shame-oriented cultures recognize grace as the key and shame as one of the main hindrances to mission. There are still too many churches – and consequently too many families – caught up in shame.[49]

When we love, God's grace opens our eyes to the future as well. When grace has turned into an operating principle within our family, we will also have hope for the future, for we know that nobody will give up, nobody will be abandoned. And although we know our shortcomings will not be swept under the carpet and our wrongdoings will be confronted, we also know that our sins and mistakes will not be the end of our relationships. Whoever has

---

46. Marshall, *Gospel Connection*, 81.
47. Marshall, 85.
48. Cha and Jao, "Reaching Out," 234.
49. Kenneth Fong, *Insights for Growing Asian-American Ministries* (Rosemead, CA: EverGrowing Publications, 1990), 93.

encountered God's compassion and grace knows him to be a God of hope too (Rom 5:1–5) and that anyone can become a new person "in Christ," for "the new creation has come: the old has gone, the new is here!" (2 Cor 5:17). It is within such fellowships of grace that new beginnings are possible and thus we will actually live the good news. Grace then becomes an operating principle among us. Consequently, any missional church will put the emphasis on grace within its family ministries, knowing that it is God's grace that opens the hearts of people and gives them the courage to join the church.

Fellowship and Dialogue as the Lifestyle of Any Relationship

Early church outreaches took place in the privacy of homes, bringing the gospel to whole families, and had its roots in a shared experience of God's glory.[50] Sharing experiences together was central. And nowhere else do we share our lives as closely as we do within our families: here, we share our experiences openly and naturally on a daily basis. We live in a kind of goldfish bowl, which quickly brings to the surface our real attitudes and behaviours. It is difficult to keep secrets, and our lives are quickly proven to be real or phoney. Here, we needn't *give* our testimonies, as our lives *are* a testimony for all to experience. Here within the family we know each other so well that any changes that aren't real are quickly recognized. I have often heard non-believers say about their relatives who have just found Christ: "I know my son/husband/wife. Let's see where this religious fancy leads to – I guess it won't take long. And I bet it won't make any difference as no one can change him/her." Such statements tell me a lot about a frustration that is probably not a recent issue. In contrast, when the impossible is happening – when someone really changes through Christ and the new faith does not fade away but grows – people become interested and are attracted to hear more. Thus, shared lives open the door for talking about and sharing the gospel.

In addition, the loss of fellowship and community is often connected to the loss of identity. In many cultures around the world, children and young people are not granted much influence or authority, which often contributes to their rebellion against their families and cultures when they get older. Such rebellion in turn causes deep personal identity crises. So our churches become highly attractive if our fellowships are less hierarchical and more "somatic" –

---

50. Marshall, *Gospel Connection*, 82.

that is, when we regard our communities as collectives as part of the body of Christ.[51] And families play a central role in this somatic approach.

However, there is an enormous need for us to grow in sharing life and in true fellowship. For example, instead of talking to each other we watch TV; instead of having face-to-face fellowship we stare at screens and swipe on our electronic devices. For the average Christian family, "fellowship" at most means eating dinner together. How can we be his witnesses that way? Therefore, missionary churches should support their families by helping them to grow socially and spiritually, which is a prerequisite for attractive evangelism.

God's Word as the Foundation of Any Relationship

Outreach is all about proclaiming and manifesting the gospel of Christ as we find it in Scripture. Whenever people have positive experiences of Christians and can link them to God's Word, the Bible will gain importance in their minds. Yet this is only possible when we as Christians know his Word well, when the Bible plays a central role in our everyday lives and is alive in our family rituals. It should be natural to ask for God's will first in our daily family lives – searching for it in his Word before looking anywhere else. Our children should be proud of having a Bible at home, which will give them the desire to read it and live by it. I remember once overhearing an interesting battle among boys in a schoolyard: each of them tried to outplay the others based on boasting of his father's possessions. Suddenly one boy said, "My dad has a lot of Bibles in different languages – he's got a whole collection. And I've got my own Bible too." Quickly this boy became the Bible expert among his classmates.

Any missionary church knows that people are ultimately convinced by God's Word. "For the word of God is alive and active. Sharper than any double-edged sword, it penetrates even to dividing soul and spirit, joints and marrow; it judges the thoughts and attitudes of the heart. Nothing in all creation is hidden from God's sight. Everything is uncovered and laid bare before the eyes of him to whom we must give account" (Heb 4:12–13). Thus, churches train their members and their families to read and apply God's Word in the midst of their daily lives. Families especially need support to be able to read God's Word at home together with translations suitable for their age groups, lives and needs. Missionary churches and family ministries will put the emphasis on adequate Bible study at home.

---

51. For the call for somatic fellowships, see Peter Cha's demands for such ministries among Korean students in the USA in Cha and Jao, "Reaching Out," 236.

These five attributes are key to reaching the world and fulfilling our calling, so it must be the key focus in churches to coach and pastor families in these areas – and in other areas too, offering, for example, marriage counselling, fellowship training, answers to educational issues, practical help when sharing house and home, leisure programmes, and so on. Any church that aims at equipping the saints should not take these family issues lightly but take pastoral responsibility for them. If we want to reach outsiders, if we want to change families, societies and nations, we must start with the insiders and pastor our families!

How Your Church Can Become a Family-Centred Evangelistic Church

In order for our churches to be those that reach whole families, we first need to take four main decisions, as defined by George W. Peters:

1. Understand and accept God's mandate and the biblical role model to reach whole families, and align our methods for outreach along that standard;
2. Focus our mission efforts on reaching and equipping our own families first;
3. Focus on ministering to parents;
4. Transfer our outreaches back into our private homes.[52]

I would add a fifth point:

5. Involve children in our mission, by both reaching out to them and empowering them to be missionaries in their own right.

We Need to Understand the Biblical Mandate

Churches will only invest time and money in missionary family ministries when they comprehend how central homes and families were in the mission of the early church as described in the New Testament. Indeed, for some churches, this will mean a paradigm shift in how they perceive evangelism to take place. We are in great danger of *"constructing"* our ideals about mission, as Bosch

---

52. George W. Peters, *Evangelisation: Total, durchdringend, umfassend* (Bad Liebenzell: VLM, 1977), 178–180.

once said so accurately.[53] When we allow our concepts to be stretched we soon see how important families are for outreach.

Some church historians are convinced that Christ's church grew so rapidly during the first centuries after Pentecost because of the authentic testimony of the early Christians – how they treated each other and their neighbours and how they cared for the poor and needy. Their good works spoke louder than their words. German Lutheran Carl G. A. von Harnack describes a "language of love"[54] spoken by Christians when reaching non-believers for the Lord. And German theologian Karl Hartenstein, who worked for an international mission ministry, defined mission as the "church's calling to witness."[55] This mandate to witness with our very lives applies to the Christian home, too, for it is here that we live most closely together, that we know one another better than anyone else, and that we recognize changes most quickly and in the most transparent way.

If we want to motivate churches for this kind of outreach and church families for family-focused mission we need to teach them from Scripture about the interrelationship between family and mission. This preaching and teaching about mission should be as practical as possible and as focused on the context and environment as necessary, yet it is from the Word of God itself that churches will receive new vision for their work. In other words, we need to adopt a new apostolic approach in our preaching to open eyes to God's original intentions for mission as outlined in the Bible.

Wherever church leaders pastor their flocks by teaching and preaching, such an apostolic approach must be a strategic process. And the teachings need clear goals – learning objectives – that might be reached through personal teaching one-on-one, small-group discussion, Sunday sermons or practical outreach. No matter how we teach our folk to motivate them to become missional, our strategy must be applicable and our goals verifiable.

Family Evangelism within the Mission Programmes of the Church

When churches adopt God's family-focused mission they first need to invest in their own families, for only healthy families can make a real difference in

---

53. David J. Bosch, *Ganzheitliche Mission* (Marburg: Francke Verlag, 2011), 9.
54. Harnack, in Bosch, *Ganzheitliche Mission*, 196.
55. Karl Hartenstein, quoted in Hans Ulrich Reifler, *Handbuch der Missiologie: Missionarisches Handeln aus biblischer, historischer und sozialwissenschaftlicher Perspektive* (Nuremberg: VTR, 2009), 44.

society. Only healthy families will reach their relatives and neighbours with the gospel. Yet, as we've seen, the family as a social institution is in deep crisis today, with some even speaking of the end of the family.[56] Everywhere we witness the collapse of traditional family structures, and the social pressure on intact families has been growing. Therefore, if churches want to use the "*Lebensraum* (home and habitat) of family"[57] as a springboard for the gospel they need first to invest in their own families and family lives. And it is not enough just to proclaim that God created and desired family. German Professor of Psychology and Counselling Ulrich Giesekus states that the church has to once again dedicate itself to everything that has to do with family affairs. Giesekus calls churches to invest in the relationships between families and God, between husbands and wives, between parents and their children, and between families, their daily business and society.[58] Indeed, all family members should be a target group of church ministries and programmes if churches really want to disciple their members.[59] However, we are probably asking too much of most churches to tackle such a big task as counselling, pastoring and discipling whole families, so we might need help from outside. Fortunately, there is an increasing number of books on how to live healthy Christian family lives. There is also helpful material for families with special needs or challenges. Many denominations, church ministries, parish centres and dioceses offer agencies for family affairs or family assistance. Though the aspect of family mission is still missing in such centres, there is much else that we still need to learn.

All Souls Church, an Anglican church situated right in the centre of London, defines itself as a family-friendly missionary church. Each Sunday, they run five worship services, with an average attendance of more than three thousand people. Reflecting the population of London itself, church visitors come from all ethnic and national backgrounds. Therefore All Souls offers Sunday services with their own distinct characteristics, such as a Spanish-speaking service for Latin Americans and an African worship service. When I interviewed All Souls mission pastor Anna Bishop she explained to me,

> Due to London's job situation 70 percent of our church members leave us after three or four years in order to live somewhere else.

---

56. See, for instance, Ulrich Giesekus, *Familien leben: Spielregeln für Eltern und Kinder* (Wuppertal: RB Brockhaus, 1994), 14.

57. Edith Schaeffer, *Lebensraum Familie* (Kassel: Oncken Verlag, 1976).

58. Giesekus, *Familien leben*, 22–30.

59. Lawrence Richards, *Christian Education: Seeking to Become Like Jesus Christ* (Grand Rapids, MI: Zondervan, 1975), 129.

> That's why we put all our efforts into training them as missionaries to prepare them for their lives elsewhere. And they are all very interested in mission! We want each one of them to be a good witness for our Lord Jesus Christ – no matter what age or family status they might have. We want singles and couples to serve Jesus. And when they have children we want the whole family to serve the Lord. That's why we put such an emphasis on family work and children and youth ministries.[60]

All Souls has already commissioned more than fifty missionaries, supporting them in various countries around the globe. A lot of their church members are engaged in outreach programmes throughout London, either voluntarily or full time. Every year dozens of volunteers go on short-term outreaches throughout the world, many families among them. "We always commission our missionary families onto the mission fields as whole families," says Bishop.

> The whole family is our missionary, not only the parents, not only the men. No, it's the family we train and prepare for mission together. It's all of them as a family serving God and man. And when they are sent or supported by particular mission works, we, as their church, pay attention to respective training and preparation as families by these ministries. Then when they are abroad we ask for reports to hear from all the family members – how they are and how they are doing in their lives and in their ministry.

What a great way of ministering and of interpreting mission! What a good idea to involve children as active agents in church and on the mission field, and to ask the missionary children for reports – for example, via video messages telling the children back home how they are experiencing mission, the new country abroad and its people. Using Skype, for example, church kids can even interview their friends live: "This way," says Bishop, "the children at 'home' get sensitized for mission, plus we honour the kids' great value for mission."

All Souls also offers family services on a regular basis. Mission plays an integral role there too, as missionaries from abroad as well as staff members of London outreach programmes share their experiences on such occasions. Again, this church sees the whole family of any such missionary as being involved. That's how All Souls has been growing a family-centred missionary culture – a culture focused on family and mission.

---

60. Interview with Anna Bishop, All Souls Church, London, 28 April 2015.

Families need to be prepared for outreach as well as for mission abroad. They need to be nurtured and enabled to grow, for only then will they be able to manifest and proclaim God's kingdom to the world around them. Most mission ministries agree with this concept of preparing the whole family of a missionary sent abroad – at least, in theory. Marion Knell, who works as a family cross-cultural consultant worldwide, especially in the Arab world, wrote a book on life as a missionary in which she demanded adequate preparation for the whole family facing this life: "All family members ought to receive orientation and training – not only the parents while their children are looked after."[61] How right that is. Yet, though Knell's book is full of great advice on how to survive as a family abroad, nowhere do we find practical suggestions about how to live God's calling together as a family. But there is a great need for practical help: not only as missionaries abroad, but also as any family that wants to follow God's calling together.

It is All about the Parents

All Souls pastor Anna Bishop further explains, "We encourage our families to live missionary lives by paying special attention to the parents' ministry" – because first and foremost, it is all about the parents. George Barna, founder of the Barna Group, is a fervent advocate of spiritual education for children, demanding that this must be the first priority in all churches. He is convinced that one of the keys to (children's) ministry is to recognize that it is ultimately the parents who are responsible for the spiritual growth of their children. Therefore, churches ought to support parents in this process, instead of taking responsibility for the children themselves.[62] The church's task in this regard is to train for and support the process, not lead it.[63] Following Barna's approach, our focus shouldn't be on successful children's ministries in order to win the parents for Christ but rather on equipping the parents to win their children for him.[64]

In his book *Der Erzieher als Seelsorger* (The Educator as Counsellor) German author Alfred Stückelberger summed up the educational mandate

---

61. Marion Knell, *Families on the Move: Growing up Overseas – And Loving It!* (Grand Rapids, MI: Monarch, 2001), 65.
62. George Barna, *Transforming Children into Spiritual Champions: Why Children Should Be Your Church's #1 Priority* (Ventura, CA: Regal, 2003), 98.
63. Barna, *Transforming Children*, 98.
64. See Watson, *I Believe in Evangelism*, 145.

thus: "Any education is to minister to children, which in turn means showing them that God has a plan and purpose for each of them and that he has cared for them from the beginning of their lives."[65] From the very first hour, those who are responsible for a child's growth and education "stand between God and the child."[66] As the child cannot yet hear God's directives, the person responsible has to listen to his instructions. That's how a child "experiences and gets to know God's love, care and help."[67] Yet actually, the child will only know God this way when those around live out his love and tell the child about him. Stückelberger is convinced that "When children experience God through those who love them, it lays the best foundation for religious instruction later on and it is the best we can do for them – and it will have a positive influence on their faith for the rest of their life."[68]

When a church has an effective ministry for parents, the growth of missional families is guaranteed because, simply put, most parents don't know how to raise their children according to a missionary lifestyle. They don't know how to live as missionary families in their everyday lives and through family rituals. Why would they? Today it is a challenge to raise children and teach them anything, and this seems to be the biggest challenge in church family ministry as well. Learning from positive examples will help. One such example is Willow Creek Community Church in Chicago, which offers a new concept of how to join parents' and children's ministries.[69]

Of course, missionary training for parents will not be enough. All experts who speak for missionary families also advocate ministries for children, teenagers, youngsters and adults that go beyond the average provisions.[70] We may already invest in such wonderful ministries effectively and with passion, but it is only when we join them to a combined concept of family-focused mission through our churches that we will see a substantial harvest. Church

---

65. Alfred Stückelberger, *Der Erzieher als Seelsorger* (Zurich/Leipzig: Gotthelf Verlag, 1939), 53.

66. Stückelberger, *Der Erzieher als Seelsorger*.

67. Stückelberger, 54.

68. Stückelberger, 54–55.

69. See Reggie Joiner, *Lebe orange! Gemeinde und Familie – gemeinsam stark* (Asslar: Gerth Medien, 2012); Karsten Böhm and Jonathan Bauer, *Denk orange! Für eine Generation voller Glaube, Hoffnung und Liebe* (Asslar: Gerth Medien, 2013); Reggie Joiner and Carey Nieuwhof, *Gemeinsam Kinder stark machen: Wie Freunde, Familie und Gemeinde sie in der Erziehung unterstützen können* (Asslar: Gerth Medien, 2012).

70. See, for example, Bryan Green, *The Praxis of Evangelism*, 4th ed. (London: Hodder & Stoughton, 1958), 189.

ministries that aim to be relevant to society and part of its transformation must discover the family as the basis of any of their work.[71]

Evangelism in Private Homes

Whenever we achieve a favourable result, our motivation for mission will grow. Yet we will only gain experience when we actually do it. When churches train their families for mission only in theory, they will get stuck sooner or later. Hence, whenever we truly assign a missionary role to our families we will need to create space for their outreach and learning. And our church structures may be either a help or a hindrance in this.

Church cell groups, for example, have proven effective in integrating whole families into the mission programmes of churches. Yet such groups can quickly become cosy fellowships and introspective meetings. We need to watch out that such groups do not meet forever simply for themselves. Yet it costs time, space, inspiration and trained staff to grow missionary cell groups. They won't become missional purely by themselves, and it is not enough to organize church into smaller groups.

On the other hand, there's a danger that our folk become alienated from the congregation when we shift outreach solely into the private homes of families. Experts on evangelism point out that the church (our congregations and buildings) has a negative image in society anyway. That means it is important that outsiders associate our home groups with the local church. Otherwise, these people we want to reach will never be seen in church, let alone become members or insiders. Whenever private homes stay disconnected from their local congregations, they do not help grow healthy churches.

Children Make Friends Very Easily

Children are natural missionaries. They don't usually share the social fears of grown-ups. They speak about things they are excited about. They connect easily: just watch children meet other children – they quickly start playing together. Children are curious; they want to know everything about their neighbours – why and how they are who they are. They cannot be fobbed off with clichés or satisfied with evasive answers. Whenever you invite children to your home, they will come. And if you let your children be who they are and do what kids do, soon your whole neighbourhood will know everything

---

71. See, for example, Nazir-Ali, *From Everywhere*, 118–120.

about you! Hence, when we raise our children in an atmosphere of sharing Jesus naturally, it is the best door-opener for the gospel of Christ.

Take, for example, the story of little Tina. She had witnessed again and again how Michaela, her friend next door, was rebuffed by her mother who was suffering from severe headaches. So one day, Tina asked her friend's mother, "Why don't you pray? My mummy always prays when she's got a headache, and then she gets better."

"I prefer taking painkillers instead," was the woman's abrupt reply.

But Tina wouldn't let go: "But you always have a headache. The pills don't help you."

"I don't want to discuss this now, Tina," the neighbour retorted, and sent her home.

When she got home, Tina immediately mobilized her whole family to pray and she shared her prayer request in Sunday school. In fact, the little girl ended up telling pretty much everyone she met about her poor neighbour's headache, and everyone was asked to pray for healing. So, when the two girls met again to play, Tina naturally asked Michaela to pray with her for her mother.

"But Mummy doesn't believe in God like you do," Michaela said hesitantly.

Yet Tina countered in a friendly manner, "But it won't do any harm either if we pray for her." And instantly she started to pray.

After finishing, Tina encouraged her friend to do so too. "I don't know how to," Michaela responded; "I've never prayed before."

"It's easy," replied Tina. "You just talk to God as you do to your best friend. Like you talk to me, for example."

Only a moment later, Michaela was praying to God. After all, it was her mum who was suffering from severe pain. "And, please God, make Daddy come back home," she added. So now Tina also knew about Michaela's dad having left home after an argument – and that this was maybe a reason for the headache.

It didn't take long before Tina's family and the whole church were informed about the difficulties this family was going through. Word finally reached Peter, who realized that Michaela's father was a colleague of his at work. So Peter spoke to the man. His colleague was astonished: "How come you know about my private life?" He was amazed by Peter's response:

"I heard it from my three-year-old: every night my son prays that his friend Michaela's daddy will come back home. Your daughter's missing you a lot, and your wife seems to have developed bad headaches because of this conflict."

The man asked, "But how on earth does your little son know about all that?"

Peter explained, "Well, he heard it from the children at Sunday school. The kids and our whole church are praying for you."

That same day the man returned home. Michaela jumped into her father's arms. And her parents had a long talk that night. Finally, the couple reconciled.

"Do you know why I've come back?" the husband asked his wife, and he told her the story of the praying children. Instantly she understood:

"That must have been Tina, our neighbour's girl. She's Michaela's friend – it's nice how they play together. The other day, Tina talked about my headache, suggesting I should pray. Her family probably goes to the same church as Peter."

The next day, the couple took the two girls aside to thank them. "Your prayer helped a lot, Tina. Thank you."

"But Mummy, I prayed too," Michaela interrupted.

"Well, thank you, darling, as well. Daddy's going to stay and we're a lot better."

Michaela then suggested, "Can we go to that church on Sunday, Mummy? They all prayed for you there."

That's how it all began. The family did not immediately go to church, but they became friends with their neighbours. Peter invited his colleague for a barbecue. And, slowly, they opened up to talk about faith too, while Peter's whole family kept praying. What would have happened if Tina hadn't done what children just naturally do?

So how do we turn not only into missionary but family-centred churches? We need to understand our calling as local churches, we need to integrate our families into our church programmes, we need to focus on ministering to parents and we need to rediscover the missionary potential of our children.

Family Academies Would Make a Real Change

There is an evangelical church in Chișinău, the capital city of the Republic of Moldova, that calls itself the "Light of the World," and although this church was planted only twenty years ago, Chișinău's inhabitants cannot imagine their city without this local church any more. The church has grown constantly ever since it began. But the special thing about these people is that they established a family academy a few years ago as one of the church's main ministries. Nina Teplitzkaja, who wrote a book on the church, said, "Families are the foundation of any society. And whenever a society consists of healthy families, we will see healthy development. This holds true for church too. And above all we need parents as role models for the younger generation. . . . The pastors of 'Light of the World' have understood this truth, that's why we invest in families first, we support them and we integrate them as active players at all levels of our church ministries."[72] Families inside or outside the church get help here; they are supported and equipped for their family lives upon the principles of God's kingdom and according to their current needs. The family academy offers courses to prepare couples for marriage and parenthood; parents get training in raising their children; and when families face specific problems they can get counsel and coaching to become healthy.[73] The church also runs centres for early education, for therapeutic help especially for victims of family violence and sexual abuse, and for orphans and those with disabilities, among other ministries.[74]

For several years now this church's family academy has coordinated all its activities around the family. And beside various other courses, the academy offers mission training to all of its families. "We consider it of the utmost importance that our church families become active in mission and evangelism, whereby we understand any social commitment," pastor Dr Vladimir Ubejvolk explained to me.[75]

The family academy has changed the church in many respects. "Previously, we had difficulty finding any volunteers; today, it's no problem at all," Pastor Ubejvolk told me. "Both young and old people gladly join the ministry. It's part of our church culture to work on the front line." Nina Teplitzkaja confirms this: "Thank God, all families of '*Light of the World*' take part in ministries – both parents and children."[76]

Many families outside the church also seek help and attend courses offered by the academy. This way, new people keep coming to the church because at the academy they get to know church families, they become friends and they get invited to church clusters. The result is a constant rapid growth that the pastor sums up by saying, "It's our healthy families who are the best proof that we successfully reach our society."

---

72. Nina Teplitzkaja, *Zerkov sluzhit ljudjam: Istoria zerkvi "Svet Miru" v gorode Kischineve* (Kishinev: Svet Miru, 2015), 74–75.

73. Teplitzkaja, *Zerkov sluzhit ljudjam*, 75–77.

74. Teplitzkaja, 115–137.

75. Interview by Johannes Reimer with Dr Vladimir Ubejvolk, 15 May 2015, in Chișinău, Moldova.

76. Teplitzkaja, *Zerkov sluzhit ljudjam*, 77.

Questions for Reflection

1. How can your church invest in church programmes, and which ministries need to be developed in view of what has been discussed in this chapter?
2. How can your church better support parents? Which areas seem to be especially weak? Who might be able to organize this?
3. What needs to be done to strengthen families in your church? What initiatives might help?

6

Becoming a Missional Family

Beginning a Process

As human beings, we are obviously born into families. Yet our families were not born as families; rather, families grow into a unit. The same holds true for a missional family: just because we are a family – and a Christian family – we do not automatically live as missional families. We need to want to do that and we must shape our missional identity and lifestyle towards that. Stephen Covey, famous writer on management and leadership, wrote in his book *7 Habits of Highly Effective Families* that good – even great – families are off-track 90 percent of the time. They know the right path yet come back to it only from time to time.[1] Covey finds this alarming, comparing a family to an aeroplane: usually you don't get on board before planning your trip or knowing where the plane is heading. Flying randomly is risky and even dangerous. In contrast, missional families know God's plan for their lives and live according to this every day. Using Covey's metaphor, missional families know where their journey is leading, they have a travel guide at hand and they know how to navigate.

However, most families are not missional yet. They do belong to God's family, they are members of a church, they believe in God the Father, Son and Holy Spirit, and they long to live out their lives in his power. But their everyday lives give a different message. Even the Christian family has entered a state of deep crisis today – and it is the family's character and nature that is in trouble. That's why churches must help to restore the family to what God intended it to be (as seen in previous chapters), engaging both parents and their children – because the whole family is important in this process as it is the collective that

---

1. Stephen R. Covey, *7 Habits of Highly Effective Families* (London: Simon & Schuster, 1998), 9.

determines who the family is and how the family lives. Churches have great potential in supporting their families and teaching them, encouraging them and carrying them, but, ultimately, it is up to the families themselves to shape their missional culture.

If we seek to become the families God intended us to be, it will take a process of transformation. In the context of church, Alan Roxburgh, pastor, writer and consultant, and M. Scott Boren describe this process from traditional to missional church via the following five stages:

1. Discovering what missional church really means;
2. Being convinced that living as a missional church is the right track to follow;
3. Discerning where the church is at this moment;
4. Trying things out – "missional experimentation"; and
5. All church members committing themselves to live according to the missional mode.[2]

Applying these stages to becoming a missional family could run as follows:

1. Identifying God's specific vision for our family;
2. Understanding and accepting God's plan for our family;
3. Analysing our everyday life against God's plan to know where we are at;
4. Starting to realize missional ideas creatively; and
5. Making a commitment to live as a missional family – with God and the church as witnesses.

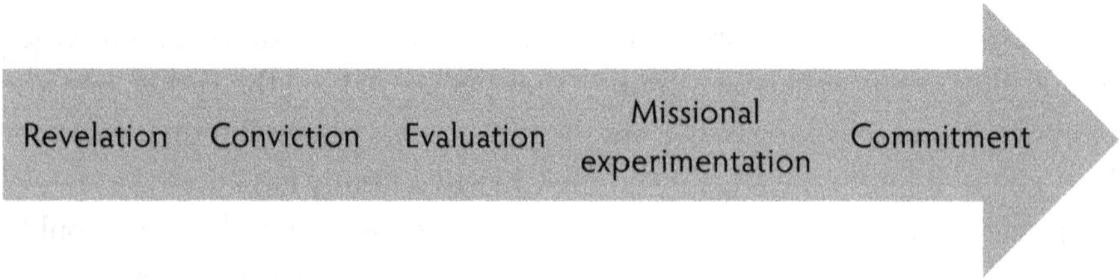

Revelation → Conviction → Evaluation → Missional experimentation → Commitment

Figure 6.1: The Transformation Process to Becoming a Missional Family

---

2. Alan J. Roxburgh and M. Scott Boren, *Introducing the Missional Church: What It Is, Why It Matters, How to Become One* (Grand Rapids, MI: Baker, 2009), 136.

Never Losing Sight of the Ultimate Goal

Missional families know God's specific plans for their lives. They have a prophetic vision for their family. They know that we tend to cast off restraint when there is no vision (Prov 29:18). Covey even speaks of a family needing a "mission statement," that is, a plan for family life that all members agree upon.[3]

People who counsel or coach families know that most family problems stem from not agreeing on the values important to each member. For example, a wife may say, "In my family we used to do it this way and it was right," while her husband disagrees: "But we have never done it that way." At that point we can watch the horizon of marital love get darker and darker. Any family will sail into rough waters when it lacks a common vision and there is no common ground for how to shape family life.

But how do we gain such a vision? From my experience as a family pastor and coach, I suggest the following five steps:

1. Find a common reference point for your family life.
2. Engage all family members in the process.
3. Write down your vision.
4. Make a covenant.
5. Celebrate each anniversary of your covenant.

Let's look at these aspects in more detail.

- *Identifying our reference point.* The first step in creating a common vision of God's particular plan for our family is that all family members need to decide to live their lives according to God's will. And we find out his will simply by reading the Bible! God reveals his dreams and will in Scripture. Hence, it is God's Word which should be the primary source to which we turn when asking how to live and shape our family's lives. Scripture will also be a good reference point for any other advice we might receive from wider family members, church, society or culture. Therefore, just as missional churches are above all Bible-centred churches and live upon values which are benchmarked against God's Word, so missional families take the Bible to be the most important reference point for their lives and values.

---

3. Covey, *7 Habits*, 72.

- *Working together on a common vision*: that is, each family member gets involved. To understand the plans God has revealed in his word, we need to turn to Scripture; therefore, it is important that we read it at home together as a family, not just listen to sermons on Sundays. Also, each family member should be involved, including younger children if they are able to join in the discussion (children at elementary school age definitely can). Our family devotions should be like a Bible study group – a home church – where we talk together about what we've understood from the Bible. Good devotional material might be helpful,[4] or maybe we could invite our pastor to join and train us. Perhaps the first chapters of this book could inspire your family's Bible study through reading the Bible passages mentioned. This stage of our transformation process will only be finished when all family members have grasped the character of the family according to God's will – that is, how to live as family together and how to be a light in this world as a whole family.
- *Writing down our mission statement.* It is a great help to write down what we've found out together by identifying a common vision for our family. It is also helpful to let each member sign this family statement. Then take a picture frame, put the statement in it and find the best place in your home to display it. You will be amazed at the power this statement will have in times of trouble and conflict. All families face such times while we live on earth – life can sometimes be a roller coaster.
- *Making a family covenant.* By signing this statement, we make a covenant creating this "family document." So why not also celebrate this covenant when adopting the statement? When we read the Bible carefully, we find indications that the family is a covenant community.[5] In a similar way, we can make an agreement in the presence of God to follow his vision and intentions for us as a family. A ceremony for formalizing a contract is something that happens throughout society, so why not celebrate a ritual when making your family covenant? Rituals are important in the life of any family, reinforcing important events and highlighting important decisions.

---

4. For example, Stephen C. Barton, *Life Together: Family, Sexuality and Community in the New Testament and Today* (Edinburgh/New York: T&T Clark, 2001).

5. For more on this, see Jack O. Balswick and Judith K. Balswick, *The Family: A Christian Perspective on the Contemporary Home* (Grand Rapids, MI: Baker, 1989), 20.

- *Celebrating our family covenant and its anniversary.* If we've made this agreement and we are a missional family, let's celebrate this covenant! Let's invite other families and tell them about it. When we have understood what the family is all about in God's eyes and when we have decided to live that way, it's worth celebrating! And let's mark the day in our calendar and celebrate its anniversaries. Maybe other families in church will join us too, and a movement to live as missional families will start. It is totally appropriate to commemorate this turning point annually. Memories nurture our renewal and give fuel to the culture of a missional church as God wants it for the *familia Dei*.

Family in a Growing Progression

Of course, once we've got a vision, it does not mean that we automatically live it out in practice. Yet it is the first and most important step towards the transformation of our family culture and life. Jack and Judith Balswick, outstanding experts in sociology and family therapy, suggest four categories that characterize the process of becoming a mature family in our everyday life: (1) covenant, (2) grace, (3) commission and (4) intimacy.[6] According to the Balswicks, *covenant*, in a nutshell, is a mutual agreement to love God and to love one another. *Grace* means we remain open to forgive and to accept each other's forgiveness. *Commission* is closely connected to our willingness to serve and to accept our ministries. And *intimacy* is about our readiness to be open – to get to know each other better and to be transparent so that others will know us well.[7]

Whenever these requirements are fulfilled the process may start along the following steps:

- Clarify and identify your background and influences.
- Start something radically new.
- Launch the process of transformation.
- Engage the whole family.

Let's look at these in more detail.

---

6. Balswick and Balswick, *The Family*, 21.
7. Balswick and Balswick, 22–31.

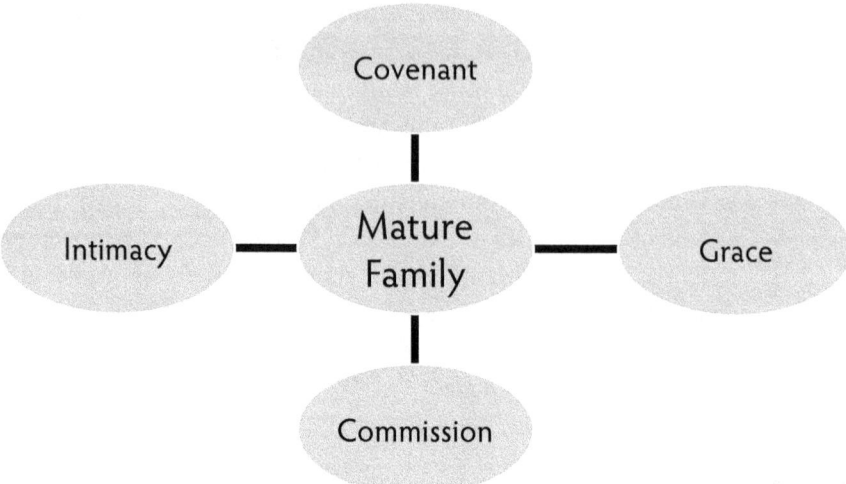

Figure 6.2: Requirements for the Process of Maturing as a Family according to Jack and Judith Balswick

Analysing Our Present Situation

The fact is that we all carry "baggage" when we start our own families. We've already been enculturated and socialized by and through our original families. We've been shaped in different ways when it comes to family life and values. So what is normal for the Smiths might be offensive for the Johnsons; what the Browns like the most, the Williamses reject. Yet their offspring are going to marry and commit the rest of their lives to each other – or they already got married years ago but are now struggling to find common ground. It is therefore vitally important to analyse our original family influences – and to do so according to Scripture and, if needed, to give up bad habits. Otherwise it will be difficult to acquire a common vision.

A Radical New Start

The Bible teaches us that marriage starts with a radical break from our original families: "That is why a man *really* leaves his father and mother and is united to his wife, and they become one flesh" (Gen 2:24; my paraphrase and emphasis). Thus, to marry means to radically leave (reject or break with) all our former paradigms. Whenever I marry a couple, I always ask two essential questions first: I ask the parents whether they are willing to let their children go, and the couple whether they are willing to leave their parental homes and spaces of influence. Only when all of them say "yes" will I marry the couple. However, such promises might turn out to have been hollow phrases only – this is the primary reason for conflict in marriage and family life. Certainly, there might be destructive influences at work other than our original family – for example, the negative influence of society, community and friends. In any case, missional families need to discern wisely, test everything according to God's Word and only hold on to what is good for their mission.

The Process of Transformation

While it's easy to describe the process of transformation, all change is difficult in practice. And it takes time! Transformation starts with the renewal of our thinking: we stop conforming to the patterns of the world and consciously adopt a biblical mindset (see Rom 12:2). This will lead to a change in our behaviour. The apostle Paul taught the church in Ephesus, who had been immersed in a culture of lies, "You were taught, with regard to your former way of life, to put off your old self, which is being corrupted by its deceitful desires; to be made new in the attitude of your minds; and to put on the new self, created to be like God in true righteousness and holiness. Therefore each of you must put off falsehood and speak truthfully to your neighbour, for we are all members of one body" (Eph 4:22–25). The Greek tense Paul is using here expresses an ongoing process: he is telling the Ephesians to keep putting off their old self, to keep speaking truthfully, to never stop but to keep exercising the truth until they *are* truthful. Any process of transformation needs our willingness to work on our character. As we will not change our character from one day to the next, we should keep reaching for the goal we have in front of us. Paul also told the Philippians:

> Not that I have already obtained all this, or have already arrived at my goal, but I press on to take hold of that for which Christ Jesus took hold of me. Brothers and sisters, I do not consider myself yet to have taken hold of it. But one thing I do: forgetting what is behind and straining towards what is ahead, I press on towards the goal to win the prize for which God has called me heavenwards in Christ Jesus.
>
> All of us, then, who are mature should take such a view of things. And if on some point you think differently, that too

God will make clear to you. Only let us live up to what we have already attained.

Join together in following my example, brothers and sisters, and just as you have us as a model, keep your eyes on those who live as we do. (Phil 3:12–17)

Any family will only grow, and maturity will only be reached, through a continual process. Change needs to be developed step by step; according to Jack O. Balswick, "the family is a developing system."[8] A family is not born overnight but needs all family members to work on their mutual relationship.

All Family Members Are on the Journey Together

Let's take the apostle Paul as a role model and follow the truth that practice makes perfect. Our transformation needs time, patience and discipline. Therefore, it is important not to be alone on such a journey – it needs to be the common goal of all family members to transform the family into a missional family. Indeed, within such a family it would demonstrate a sinful attitude for one member to tell the others, "This is only your quirk and nothing to do with me. You'd better deal with this on your own."

Markers along the Journey

Missional families are missionaries by nature. This means that *who* they are is much more important than what they *do*. This is all about the character of the family, meaning the inner being that needs to be transformed into the image of God as Paul describes in Ephesians 3:14–20. Yet, as John and Susan Yates say, character is precisely the point where families in our Western societies face their greatest crisis.[9] They add that any social programmes to develop strong characters aim at individuals only instead of whole families, which completely neglects the family's collective culture and character. Furthermore, they state that individualism nurtures "expedient or malleable or legalistic (uptight) characters."[10] An *expedient* character, according to John and Susan Yates, is someone with little interest in ethics but whose main focus is on his or her personal gain. *Malleable* characters pay attention only to what others think of

---

8. Balswick and Balswick, 35.

9. John and Susan Yates, *Character Matters! Raising Kids with Values That Last* (Grand Rapids, MI: Baker, 1992), 5–6.

10. Yates, *Character Matters!*, 11–12.

them. *Legalistic* characters follow the rules and orders others give them. We come across all three kinds of characters among Christian families, but none of them can be found in the Bible. And none of these attitudes help us manifest God's kingdom in this world, because expedient families are focused only on their own well-being, malleable families aspire only to have the right image in church and society, and legalistic families are always afraid of making mistakes.

In contrast, missional characters live and are carried by their mission to reach the world around them.[11] Such characters are developed in families that seek to become Christlike and who really want to act in accordance with God's mandate. We've already described the specific steps to be taken along that journey. Yet it is important from time to time to take stock of how far we've come. I remember how, when our children were little, when travelling through Germany they would ask just minutes after we had left, "Daddy, how long till we get there?" It was good for them to learn the signs beside the autobahn and have these markers explained. Then we were able to answer their question and keep them silent – at least for another few miles. Of course, after a while they would ask again.

In John and Susan Yates's helpful book on how families can build good character, they discuss raising good-natured children and mention the following central attributes: integrity, willingness to learn, self-discipline, empathy, humility, courage, faith and joy.[12] For me, these character traits should be applied to all family members as well as to the whole collective of the family. Applied to missional families, *integrity* means that they are committed 100 percent to God's particular plan for them. *Willingness to learn* opens space for lifelong learning, proper development and formation of personality. When it comes to *self-discipline*, we mean that families are unreservedly willing to reach their goals in a systematic manner. *Empathy* describes their conscious search to understand the people around them. *Humility* means they help others selflessly. When it comes to *courage*, we mean that families are bold enough to enter even unknown territory. *Faith* is nothing other than their unconditional trust in the family being a successful enterprise because God ordained the family in the first place. And *joy* means their healthy, happy hearts and cheerful minds celebrating God, life and themselves. All these attributes should help

---

11. For more on missional character, see Will Manchini, *Church Unique: How Missional Leaders Cast Vision, Capture Culture, and Create Movement* (San Francisco: Jossey-Bass, 2008), 151–163.

12. Yates, *Character Matters!*

and facilitate the "endeavour" of missional families, at least whenever they manifest in real life as true family *culture*.

Theology: The Biblical Criteria of a Missional Character

When we search in the Bible for the typical attributes of missional character, though, we need to turn first to Christ's Beatitudes. Erik Kolbell, psychotherapist and ordained minister, describes Matthew 5:1–12 as a "moral compass"[13] for all Christians. In these verses Jesus talks about our character,[14] before going on in verses 13 to 16 to talk about the mission to which he calls his disciples:

> You are the salt of the earth. But if the salt loses its saltiness, how can it be made salty again? It is no longer good for anything, except to be thrown out and trampled underfoot.
>
> You are the light of the world. A town built on a hill cannot be hidden. Neither do people light a lamp and put it under a bowl. Instead they put it on its stand, and it gives light to everyone in the house. In the same way, let your light shine before others, that they may see your good deeds and glorify your Father in heaven. (Matt 5:13–16)

In the original Greek the "You are" is grammatically emphasized, meaning something more like "You really are" or "It's you, not them but you, who . . ." In addition, Jesus describes a state of being rather than just performing: he speaks of *who* we *are*, not *what* it is our mandate to *do*.[15] It was because of *who* the early Christians were that they were soon persecuted for their faith.[16] Of course, it was not only the church's nature but also the mission which gave offence; but it is who we are that makes us live our lives and our mission accordingly. So, who are we? We are the salt and the light of the *cosmos*, so Jesus says we are here for the sake of the whole earth! He describes not only our nature here but also our calling, for both salt and light are essential elements needed for all life on earth. Hence, both reveal how important we are for life itself. And God

---

13. Erik Kolbell, *What Jesus Meant: The Beatitudes and a Meaningful Life* (Louisville/London: Westminster John Knox, 2003), 12.

14. For more on this, see, for example, Mark A. Powel, "Matthew's Beatitudes: Reversals and Rewards of the Kingdom," *Catholic Biblical Quarterly* 58 (1996): 460–479.

15. Professor Robert H. Gundry disagrees here – see Robert H. Gundry, *Matthew. A Commentary on His Handbook for a Mixed Church under Persecution*, 2nd ed. (Grand Rapids, MI: Eerdmans, 1994), 68.

16. Gundry, *Matthew*, 69.

is all about life; he desires life and he wants his creation to live. Life is God's first mission and the family is his guarantee to keep this promise of ongoing life. Therefore, missional families are privileged to be the salt and light of the world. Let's explore this in more detail.

Salt is a basic element of life. If our bodies lack salt, we will become ill and ultimately die. That's why salt has always had such a great religious meaning. We find it in the Old Testament: the people of Israel had to sprinkle salt on some of their offerings and even sacrifice salt (Lev 2:13; Ezek 43:24; Mark 9:49). God ordered that salt be added to the blend of incense (Exod 30:35). Hence, in Old Testament times it was impossible to celebrate holy services without salt (Ezra 6:9; 7:22). Salt was the symbol of purity and purification. The prophet Elisha healed the bad water of Jericho by throwing salt into the spring (2 Kgs 2:19–22). Salt was to cleanse and to protect from decay.

Can salt lose its saltiness? Technically not, unless we are talking about the salt which was obtained from the Dead Sea.[17] The people of Palestine used salt from the Dead Sea ever since they lived there. The Dead Sea "salt" consists of 33 percent salt along with other elements such as chalk and magnesium. Through a process of evaporation and washing, the elements could be separated. The salt was then used for cooking, but the other elements were used for building, for instance, to repair floors. So this kind of "salt" would literally be trampled on the ground because it was saltless.

Contrary to salt, the light of the world refers to God himself (John 8:12; 12:46; 1 John 1:5). At the same time, it was Israel's calling to be a light to the nations (Isa 51:4–5). God's people were not, however, able to live up to this mandate. It was only later that Christ brought God's light into the world (John 1:4–5, 9; 12:46). His disciples were later called "children of the light" (1 Thess 5:5; cf. Eph 5:8) as they carried the light of the gospel into the world: "the light of the gospel that displays the glory of Christ, who is the image of God" (2 Cor 4:4). Professor Donald A. Hagner is convinced that when Jesus calls the disciples "the light of the world" he is actually saying that as receivers of the kingdom they represent the truth of salvation which has come into the world.[18]

In calling us salt and light, Jesus passed on his life's vision to his followers. Let's try to catch his vision for us as missional families. Note that Jesus did not only speak about his vision, but he also gave his disciples authority to actually be able to live out this task.

---

17. Donald H. Hagner, *Matthew 1–13*, Word Biblical Commentary 33a (Nashville: Thomas Nelson, 1993), 99.

18. Hagner, *Matthew*, 100.

But just before Jesus gave this important mission statement we find the famous Beatitudes in Matthew 5:3–12, eight blessings for specific character attributes. In other words, here Jesus describes how his disciples would be equipped to be the salt and light of the world:

> Blessed are the poor in spirit,
>> for theirs is the kingdom of heaven.
>
> Blessed are those who mourn,
>> for they will be comforted.
>
> Blessed are the meek,
>> for they will inherit the earth.
>
> Blessed are those who hunger and thirst for righteousness,
>> for they will be filled.
>
> Blessed are the merciful,
>> for they will be shown mercy.
>
> Blessed are the pure in heart,
>> for they will see God.
>
> Blessed are the peacemakers,
>> for they will be called children of God.
>
> Blessed are those who are persecuted because of righteousness,
>> for theirs is the kingdom of heaven.
>
> Blessed are you when people insult you, persecute you and falsely say all kinds of evil against you because of me.
>> Rejoice and be glad, because great is your reward in heaven, for in the same way they persecuted the prophets who were before you.

Here Jesus used a stylistic tool – beatitudes – known to his audience from the Old Testament. Donald Hagner even highlights the close connection between this passage and Isaiah 61:1–2 and Luke 4:18.[19]

Christ starts each Beatitude by declaring that his disciples are "blessed," *makarioi*. *Makarios* means being in a state of utter bliss and contentment, and complete satisfaction for all eternity.[20] The blessed belong to God's kingdom, and this state of being blessed will certainly show in our behaviour. Interestingly, in the ancient world, bliss was ascribed to the gods; a "blessed state" was spiritual and godly in Greek eyes. When we are *makarioi* we have reached the state where fate cannot harm us any longer. Beatitudes in the Old

---

19. Hagner, 92–93.
20. Hagner, 91.

Testament wisdom literature (see Ps 1:1 or Eccl 3:19–23) showed that the way we live has consequences for how we feel – in other words, there is a close connection between what we do and what we will harvest. Therefore, when we've reached the state of *makarios* described by Jesus, we will act out of this bliss and will have abundant life, salvation and blessing! And this connection is irreversible; these Beatitudes will automatically lead to their respective manifestations in life.[21]

It makes perfect sense to interpret Christ's Beatitudes as biblical attributes of a missional life: when we are *makarioi* we are the salt and light of the world. So let's take a closer look at each of these blessings.

Surrender: Depending on God Alone

Jesus starts with "Blessed are the poor in spirit, for theirs is the kingdom of heaven" (Matt 5:3). The Greek text for "poor in spirit," *ptochoi to pneumati*, is not easy to understand and has been interpreted in different ways.[22] What does it mean to be "poor in spirit"? Some have interpreted "the poor" in a literal and physical sense, dropping the "in spirit" so that it signifies the needy and impoverished. This interpretation fits the Beatitudes as recorded in the Gospel of Luke, where we find supplementary verses: "Blessed are you who are poor, for yours is the kingdom of God. . . . But woe to you who are rich, for you have already received your comfort" (Luke 6:20, 24). Luke leaves out the phrase "in spirit" as well, but is it really legitimate to drop it from the verse in Matthew? Certainly not. The passage in Luke appears in a different context and should be interpreted accordingly. In contrast, Matthew reports Jesus talking about those who are needy, but also about the "poor in spirit"![23]

Other interpretations suggest that the "poor in spirit" refers to people who have realized how little they know, how little they are capable of. Still others interpret the "spirit" to refer to God's Spirit; then the "poor in spirit" would mean those who know how poor they are before God. But why not combine these latter two approaches? "Poverty in spirit" would then describe our profound lack of sufficiency before God. The fact is that we owe everything to God's Spirit – everything we know and all that we are. When we are poor in

---

21. For more on this, see Eduard Schweizer, *The Good News According to Matthew* (London: SPCK, 1984), 80–85.

22. For discussion on this, see, for example, Hagner, *Matthew*, 91–92; Schweizer, *Good News*, 86–87; Gundry, *Matthew*, 67–68.

23. Yet literal poverty is indeed still a factor; see Schweizer, *Good News*, 86–87; and Hagner, *Matthew*, 91.

spirit we realize our total disqualification: we are poor before God because we are poor without his Spirit! We have stopped trusting in our own capabilities, intellects, competences and opportunities. We know for sure that we are nothing without God and we have nothing without him! Hence, this is an attitude, a state of heart, and not a material state in life. Erik Kolbell is convinced that poverty in spirit, according to Christ's teaching, the Psalms and the rabbinical tradition, does not mean rejection of material possessions but repudiating all the powers that try to control our lives and dictate how we ought to be.[24]

Of course, you can be poor but impudent at the same time. Some needy people fall into criminality in that way, following the conviction: "I'm poor, and you owe me something, so I'll avenge myself." In contrast, those who are "poor in spirit" do not seek revenge or crave more because they see themselves through God's eyes, they know about their inadequacies before him. And they live in his presence, taking his point of view on their lives, their gifts, and their hearts, minds and deeds. They do not allow anyone or anything to guide and influence them except God himself.

It is this state of living that gives them possession of the kingdom of heaven! Jesus says, "for theirs is the kingdom of heaven" (5:3). The kingdom of heaven, according to Matthew, is synonymous with the kingdom of God, which is the realm and kingdom of the righteous King. Jesus came to proclaim God's kingdom, God's authority and the good news (Mark 1:14–15). This coming kingdom was what Jesus taught the disciples to pray for (Matt 6:9–10) and it was this kingdom which they should seek first, aligning their lives with him: "But seek first his kingdom and his righteousness, and all these things will be given to you as well" (Matt 6:33).

So Jesus says to the poor in spirit that the kingdom of heaven is theirs: they do not have to wait for it, it is already theirs now! It is not a vague hope, a cheap comfort, or something to put off for a day in the future – Jesus states something that is real today. The poor in spirit live in his kingdom under God's authority *now*. And so they have access to his supernatural power.

As we confide in God, he is our protection and shield. As we trust in him, he is our comforter and helper. Jesus said to the apostle Paul, "My grace is sufficient for you, for my power is made perfect in weakness" (2 Cor 12:9). And Paul even proclaimed, "I can do all [things] through him who gives me strength" (Phil 4:13). Coming back to our mission, all of us who follow Christ are to be the salt and light of this world. But can we ever fulfil this huge task? Yes we can, when we know in our hearts that it is not all about us but about God.

---

24. Kolbell, *What Jesus Meant*, 30.

And to him, all things are possible! When our minds as well as our lives grasp this truth, we will be amazed what the "poor in spirit" are really capable of.

How do we enter this bliss? What do we have to do to get there? Paul tells the Philippians to have the same mindset as Christ Jesus (Phil 2:5). Even our Lord lived poor in spirit – literally poor, as he was anything but rich and once told his disciples, "Foxes have dens and birds have nests, but the Son of Man has nowhere to lay his head" (Matt 8:20). Yet he had chosen to live like that, as we read in Philippians 2:5–11:

> In your relationships with one another, have the same mindset
> as Christ Jesus:
> who, being in very nature God,
>   did not consider equality with God something to be
>   used to his own advantage;
> rather, he made himself nothing
>   by taking the very nature of a servant,
>   being made in human likeness.
> And being found in appearance as a man,
>   he humbled himself
>   by becoming obedient to death –
>   even death on a cross!
> Therefore God exalted him to the highest place
>   and gave him the name that is above every name,
>   that at the name of Jesus every knee should bow,
>   in heaven and on earth and under the earth,
>   and every tongue acknowledge that Jesus Christ is Lord,
>   to the glory of God the Father.

How did Jesus make himself nothing? He did so in three steps:

1. Jesus knew who he was, yet he did not consider equality with God something to be used to his own advantage. Jesus knew his origins. And he knew God's power and possibilities – that's why he could make himself nothing. As far as we are concerned, this means that the less we know (of) God, the more we will hold on to the little we have. If we only knew how powerful and amazing our God is, it'd be easy for us to have great faith.

2. Jesus made himself nothing out of obedience. God had a plan for his Son, that he would save the world through him. Jesus did not become poor for poverty's sake but for our sakes! As far as we are

concerned, this means that the less we know our specific task(s), the more difficult it is to let go of things; in which case we will hold on to our possessions yet still become poorer.

3. Jesus had hope for his exaltation to come: he expects all creation to bow the knee before him. Jesus knew the hope of his existence, and that's why he was able to make himself nothing: he knew the great riches awaiting him. As far as we are concerned, this means that the less we know of our inheritance, the more we will hold on to earthly things – which could mean holding on to our family members as well.

Empathy: Suffering with the Afflicted World

Next, Jesus promises bliss and blessing to another surprising group of people: "Blessed are those who mourn." But sorry, Lord – when people are mourning, they certainly are not happy and blessed! Those who mourn are low-spirited because they are coming to terms with a great loss – they have just lost a loved one. And that awakens feelings of helplessness, fear and depression. Indeed, if our mourning becomes extreme it can lead to irreversible psychological damage. Why would such mourning lead to bliss? And note that we are talking about continuous mourning, as the Greek grammar here describes a permanent state. Is Jesus referring to eternal mourners?

The Greek term *pentos* means to lament or groan about undesired conditions of life. Those who mourn, the *pentountas*, bewail an undesirable state apart from God's will. The same Greek word is used when Jesus groaned in a kind of apocalyptic lament: "Woe to you who are well fed now, for you will go hungry. Woe to you who laugh now, for you will mourn and weep" (Luke 6:25).

Paul also uses this word when he laments the lack of remorse in the church in Corinth. He says, "It is actually reported that there is sexual immorality among you, and of a kind that even pagans do not tolerate: a man is sleeping with his father's wife. And you are proud! Shouldn't you rather have gone into *mourning* and have put out of your fellowship the man who has been doing this?" (1 Cor 5:1–2). In his second letter to the Corinthians (2 Cor 12:21) Paul expresses his concern that he might be "*grieved*" over many who have not repented of their sins. In Mark 16:10 we read about the Easter message conveyed to those "*mourning* and *weeping*." And we see that "torment and *grief*" is a consequence of God's judgment (e.g. in Rev 18:7).

Therefore we can say that when Jesus talks about "those who mourn," he is referring to people who have realized the desperate state they are in and who are suffering as a consequence.[25] When discussing this verse, Bible commentaries also refer[26] to Isaiah 61:1-3:

> ... because the LORD has anointed me
> ... to proclaim good news to the poor ...
> to comfort all who mourn,
> and provide for those who grieve in Zion –
> to bestow on them a crown of beauty
> instead of ashes,
> the oil of joy
> instead of mourning,
> and a garment of praise
> instead of a spirit of despair.

The prophet Isaiah announced that the Messiah would comfort all those who mourn. And indeed, we are all too familiar with grief here on earth. However, Isaiah talks about comfort for those who grieve in Zion: it's in Zion that they were mourning, not just anywhere, and this has a deeper meaning. In the days of Isaiah the people of Israel were lamenting their condition because they had lost their temple that had been built on Mount Zion as Jerusalem had been overrun by the enemy. People mourned and wept because they wouldn't see God's almighty power move among them anymore. The Old Testament prophets lamented this. So here we are talking about the grieving of God's people at the terrible condition they are in. They mourn and suffer because God's power and presence had left Zion, leading to the disaster and destruction wrought by their enemies.

When we acknowledge the close connection between these laments and "those who mourn," it's clear that Jesus is not talking about the weeping that is typical following the loss of a loved one. Rather, he refers to people who have a deep awareness that our world is forsaken, who grieve that this world does not know God's awesome power, and to hearts broken over the world's misery. He talks about people who can't live their lives as if it's "business as usual" while their neighbours are divorcing; people who are not able to overlook the poor in their towns; people whose hearts are moved by the needs around them. "Those

---

25. For more on this, see Karl-Ernst Apfelbacher, *Selig die Trauernden: Kulturgeschichtliche Aspekte des Christentums* (Regensburg: Friedrich Pustet, 2002).
26. Schweizer, *Good News*, 90.

who mourn" have a passion for the lost and needy that won't let go. Martin Luther translated these words as "*Selig sind die da Leid tragen*" – literally, "Blessed are those who carry (are burdened with) mourning," which parallels the English expression in Paul's call that we should "carry each other's burdens" (Gal 6:2). So "those who mourn" actually have mercy and compassion. They are burden-carriers: they do not weep for themselves but for the perilous state of others. They grieve and suffer when there's no hope and change for the people around them.

These are the ones Jesus is blessing with the promise that they will be comforted! The original word in Greek is *paraklesis*, which is directly related to the *parakletos* – the Holy Spirit. This name is often translated in some Bible versions as the Comforter (John 14:26; 15:26). Blessed are we when we are comforted by the Holy Spirit himself! Blessed are we when we get to know his power, as the Holy Spirit is the Lord of ministry in the new covenant (2 Cor 3:17). Wherever the Spirit is active, people are convicted of their sins, and judgment and righteousness are brought into the world (John 16:8). Therefore Jesus blesses those who suffer from the world's forsakenness and godlessness; he promises that we will be filled and equipped by the power of his Spirit. In this way we will be part of his transformation of the world and we will witness his signs and wonders.

But truthfully, who among us is really mourning for the people around us who are on their way to hell? And who still has a soft heart that mourns the many divorces we see today? We've all become numb to that, haven't we? Who among us weeps about the growing addiction problems in our society, as people struggle to cope with their lives? Nevertheless, there may be a connection between our broken hearts and the miracle of renewal among those around us. Jesus clearly says in these verses that there is!

This leads us to the important question: how can we develop such passion? Look at how Jesus prepared his disciples for their mission:

> Jesus went through all the towns and villages, teaching in their synagogues, proclaiming the good news of the kingdom and healing every disease and illness. When he saw the crowds, he had compassion on them, because they were harassed and helpless, like sheep without a shepherd. Then he said to his disciples, "The harvest is plentiful but the workers are few. Ask the Lord of the harvest, therefore, to send out workers into his harvest field." (Matt 9:35–38)

Note that Jesus had compassion when he saw the crowds: in other words, because he had eyes that were opened to the world and their needs around him, he could weep for them. He sent out his disciples to do the same: to *see* the harvest and pray for workers. Only when we see our neighbours and their needs will we develop compassion for them. And only when we intercede on their behalf will we cultivate a passion that lets us reach out and be used by the Holy Spirit. And, if we want to see and experience, we need to get close to people; we need to mingle with the crowds. That's what Jesus did, going from house to house, and being out in the market place.

Missional families live their lives right where people are. They mingle; they don't keep out of their neighbours' way but see them and suffer because of their unsaved condition.

Kindness: Renouncing Any Violence

Take any society in this world: wherever people live, they are confronted with the big issues of power, might and violence. In the family too, it might be all about power, and Christian families are no exception; take, for example, the age-old discussion about who has the final say in a decision. Yet in his third Beatitude Jesus praises the total renunciation of violence, saying, "Blessed are the meek, for they will inherit the earth." And he stops his disciples fighting over who will be the greatest in heaven and sit next to the Master, telling them,

> The kings of the Gentiles lord it over them; and those who exercise authority over them call themselves Benefactors. But you are not to be like that. Instead, the greatest among you should be like the youngest, and the one who rules like the one who serves. For who is greater, the one who is at the table or the one who serves? Is it not the one who is at the table? But I am among you as one who serves. You are those who have stood by me in my trials. And I confer on you a kingdom, just as my Father conferred one on me, so that you may eat and drink at my table in my kingdom and sit on thrones, judging the twelve tribes of Israel. (Luke 22:25–30)

Here we see that Jesus taught about serving and not about ruling. However, by our very nature, humankind will react violently to violence, following the principle "eye for eye" that we read of in Exodus 21:23–25: "But if there is serious injury, you are to take life for life, eye for eye, tooth for tooth, hand for hand, foot for foot, burn for burn, wound for wound, bruise for bruise." Jesus took this law much further: "You have heard that it was said, 'Eye for eye, and tooth for tooth.' But I tell you, do not resist an evil person. If anyone slaps you on the right cheek, turn to them the other cheek also" (Matt 5:38–39). The

Lord taught his disciples not to take revenge and not to give in to hatred, but to renounce any violence – for love: we are to meet even evil with love, and we are to love our enemies (Matt 5:44). Such an approach is not possible in our own strength. Therefore, we need this state of blessedness we have talked about and the shalom given by God; we need to be brought into his presence and stay close to him in order to be able to live up to Christ's standard.

This third Beatitude is about the meek – people who totally renounce any violence. The original Greek word *praeis* means meakness, gentleness, benignity, placidness, blandness,[27] and it was used, for example, to describe kind and comforting words, healing or pleasant plants and animals. It is often used in the Old as well as the New Testament. English Bibles translate it here as "meek," but it is also translated as "gentle" when Christ describes himself as *praeis* in Matthew 11:29: "Take my yoke upon you and learn from me, for I am gentle and humble in heart, and you will find rest for your souls." Meekness or gentleness is one of the character traits of Christ as Jesus fulfilled the prophecy of being the *praeis* king described by the prophet Zechariah. In Matthew 21:4–5 we read, "This took place to fulfil what was spoken through the prophet: 'Say to Daughter Zion, "See, your king comes to you, gentle and riding on a donkey, and on a colt, the foal of a donkey."'" And in Galatians 5:23 we read that the same *praeis* is the fruit of the Holy Spirit as well.

A meek and gentle person renounces any violence or manipulation. When we are *praeis*, we trust only in God's power and strength and we count on his aid and kindness. Paul explains meekness well when he writes to the Romans, "For by the grace given me I say to every one of you: do not think of yourself more highly than you ought, but rather think of yourself with sober judgment, in accordance with the faith God has distributed to each of you" (12:3). Hence, people with such a gentle and humble attitude seek no self-justification. They let their lives give testimony; they let their deeds speak instead of their arguments.

Christ is the best example of this gentleness. When the disciples of John the Baptist ask him whether he is the promised Messiah, the Lord's answer is gentle: "Go back and report to John what you hear and see: the blind receive sight, the lame walk, those who have leprosy are cleansed, the deaf hear, the dead are raised, and the good news is proclaimed to the poor. Blessed is anyone who does not stumble on account of me" (Matt 11:4–6). Jesus doesn't argue with words, he simply lets his deeds speak for him!

Psalm 37:1–11 is an Old Testament parallel to the Beatitudes:

---

27. Hagner, *Matthew*, 92.

Do not fret because of those who are evil
  or be envious of those who do wrong;
for like the grass they will soon wither,
  like green plants they will soon die away.

Trust in the Lord and do good;
  dwell in the land and enjoy safe pasture.
Take delight in the Lord,
  and he will give you the desires of your heart.

Commit your way to the Lord;
  trust in him and he will do this:
he will make your righteous reward shine like the dawn,
  your vindication like the noonday sun.

Be still before the Lord
  and wait patiently for him;
do not fret when people succeed in their ways,
  when they carry out their wicked schemes.

Refrain from anger and turn from wrath;
  do not fret – it leads only to evil.
For those who are evil will be destroyed,
  but those who hope in the Lord will inherit the land.

A little while, and the wicked will be no more;
  though you look for them, they will not be found.
But the meek will inherit the land
  and enjoy peace and prosperity.

Meek people receive their identity and value from God. They don't need to be violent as they trust him to take action – they are convinced that good will have the victory in the end. They don't need to suppress others but instead heap good works on the evil one's head. In Proverbs 25:21-22 we read: "If your enemy is hungry, give him food to eat; if he is thirsty, give him water to drink. In doing this, you will heap burning coals on his head, and the Lord will reward you."

What is the reward for those who are meek? Jesus promises that "they will inherit the earth." So renouncing control leads to possessing all the earth![28] This might sound odd but it makes perfect sense. It was God's original plan for humankind to rule the earth. In Genesis 1:28 we read: "God blessed them

---

28. For more on this, see Schweizer, *Good News*, 90–91.

and said to them, 'Be fruitful and increase in number; fill the earth and subdue it. Rule over the fish in the sea and the birds in the sky and over every living creature that moves on the ground.'" Hence, if we are meek in character we are given back our original charge. God will not take us from the earth but will hand it back to us. And those who are meek are stewards after his own heart!

When we grasp this, we cannot hold on to desires to quit this planet and rid ourselves of any responsibility for this earth, as is thought by some Christians. On the contrary, when we take our Lord seriously and we meekly submit to his mandate, we cannot but willingly accept our responsibility for our planet and live accordingly. Of course, godly stewardship should be free from any violence against creation and avoid any depletion of the earth's resources; in contrast, "whoever believes in [him], as Scripture has said, rivers of living water will flow from within them" (John 7:38). Nothing on earth is as strong as water. The Chinese philosopher Laozi stated, "There is nothing on earth that is softer, nothing that is weaker than water. Yet, neither is there anything that can shape the hard-hearted as water does. And conversely, nothing will ever be able to change water."[29] Notice that the power and effect of water lies in constant gentle repetition; in the end it can sculpt even the hardest stone.

It is this gentle, powerful love of Christ that missional families will follow, so issues of might and power turn into issues of love. Their relationships are defined by meekness towards each other and also towards their neighbours. They submit to each other instead of demanding submission (see Eph 5:21–32).

Self-Denial: Totally Committed to Justice and Righteousness

The fourth Beatitude is another challenge: "Blessed are those who hunger and thirst for righteousness, for they will be filled" (Matt 5:6). When we are hungry and thirsty we will be content in bliss: this seems like a paradox, doesn't it?

Jesus does not refer to an arbitrary craving here, nor to random hunger and thirst. It is about those who hunger and thirst for *righteousness* – a key term in his teachings: five times he refers to it alone in his Sermon on the Mount, twice here in the Beatitudes (vv. 6 and 10). Christ warns his disciples in the same chapter, "For I tell you that unless your righteousness surpasses that of the Pharisees and the teachers of the law, you will certainly not enter the kingdom of heaven" (Matt 5:20). In Matthew 6:1 he says, "Be careful not to practise your righteousness in front of others to be seen by them. If you do, you will have no reward from your Father in heaven." And as if God's kingdom

---

29. Taoteking, "Saying 78," http://www.tao-te-king.org/78.htm, accessed 21 January 2020.

was condensed in this term, Jesus tells his followers, "But seek first his kingdom and his righteousness, and all these things will be given to you as well" (6:33).

Apparently, righteousness plays an important role. It is mentioned in fundamental statements made by Jesus: for example, that righteousness determines our participation in his kingdom, and seeking righteousness is to be the absolute priority in the lives of his disciples. So we can conclude that this fourth Beatitude opens an important door to life as God intended it to be. But what is this righteousness?

When the Bible talks about righteousness it refers to right deeds. Hence, a righteous person is someone who does the right thing in God's eyes. In Malachi 3:18 we read, "And you will again see the distinction between the righteous and the wicked, between those who serve God and those who do not." The apostle Paul compares the life of the righteous person with the life of a sinner, quoting Psalm 14:1–3, and reaches the sad conclusion "There is no one righteous, not even one" (Rom 3:10). It becomes clear that it is out of the reach of any human being to live in true righteousness, always doing the right things according to God's will. Therefore, it was his faith that was credited to Abraham as righteousness, not his own right deeds (Rom 4:3–5). Our hope for doing the right thing is only in God, for he is our righteousness. The prophet Jeremiah proclaims God's name to be "The LORD Our Righteous Saviour" (Jer 33:14–16). Our hope is in his promise to take action on our misery – a promise we find in Isaiah: "I am bringing my righteousness near, it is not far away; and my salvation will not be delayed. I will grant salvation to Zion, my splendour to Israel" (Isa 46:13). And indeed, God kept his promise. As human beings were not sufficient, God sent his Son, Jesus Christ, who became our righteousness for us (1 Cor 1:30). It is Christ who justifies us (Rom 3:26), and those who turn to him become a new creation and "the righteousness of God" (2 Cor 5:17, 21). When we hunger and thirst for righteousness we basically wait on God's initiative to change our misery.[30]

Hence, righteousness is a state that follows justification. Only when we are justified can we live righteous lives. And we ought to live righteously because faith by itself, if it is not accompanied by action, is dead (Jas 2:17).[31]

Yet what exactly are those right deeds? What is right action according to God's will? What's fair, just and right in his eyes? It's good to ask such questions, for this is probably exactly what Jesus meant by hungering and thirsting for

---

30. Schweizer, *Good News*, 91.
31. For further discussion on the link between righteousness and justification, see Hagner, *Matthew*, 93.

righteousness: asking and checking whether our actions are right in *his* eyes before we proceed with them. For as we are new creations in Christ, "we are God's handiwork, created in Christ Jesus to do good works, which God prepared in advance for us to do" (Eph 2:10). We are hungry and thirsty when we become passionate to live according to our calling.

On the one hand, this means living a life according to God's commandments, a life aligned with his compassion and care for our neighbours in need – as we all know his will for us in general. On the other hand, it means living out our very personal callings that God has for each one of us. That's why God "himself gave the apostles, the prophets, the evangelists, the pastors and teachers, to equip his people for works of service" (Eph 4:11–12). In short, we are different and we have different callings; hence, to live our lives in righteousness according to God's will does not mean the same thing for all of us. Living a righteous life does not mean following a list we all have where we simply tick off our duties. On the contrary, when we live by his Spirit, it's all about freedom in him – and this, by definition, excludes any unfair, fleshly act, as Paul writes to the Galatians: "So I say, live by the Spirit, and you will not gratify the desires of the flesh" (Gal 5:16). We will refrain from any sin and live our lives in righteousness under the guidance of God's Spirit. For this reason, Paul kneels before God asking to be transformed in his inner being into the likeness of God and to his fullness through the Spirit (Eph 3:14–15). That's the only way we can handle a life of righteousness! Jesus promises blessings to those who really hunger and thirst for this transformation.

Therefore, all who follow Christ face two tasks: first, with eyes opened to the world around us, we are confronted with the challenge of how this world may be brought back under God's reign. How should we deal with the unjust and unfair situations we all face everywhere? Christ's disciples should hunger and thirst to find answers to that question – with their hearts always troubled by the injustice they see, finding their rest and peace only in God himself – even if this means persecution and harm while actively seeking God's justice. After the eighth Beatitude Jesus makes a sort of postscript comment: "Blessed are those who are persecuted because of righteousness, for theirs is the kingdom of heaven. Blessed are you when people insult you, persecute you and falsely say all kinds of evil against you because of me. Rejoice and be glad, because great is your reward in heaven, for in the same way they persecuted the prophets who were before you" (Matt 5:10–12).

So the real question is: how can we personally and specifically find answers to the challenge of our unjust surroundings? We shouldn't rush into blind activism but rather find specific deeds of righteousness. When we seek to be the light of the world we need to shine in a specific place with our light focused in order to pierce the darkness.

Those who long to live according to God's will in every aspect of their daily lives are promised that they "will be filled." If we are hungry and thirsty for a life given by God under the guidance of his Spirit, it will certainly pay off! We will experience God putting us in the right places and our lives being an anchor of justice for those around us. And we will live righteously without struggling and fighting for righteousness, because our lives will reflect the "truth": He who desires what God desires may wish for all he wants.

Missional families want to live their lives according to God's righteousness. Every situation they face makes them hungry and thirsty for him to tell them what to do for the people around them. And they won't find peace until they have done so practically.

Compassion: The Main Motivation Is Mercy!

In his fifth Beatitude Christ seems to quote passages from the Old Testament: for example, Proverbs 14:21 says, ". . . but blessed is the one who is kind to the needy," while Jesus says, "Blessed are the merciful, for they will be shown mercy" (Matt 5:7). Mercy and compassion mean showing unconditional love and a devotion we have not deserved. We are not naturally merciful. Mercy and grace are rather part of God's unique character, because he *is* love (1 John 4:7) and he is "a compassionate and gracious God" – that's how his people knew him (Exod 34:6) and what they praised him for (e.g. in Ps 103:8). Jesus taught his listeners about the loving and gracious Father – for example, in the parable of the lost son: every day the father waits for the return of his son, who has squandered all his money, and when the son returns his father forgives him and restores him (Luke 15:11–32). This is God's mercy, compassion and grace stretching out to everyone who turns back to him. We don't deserve the grace that released us from sin's slavery (Eph 2:4–5). We don't deserve to be made God's heirs (Eph 1:18).

God is full of mercy and grace. And if we have a personal relationship with him, his compassion will capture our hearts as well. Jesus demands compassion of those who claim to know God. In the well-known parable of the good Samaritan (Luke 10:25–37) Christ makes it very clear that it is not religion and piety that make us compassionate people. Only those are merciful who participate in God's nature since God is full of grace (2 Pet 1:4). Only those born of God – who is love – are able to love as he does (1 John 4:7). It is God's compassion that makes us compassionate. God is not able to look away and pass by the misery of his creation, and neither can the "good Samaritans" walk by. It was the righteous man Job who declared, "I rescued the poor who cried for help, and the fatherless who had none to assist them. The one who was dying blessed me; I made the widow's heart sing. I put on righteousness as my clothing; justice was my robe and my turban. I was eyes to the blind and feet to the lame. I was a father to the needy; I took up the case of the stranger" (Job 29:12–16).

"But this is too big a task," you may interject. Actually, I do not agree, because when we live and act in God's compassion, we reap his compassion ourselves. Jesus says that the merciful "will be shown mercy." In Proverbs 11:25 we read: "A generous person will prosper; whoever refreshes others will be refreshed." David sang in Psalm 41:1–3, "Blessed are those who have regard for the weak; the LORD delivers them in times of trouble. The LORD protects and preserves them – they are counted among the blessed in the land – he does not give them over to the desire of their foes. The LORD sustains them on their sick-bed and restores them from their bed of illness."

Missional families know about their ministry of compassion. Grace and mercy determine their actions. And they know that nothing they give will be in vain: God himself will restock their resources. God's promise as given by Paul to the Philippians is true for us as well: "And my God will meet all your needs according to the riches of his glory in Christ Jesus" (Phil 4:19).

Sanctification: Keeping Our Hearts Pure

In his sixth Beatitude Jesus talks about our hearts: "Blessed are the pure in heart, for they will see God" (Matt 5:8). We can only live our lives according to our callings when our hearts are pure. Only the pure in heart will see God, thus taking direction from him.

Why are our hearts that important? Biologically, it is simply explained: we all know that this central organ supplies our body with blood which in turn supplies all other organs and body parts with everything we need. When our hearts become sclerotic or blocked somehow, our lives are in danger! So we can understand Christ's metaphor of an impure heart.

But what exactly does Jesus mean by "heart" here? When Scripture talks about our hearts, it means the centre of our being. It is the "location" of our passions and desires, of wisdom and sense. We know of Solomon receiving "a wise and discerning heart" from God (1 Kgs 3:12). However, the human heart is also the dwelling place of evil thoughts and evil desires which bring our lives into trouble (Gen 6:5; 8:21). Jesus explained, "For out of the heart come evil thoughts – murder, adultery, sexual immorality, theft, false testimony, slander" (Matt 15:19).

Thus, there's nothing we ought to watch more than our hearts: "Above all else, guard your heart, for everything you do flows from it" (Prov 4:23). The state of our hearts determines our lives – whether we live blessed and good lives or whether we live unhappy, evil and ruined lives.

If we really wish to follow in Jesus's footsteps, we need to have sound hearts. Yet our hearts are not pure! Proverbs 20:9 says: "Who can say, 'I have kept my heart pure; I am clean and without sin'?" Clearly this question is rhetorical, for the answer has to be "Nobody can!" That's why people ask God to purify their hearts – as David prays in Psalm 51:10: "Create in me a pure heart, O God, and renew a steadfast spirit within me."

What does it mean to have a "pure" heart? The Greek word for "pure" in Matthew 5:8 is *katharos* which speaks of moral purity, of a heart cleansed from any filthy sin. But the Greek term also describes a heart that is undivided, unadulterated and focused. A pure heart has no hidden agenda, no questionable motives. This is a heart after God's heart – or, to be more precise, a heart soaked and filled by God's love and character!

So it cannot be down to any human achievement to have or get such a heart; rather it is God himself who purifies and cleanses our hearts: "But if we walk in the light, as he is in the light, we have fellowship with one another, and the blood of Jesus, his Son, purifies us from all sin" (1 John 1:7). A heart that is pure, a heart that believes, is able to accept the gospel (Rom 10:9). And whoever accepts the gospel of Christ accepts the Lord himself, making him or her a new creation (2 Cor 5:17) with a pure heart (1 Tim 1:5). Only then will we produce a good crop as a natural consequence (Luke 8:15).

God wants us to live our lives according to his will, which means loving him and our neighbours as ourselves. When Jesus was asked about the greatest commandment he responded by quoting God's command in the Torah: "'Love the Lord your God with all your heart and with all your soul and with all your mind.' This is the first and greatest commandment. And the second is like it: 'Love your neighbour as yourself'" (Matt 22:34–40; cf. Lev 19:18; Deut 6:5). We can only truly love when we love with all our heart. A pure heart is whole – it is undivided and thus able to focus completely on God and on our neighbour, with no room left for self-centredness.

Christ's promise for those with a pure heart is that "they will see God"! They will experience God in their everyday lives. Only when we experience God, when we know him personally, are we really able to serve him. Only the pure in heart are able to do his will (Eph 6:6). Only this way can we fulfil his mandate of being the light of the world as we see him move and because we follow him. For Jesus is the light of the world and he loves moving in the dark places of this world. Therefore, he who sees God is able to see his or her own assignment. When we follow him, we are under his command and thus fulfilling our mandate. In this way God's kingdom becomes a reality on earth (Matt 6:10).

Missional families know that their identity and calling come from God himself. They want to do what he wants to do in this world. Yet to discern and comprehend that in detail, they need pure and sound hearts. That's why missional families look first to have their hearts cleansed and kept pure before him.

Peacemaking: Bringing about Peace

"Blessed are the peacemakers, for they will be called children of God," Jesus says in his seventh Beatitude (Matt 5:9). Christ's disciples are to be peacemakers. The Greek word *eirenopoioi* – literally, those who bring about peace – refers to people who are actively committed to restoring peace between quarrelling or battling parties. And Christ promises bliss to those who bring peace to others, to those whose lives are peaceful, as God is a "God of peace" (Rom 15:33). To be able to do that we need to be close to his character; we need to become like God. Any peace we can bring about can only be the peace we have from God ourselves. Jesus knew that and made sure his disciples would have his peace. He often greeted them with the words "Peace to you" and he told them, "Peace I leave with you; my peace I give you. I do not give to you as the world gives. Do not let your hearts be troubled and do not be afraid" (John 14:27). Jesus gave them a peace that cost him greatly: Paul writes that it is through the cross that we are "reconciled . . . to God" and that by the cross "he put to death [our] hostility" (Eph 2:16). God desires peace and reconciliation between his beloved creation and himself. Paul continues in verse 17 by saying that Jesus "came and preached peace to you who were far away and peace to those who were near." Therefore, as his disciples we are called to be ambassadors of his reconciliation (2 Cor 5:18–20).

Peacemaking is a ministry and task given by our Lord. Peacemakers do the right thing; they act within God's will and bring about peace in perfect accordance with their nature as his children. For peacemakers "will be called children of God," Jesus says. The prophet Isaiah proclaimed that "the fruit of that righteousness will be peace" (Isa 32:17). And the apostle James writes, "Peacemakers who sow in peace reap a harvest of righteousness" (Jas 3:18).

Of course, as human beings we remain limited even though following Christ's peace. Already among the early Christians we find disputes and controversies, dissensions and even divisions. Paul had to address the Corinthians as follows:

> I appeal to you, brothers and sisters, in the name of our Lord Jesus Christ, that all of you agree with one another in what you say and that there be no divisions among you, but that you be perfectly united in mind and thought. My brothers and sisters, some from Chloe's household have informed me that there are quarrels among you. What I mean is this: one of you says, "I follow Paul"; another, "I follow Apollos"; another, "I follow Cephas"; still another, "I follow Christ." (1 Cor 1:10–12)

It is human to have different opinions, it is normal to face conflict and discord, and it is typical for us to try to win disputes and to argue at times. However, all of this should not determine or rule our churches. For discord and dissension are acts of our flesh (Gal 5:19–21), and as Christians we should not be ruled by our flesh but by God's Spirit, bringing forth good fruit (note that peace is among the fruit of the Holy Spirit as described in Gal 5:16–23).

The apostle Paul tells the Philippians,

> Therefore if you have any encouragement from being united with Christ, if any comfort from his love, if any common sharing in the Spirit, if any tenderness and compassion, then make my joy complete by being like-minded, having the same love, being one in spirit and of one mind. Do nothing out of selfish ambition or vain conceit. Rather, in humility value others above yourselves, not looking to your own interests but each of you to the interests of the others. (Phil 2:1–4)

Being peaceable is possible for us when we deny our own glory and selfish ambition to seek the interests and well-being of others. Paul himself had to learn this lesson the hard way. He started his second missionary journey after taking a wilful decision, not listening to the counsel of his friend and mentor Barnabas. They ended up disagreeing and finally had to separate, which turned out to be an obstacle to the work of the Holy Spirit. Only when Paul reached Troas did he come to his senses, maybe because he was reminded of Christ's words "I am not seeking glory for myself" (John 8:50). When the apostle got back on the right track we read of a happy ending, as Luke reports Paul saying, "It seemed good to the Holy Spirit and to us" (Acts 15:28), referring to

Barnabas, himself and their companions. It is not about our own opinions and our being right, but it is all about the Holy Spirit and his guidance. And God's Spirit desires our unity, God's peace and righteousness, "so that the world may believe that you have sent [Jesus Christ]" (John 17:21). Later in his ministry, Paul would urge the churches of Christ to "make every effort to do what leads to peace and to mutual edification" (Rom 14:19).

Missional families are beholden to God's character, and God is love and peace. Thus, missional people will bring about peace and seek peace with their neighbours, their brothers and sisters in Christ – indeed, as far as it depends on them, everyone (Rom 12:18). They will make every effort to live at peace with everyone (Heb 12:14). Missional families are peaceable peacemakers.

Boldness: The Courage to Swim against the Tide

Jesus finishes his Beatitudes by encouraging his disciples to know his bliss in the midst of resistance and persecution to come. When Matthew wrote down his account of these words he knew exactly what Jesus had been talking about because his church had already faced persecution and hardship: "Blessed are those who are persecuted because of righteousness, for theirs is the kingdom of heaven," Jesus had told them (Matt 5:10). Blessed are those who are bold and have the courage to do anything for Christ's sake and his righteousness, even if they will be persecuted for sticking to their mandate in this world. Christ himself had to face resistance and persecution, and he did not promise his disciples an easy life: "Remember what I told you: 'A servant is not greater than his master.' If they persecuted me, they will persecute you also. If they obeyed my teaching, they will obey yours also" (John 15:20). The early church was persecuted the instant they preached the gospel and manifested God's kingdom for all to see in Jerusalem (Acts 4). Soon many of them had to flee the city. Living as a Christian has always meant living a life under threat. Jesus highlighted this by finishing his blessings with these words to his disciples; for the Lord meant them personally to the disciples who were present then (Matt 5:11–12).

So Christ's followers were warned that their testimony would raise controversy. They knew that they would be contested. But through these troubles they would become stronger. The apostle James writes to his persecuted brothers and sisters, "Consider it pure joy . . . whenever you face trials of many kinds, because you know that the testing of your faith produces perseverance. Let perseverance finish its work so that you may be mature and complete, not lacking anything" (Jas 1:2–4).

Persecution and trial for righteousness' sake will not harm our testimony; on the contrary, it will strengthen us: we will become more mature and even richer in order to complete the work that Christ began. Those who are bold will win the victory in the end!

Missional families are inspired by the courage praised by Jesus here. They let this boldness infect them to swim against the tide.

The Whole Family Is on This Journey

Christian families who are looking for their missional identity need to take note of Christ's Beatitudes. They should take this part of his teaching as a reference point to measure their growth in becoming more like him, for these eight character traits show their development towards a culture that reflects God's heart and mission. So again, this is about whole families who surrender to God and depend totally on him, who are empathetic and kind, who live in self-denial and out of compassion, who keep their hearts pure, who are peacemakers and who are bold enough to swim against the tide. If we cultivate such a culture among us and raise our children accordingly, we will soon witness God's support and blessing on our whole family. And we will see how he uses all of us to build his kingdom in this world.

Creating a General Framework

Any social institution needs a good framework to function well and ultimately to survive. This holds true for the family as well. Therefore, it is no surprise that we find a lot of teaching on structure and a framework for family life in Scripture. The fewer systems and structures families maintain, the weaker they get, and consequently, their influence on society dwindles. In contrast, strong and successful families emphasize frameworks that sustain their values.[32] Such frameworks start, for example, with our daily schedule (when we get up, when we wake our children, how we spend our time), and with our schedules making room for quality time and fellowship (do we have regular time to play with our children, quality time to talk and do things together, etc?). If parents lack quality time with their children, they will not develop relationships of mutual trust. When the children are grown up, they may sum up their childhood in one fatal sentence like: "My father never had time for me" or "Dad doesn't know me at all; why should I listen to him now?"

---

32. Covey, *7 Habits*, 136–137.

Missional families seek to install frameworks in their everyday lives that are inspired by God's mandate and mission. In practice, this means that they need time (1) for God, (2) for each other, (3) for fellowship with other Christians at church and (4) for people in their community.

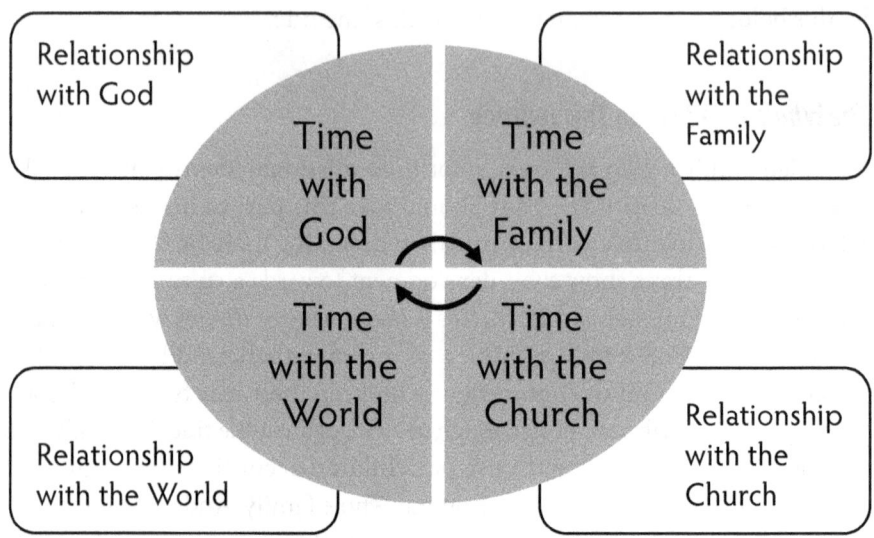

Figure 6.3: A Family Schedule Linked to Basic Relationships

Each of these four relationships is equally important for a missional family, as each realm reflects its calling and identity. Consequently, we should make quality time and space available for each of these four spheres of relationships. If our daily lives are too busy and neglect any of these, we will soon be in trouble. Certainly, our daily duties – our jobs, school, and so on – will consume most of our time and energy. Yet, when it comes to the rest of our day, we should schedule our time wisely for all four realms. And the important thing is not the amount of time we spend in each area, but the quality of that time.

Let's take a closer look at each of these four spheres, starting with our quality time with God. How do we invest in our relationship with him? When and where do we spend time with God as a couple? As a whole family? How often do we pray together? How do we manifest in our daily lives that we depend totally on him? It is not enough to think about these questions once or to listen to a good sermon about this; we need to actually do it – to spend time with God together on a regular basis. Children react very sensitively to whether God has a place in their family or not. Regular devotions as a family, regular family prayer times, Bible study together and discussions about the Sunday sermons are some of the many ways of becoming a kind of home church as a family.

My friend Sebastian told me,

> In my family there was nothing that my dad would not turn into a concern before our God, or at least an issue linked to him. If anything bad happened in the world, we could be certain that our parents would gather us together to intercede for that matter. Whenever there was something good happening in our neighbourhood we would sit together and praise God and thank him on behalf of our neighbours. And certainly, any matter concerning our own family members or our own little church would be brought before him. It has been our family culture to involve God in anything concerning our life, so today it's second nature to think of him first and pray whenever anything happens. This is no battle or religious struggle for me, it is part of my nature – God is part of my very existence in this world.

Sebastian's parents gave him a wonderful treasure. He has grown into a man who counts on God anywhere he goes. Why? Because when he was younger he experienced his family actively and authentically living in God's presence. Sebastian was raised in a missional family.

Missional families are not only connected to God, maintaining a good relationship with him, but they invest in positive fellowship with each other as well: in how they treat each other, how they show their love and affection, how they communicate, how much time they spend together, whether they have fun – in short, being happy together as a family. Happy families are attractive witnesses for the gospel of Christ. Therefore, we must invest in quality family time: we need private time and space for ourselves, for our individual relationships and for all family members to grow spiritually and to develop healthy personalities. We need time to learn, to make plans, to dream, to solve problems and to have fun together. We need time when we meet all together and we need private time individually; for example, the parents need to spend quality time as a couple, there needs to be special time for father and son, mother and daughter (and father and daughter, and mother and son), and even siblings need time together alone.[33] If we do not invest quality time in our relationships our family will be in danger of unravelling and falling apart.

---

33. For wonderful examples, see Covey, *7 Habits*, 137–166.

Members of a missional family have made a covenant with one another for one another. They feel responsible for each other. They perceive themselves to be a collective, a unity, a social unit, "one family" before their God. This takes time and consideration.

Yet, third, any missional family is also part of God's family – part of the global body of Christ and part of a local church. Here, missional families find their "spiritual relatives," their role models and teachers; here they receive encouragement and are called to serve other "spiritual family members." Here at church families grow, and this also needs time and space. So if we really want to live out church according to God's heart and serve him, it might not be enough just to attend the Sunday services.

And, fourth, missional families know their obligation and responsibility for the world around them. The family is the core of culture and society; therefore missional families have their hands full as God's primary agents for his mission to reach the world. We need to make time and space for our neighbours, friends and colleagues – and even for our enemies. If we limit our time in this realm we are not being faithful to our mandate.

It may seem that these four aspects – our devotional time, our fellowship as a family, our commitments in church and our reaching out to the community – are in competition with each other. Is it really possible to cultivate quality healthy relationships with all these people? Indeed, we might not sustain all of these at the same time,[34] and it is certainly not possible without being well organized. Therefore, missional families will establish good frameworks and structures to avoid being crushed under the weight of so many tasks. And they will pay attention to their attitudes and hearts, which will boost their resilience.

It Is All about Our Hearts

In chapter 2 we explored the Trinitarian character of the family due to its being created in God's image. We saw that the three persons of God have a close relationship. Thus, we could say that God himself faces the same challenge of many busy and burdened families today: Father, Son and Spirit need time for one another – time for fellowship, time for creating, time for his mission in the world. Why would we think God was not busy? Think of Christ's life on earth. Jesus said, "Foxes have dens and birds have nests, but the Son of Man has nowhere to lay his head" (Matt 8:20). Jesus was always busy, mingling with

---

34. For studies on family stress and possible solutions, see Balswick and Balswick, *The Family*, 245–272.

people and hardly ever alone. In addition, Jesus was "tempted in every way, just as we are – yet he did not sin" (Heb 4:15). How could he carry out his busy ministry without being stressed and sinning?

The answer is God's very nature within himself: Father, Son and Spirit have such a close reciprocal relationship that each depends on the others. They belong to one another in such a way that no one can ever separate the Creator from the Redeemer, Comforter or Encourager. Everyone is intertwined, and his tasks are not linear. This basic principle of God's Trinity and close interdependency is the solution for missional churches, providing peace and harmony in the midst of busy lives with all their challenges. Stephen Covey writes about this win-win principle in the family as the guarantee for a successful family life:[35] as we can be sure that we also will benefit from any investment of our time in God, our neighbour and even our enemy, it turns out to be a gift to ourselves; and when we recognize this, our burden gets lighter. That's how the Lord defined how we would follow him, explaining to his disciples,

> All things have been committed to me by my Father. No one knows the Son except the Father, and no one knows the Father except the Son and those to whom the Son chooses to reveal him.
>
> Come to me, all you who are weary and burdened, and I will give you rest. Take my yoke upon you and learn from me, for I am gentle and humble in heart, and you will find rest for your souls. For my yoke is easy and my burden is light. (Matt 11:27–30)

When we take up his mandate (his yoke) we will find rest for our souls, as his mission is about who we are and not what we do. Jesus manifested his own mission on earth by his whole person. That's why his name is "above every name, that at the name of Jesus every knee should bow, in heaven and on earth and under the earth" (Phil 2:9–10). And we as Christians, in our relationships with one another, should have the same mindset as Christ Jesus (Phil 2:5).

That holds true for us as families, too. Our mission is not a performance; it is not about what we do but rather is a gift of God. And we will be strengthened as a whole family whenever we spend time with our God, whenever we spend time together, whenever we are committed in church and whenever we serve the world. Any family following in God's footsteps will be blessed!

Elsa, a mum of three lively boys, told me,

> This revelation really set me free because for such a long time I had lived in self-pity, seeing myself as the greatest victim on

---

35. Covey, *7 Habits*, 169–170.

earth. Everybody seemed to want something of me: my family, my husband, the church ... as well as all those sermons calling for more commitment to reach our town – to evangelize the whole world. I couldn't hear that any more; my nerves were on edge. I used to hit the roof for no reason and soon I got depressed. Eventually we had a seminar in church about living a holistic lifestyle. And all of a sudden I realized that it is good when I spend time with my boys – as this is how God is pleased with me. And this is how I get prepared to reach the world; because there are mothers out there who don't know God, to whom I can be a witness of living a good life with three active, happy boys. I realized it is good to spend time with my husband, for this is pleasing to God, and our family is in good shape and my husband is better off – better prepared to fulfil God's tasks. It is good to have fellowship in church, for there I learn to have self-discipline and I can find peace; and I can also be a testimony to my brothers and sisters in Christ. And together we are better witnesses to the world. And it is good to help out at the local kindergarten and even meet my neighbours at the coffee shop from time to time. That's how I can serve people: they watch my life and get a taste of my faith. And this is mission! All of a sudden I realized that I had lived the life of a missionary all along! I had just not known that fact, which made me more and more tense. Finally grasping this truth unleashed hidden powers in me. Today I am busier but less stressed out than ever. I enjoy being God's child and being mum of three great boys, the wife of a wonderful busy man, on the staff of a good church and an active citizen in our community. And as everything goes hand in hand the burden has gone and I enjoy my life again.

This is how it should be in a missional family!

The Immune System of a Missional Family

When we start living our lives along this integrating principle we will learn the art of synergy, that is, the benefit of what Covey calls the calculation $1 + 1 = 3$.[36] When our different tasks coincide we can accomplish more by doing

---

36. Covey, 249–251.

them together than one after the other. Synergy effects can become even more effective in our family when we tackle things together with all family members or even with our friends.

For example, mothers often go to the playground with their toddlers. Their primary task is to let the children play and run riot (I'd prefer to say, to get some fresh air!). Most kids like playing with other children – they love connecting, and soon they become close friends. As the mothers watch their children play they might chat with other mothers watching their children. It starts with a bit of small talk and maybe a friendship develops. In this way one task – the care of children – is combined with another one – friendship evangelism: the mothers are involved with their own kids but at the same time they can take this opportunity evolving from their childcare. And maybe they can then invite all the children for ice cream in their garden, and even the neighbours will join them; in this way, they have been successful in mission without any extra effort.

Mascha reports,

> I'm so amazed by our God. He is so good at handling several things at the same time and making room for divine appointments. Our children made so many friendships in our neighbourhood. They are the best missionaries. I got to know my wonderful neighbourhood mums and we share in childcare. So, once a week I have time to myself. And together we started a mums and toddlers group at church. Everybody is happy about my commitment. One of my neighbours, Helena, is a tax consultant. She offered to do my tax return, which helps a lot as it always takes me days. Now I even have time to continue my studies together with another neighbour. She helps me learn maths. Even our husbands have become more mindful and affectionate. My husband who is not a believer joins us for church services because our neighbours are coming. Sharing life with other people is fun this way.

Stephen Covey states that synergy sets free a lot of capacities. It leads to new ideas and connects people on different levels. In addition, it helps recharge our emotional batteries, because when we work side by side creatively, our relationships will become deeper.[37]

Synergy evolves when we delegate tasks to our family members and to people in our mission field, bringing us into close contact with them. We reach out to the world together with people from the world, instead of just going on

---

37. Covey, 260.

mission: we serve *with* them instead of just ministering *to* them. Believe me, non-believers want to get involved.

In his wonderful book *How to Reach Secular People*, George G. Hunter III explains that effective communicators don't try to do all the communication themselves. They know that faith is received rather than taught. Whenever people get involved, faith is passed on through their participation in the faith project. That's why we invite seekers to be active participants in our fellowship as well as in our outreaches and our ministries in church. Many people come to faith within months that way.[38]

Hunter quotes a pastor Harnish, who says the same thing based on his experience. Harnish was raised with the concept that people first have to accept Jesus as Lord, then they learn to read the Bible, next they become members of a Christian fellowship and after that they learn to serve God in the world. Today, he observes that it's the other way round: people participate in serving the world, then they start asking theological questions, and only then do they commit their lives.[39]

Ideally, churches shape their outreach according to the people they want to reach. As Swiss Protestant theologian Karl Barth once said, church is a "fellowship for the world."[40] And German theologian and Nazi martyr Dietrich Bonhoeffer said: "The church is the church only when it exists for others."[41] He continued by saying that the church must shape society and be part of its community, and should do so "not dominating, but helping and serving."[42] These words from Bonhoeffer have been quoted frequently by both Catholic and Protestant churches throughout the world. However, this idea of a "church for others" also has loopholes. In his reflections on Bonhoeffer's claim, German missiologist Theo Sundermeier points out that it was in a liberal and humanistic context that Bonhoeffer demanded such a church.[43] And in such a context the church is in danger of becoming pro-existent – that is, it exists in order to serve others and their needs. But this may lead to a serving church

---

38. George G. Hunter III, *How to Reach Secular People* (Nashville: Abingdon Press, 1992), 99–100.

39. Harnish, in Hunter, *How to Reach*, 100.

40. Karl Barth, *Church Dogmatics IV/3* (Edinburgh: T&T Clark, 1962), 762–763.

41. Dietrich Bonhoeffer, *Letters and Papers from Prison*, enlarged ed. (London: SCM, 1971), 382–384.

42. Bonhoeffer, *Letters and Papers*, 382.

43. Theo Sundermeier, "Konvivenz als Grundstruktur ökumenischer Existenz heute," *Ökumenische Existenz Heute* 1 (1986): 62–63. See also David J. Bosch, *Ganzheitliche Mission* (Marburg: Francke Verlag, 2011), 384.

turning into a fellowship of those who have all the answers and have power over those "others." We find many examples in church history of the church gaining control over those who were needy by serving their needs. Therefore Sundermeier suggests that the call of the church is to exist with outsiders rather than existing for outsiders.[44] This means that instead of talking about pro-existence we should talk of co-existence.[45] Gourdet, missiologist in South Africa, offers a similar idea, observing that we need to identify with people, and in order to do that we need to authentically participate in their lives – which in turn means we need to work with them instead of working for them in order to reach them.[46] We need to get close enough to find effective ways of communicating the gospel; to find such ways we must learn *from* but also *with* the people concerned.[47] Any successful evangelism will come through sharing our lives with those we want to reach.[48] In addition, we can only pass on Christ's gospel in an open space where everyone may share his or her story with freedom.

Certainly, becoming involved with people in this way brings its own challenges. For these people are, by definition, different! They feel and think differently and at times will come up with ideas we may find strange. Only when we've learned to love them and come to appreciate their differences as gifts and enrichment for ourselves will we truly be able to work together and let them really enter our world. But whenever we see others as a danger and as our rivals, we will not experience any synergism; rather, we will face conflict and lose energy through friction.

As Christians we know that we were all baptized "by one Spirit so as to form one body" (1 Cor 12:13). We know our giftings and competencies. And we know that we need each other because we need the gifts and competencies of our brothers and sisters: no one person unites all the gifts and acts of service. It is only together that we manifest the fullness of God's work and power for the common good (1 Cor 12:4–7). Because of this unity it should be easy for us as Christians to share our lives with others – especially within our

---

44. Sundermeier, "Konvivenz," 62–63.

45. Sundermeier, 65.

46. S. Gourdet, "Identification in Intercultural Communication," *Missionalia* 24, no. 3 (1996): 407–410.

47. David Hesselgrave, *Communicating Christ Cross-Culturally: An Introduction to Missionary Communication* (Grand Rapids, MI: Zondervan, 1991), 46.

48. For example, Jacob A. Loewen, *Culture and Human Values: Christian Intervention in Anthropological Perspective* (Pasadena, CA: William Carey Library, 1977), 36; or Gourdet, "Identification," 407.

families – provided we know our own gifts and competencies, including our limitations, and provided we know the gifts and competencies of all family (church) members as well. Knowing that (and where) others are better than ourselves, we can be confident in their engaging in our lives with great freedom. If people are not afraid to share their lives, they can make room for a culture of "togetherness" according to the biblical pattern of *koinonia*.[49] In this way we will belong to a fellowship where people both care for one another and challenge one another. In such a fellowship we will be able to deal with the usual tasks as well as dare to walk in new ways. Such fellowship is like the human immune system: whenever it is strong, all the individual body parts will resist sickness and overcome breakdown; but whenever it is weak, they will develop badly and undergo stress. Missional families are immune to such harm as they mainly focus on good fellowship and walk in their spiritual gifts.

The Character and Culture of a Missional Family

We have noticed that neither missional character nor culture falls automatically from heaven. Missionary success is not guaranteed simply by emphasizing the family itself. We find evidence for this when we look at international studies of countries where the church of Christ is fought politically and forced to withdraw from the public space and meet within homes.[50] For example, Todd Jameson explored the situation of the home churches in Muslim Central Asia. He found these churches struggling to live as missional families despite diligent attempts by different missionaries to train missional families and to implement this concept nationwide. We conclude (again) that it takes time to shape a missional culture. As with any new culture, we adapt to the culture of God's kingdom through an ongoing process of transformation. Hence, we need to invite God to work with our families, or, even better, "let him bless our families," as Rev Dr John Killinger suggests.[51] This way, and only this way, our families will become who they are in God's eyes already – the prime mission agents in the world.

---

49. The Greek word *koinonia* (fellowship) means a mutual fellowship of enriching one another, e.g. Acts 2:42.

50. David Greenlee, "Growing Churches in Resistant Areas," in *Extending God's Kingdom: Church Planting Yesterday, Today, Tomorrow*, ed. Laurie Fortunak Nichols, A. Scott Moreau and Gary R. Corwin (Wheaton, IL: Evangelism and Mission Information Service, 2011), 219.

51. John Killinger, *Letting God Bless You: The Beatitudes for Today* (Nashville: Abingdon Press, 1992), 129–135.

Questions for Reflection

1. What would the consequences be for your personal development if your whole family bore all the responsibilities together as a unit, instead of each member carrying the weight alone? What would this do for your life as a father or mother, as parents or as children?
2. Apply the new thoughts and insights of this chapter to your own family and to the missional family ministry of your church. As far as Christ's Beatitudes are concerned, what difference should they make to how you live with your neighbours, your work colleagues, the parents of your children's friends at school or kindergarten, and so on?
3. How do you live out your faith as a couple? How does your spiritual life manifest itself? Do you share time in worship, intercession, devotions and Bible discussions?
4. How do your children know you live a missional life?

7

Family Mission in Practice (1)

As God, Even So Family

Let's talk about family mission in practice. Where and how can a Christian family really engage in mission for God? As we have seen so far, mission means that we are fully committed to living our lives in accordance with God's will, and that we do so in word and in deed.[1] God is missionary: the Father created the earth, the Son saved the world, and all the while the Spirit is shaping his kingdom. Hence, we cannot dismiss this Trinity of God's mission without consequences. If we stop honouring the Creator we will disregard and neglect his creation too, and we will lack motivation to work for the salvation of the earth and life on earth. If we lose sight of his Spirit, the Great Designer of all life, we will find ourselves alone and will work out of our own strength and our own intellects. But who are we, with our minuscule power, when left alone in this great universe? What can we do by ourselves?

If we really want to take part in God's mission we would be wise to follow his plan. Otherwise we risk doing anything but his mission. And family mission is no exception. The family is to follow God in his whole nature and live accordingly.

Church growth author George G. Hunter III, in a book on how to reach non-believers, describes a range of steps we should take to share the gospel more effectively.[2] In the first instance, Hunter emphasizes the content of

---

[1]. For more on mission, see Johannes Reimer, *Die Welt umarmen: Theologie des gesellschaftsrelevanten Gemeindebaus*, Transformationsstudien 1, 2nd ed. (Marburg: Francke Verlag, 2013), 195–197.

[2]. George G. Hunter III, *How to Reach Secular People* (Nashville: Abingdon Press, 1992), 91–97.

our outreach, and it soon becomes obvious that it is easy to implement his suggestions within a family-centred mission.

If we want to reach non-believers today, we need a theology that is close to real life instead of the complicated mental games sometimes displayed in church sermons. People need to be able to catch the truth in our teachings quickly, and they must be able to apply it to their everyday activities as they grasp the gospel's meaning for their personal lives. Today, whenever people need time to ponder and search the meaning of a sermon, the opportunity is already lost and they move on – we have lost them before even getting their attention. In healthy families, however, there is less preaching; instead, they live and experience their faith. Evangelism is an everyday experience; they are living testimonies of the gospel.

Hunter calls for the following six changes:

1. *Churches that want to reach non-believers need to use everyday language.* Our "Christianese" is neither tolerated nor understood. This demand is met naturally within families, because our daily family lives are usually not a sacred matter. Note that to reach this mission goal requires that we do not differentiate between our everyday lives and "holy Sunday services."

2. *Non-believers are not interested in dogmatic truths but are searching for real spiritual experiences.* Again, I see that families have an advantage here. For when we share our lives closely, we soon find out what is real and what is true of our Sunday sermons.

3. *Non-believers are not willing to reflect on nor able to ponder transcendent assumptions. They live in the here and now.* Therefore, Hunter calls us to emphasize truths connected with this life, instead of postulating transcendent assumptions. What an advantage for the family! For family life is all about living in the here and now, as our daily lives and schedules determine our daily routine. Whenever God and faith comes in, it has to do with this life now: our Lord will manifest himself in our lives here and now for all to see.

4. *Non-believers are not willing to divide their lives into separate secular and sacred categories. They regard any division negatively.* That's why Hunter calls us to live our whole lives under God's reign, which he claims to be more important than our membership of a specific religious group. Families have undreamed-of possibilities for manifesting God's life here too, if they comprehend their very lives to be an integral part of the *familia Dei*, the church, because in

this way, church life happens every day within the family, not only on Sundays.

5. *Non-believers are often focused on themselves. Self-fulfilment is one of the highest values today.* Therefore, Hunter insists that we communicate the gospel by emphasizing the value and godly calling of all people instead of preaching on sin and judgment all the time. Within our family settings, if we put the emphasis on the negative, it will soon cause isolation and alienation. In contrast, parents after God's heart encourage their children. They know about their children's faults and try to overcome them, not by constant nagging, but through nurturing and supporting them in their strength. Thus, there is great potential in families to manifest the gospel of Christ to non-believers in this aspect.

6. *Finally, we need to recognize that today, non-believers have a negative image of Christianity – of the church and us.* Hence, Hunter calls for the church to shape a positive image in society. This renewal is easier within the context of family than within the walls of a church.

In addition to the constituents of our evangelizing, Hunter emphasizes new ways in communicating the gospel, and these ways of communication are also best suited to family-centred outreach:[3]

1. According to Hunter, any good communication starts with listening instead of talking. Only when we listen and observe can we give good counsel. And again, it's in the family context that I see this principle working best.

2. We should share the gospel on neutral ground or in a setting familiar to those we want to reach, instead of dragging them into church buildings and special venues. Again, families can step in here, as family homes are not church buildings. And in their everyday lives they meet people right where they are.

3. Successful mission reaches out to people as friends instead of evangelistic targets that turn people into objects. As friends we learn to make Christ's gospel attractive and palatable to others, instead of imposing it on them. Through conventional evangelistic methods the evangelist has to be good at rhetoric to reach that goal, while the family can pull out all the stops of verbal and non-verbal communication.

---

3. Hunter, *How to Reach*, 98–106.

4. If we want to share the gospel successfully we cannot rely on the power of words and persuasion; we need the power of personal experience. Therefore our outreach should always involve and engage with people. The people we want to reach with the gospel ought to experience the gospel themselves first. That approach only works when we are open to letting them take part. Yet note that people need to share our faith in order to be able to accept it. And this again points to the family, as active participation is a lot easier in a family setting than in a church.

5. Effective communication aims at addressing people's burning issues. There is no greater harm done to the gospel than by addressing topics which are totally irrelevant. Again, the family beats any other setting here because within the home, we quickly find out what people are interested in and what they perceive as less significant. By contrast, within the setting of a public evangelistic rally, the speaker is confronted with a variety of people and different interests. Here, it is difficult to bring the gospel home for everyone. In contrast, when we share the gospel at home we can pay attention to the individual listener.

6. Successful communication is a process. It allows our dialogue partners or friends to get more and more information and gain insight at their own pace. Any paradigm shifts and new understandings also need time and space. However, typical evangelistic crusades have a tight schedule – even when done over several days or weeks – and we need to plan and organize our communication. In contrast, within the family setting it's easy to share the gospel as we live alongside each other. We know each other well and we have time to talk.

7. Reaching people with the gospel effectively is an individual process. Bryan Green is right to say that mission of the masses won't work.[4] To win people for Christ is something personal because we are calling individuals to follow him. The private home and the personal fellowship of the family seems to be the most suitable setting for this personal approach.

Postmodern evangelism is an integrating, holistic process in the midst of our everyday lives, manifesting itself in word and deed. In theological terms,

---

[4]. Green, in Hunter, 104.

we speak of the kerygmatic (proclaiming), diaconical (serving), liturgical (celebrating), political (social) and koinonial (dialogical) dimensions of fulfilling our mandate[5] to glorify God and build his kingdom.

How do these dimensions apply to the family's mandate to transform the world? Are these dimensions reserved exclusively for the church and therefore not applicable to our families? Let's explore this in more detail.

Mission Needs Our Testimony

The church's mission started on the day of Pentecost, when Jesus fulfilled his promise to send his Spirit, enabling his disciples to be his witnesses in Jerusalem, in all Judea and Samaria, and to the ends of the earth (Acts 1:8) – and indeed they were his witnesses by giving testimony about his renewing power, his salvation and his life in all its fullness.

Any mission starts with our testimony. And our witnessing will only be effective when seen and heard in public.[6] That's why Jesus told his disciples that they were the salt and light of the world, a town built on a hill and that they should let their light shine for everyone (Matt 5:13–15). Certainly, we are not from the world, but we are sent into the world. And here on earth we should be as one and should live according to God's will so that the world may believe Christ is the Saviour (John 17:16–21). And, as we saw earlier, the Holy Spirit chose the private home and the family to be the place where his testimony would speak the loudest. Indeed, Christian families have a place in society where they are most exposed and have manifold opportunities to witness to and manifest the power of the gospel of Christ. The following are some examples.

One of my church members has a neighbour who told me the story of their friendship:

> I've observed my neighbours for a long time now. I've noticed how this couple treat each other and how they raise their children. I've watched them quarrel and reconcile again. Sometimes I've even had the impression that they did not want to hide their lives from me. On the contrary! They've invited us for dinners. We've celebrated birthday parties together. We've helped each other in our gardens and with extra cleaning jobs. We've even gone on holiday together. We've become friends – really true friends. Except that

---

5. Hunter, 198–206.

6. H. L. Ellison, *The Household Church: Apostolic Practice in a Modern Setting* (London: Paternoster, 1963), 22.

their faith bothered me. No, they didn't try to drag us into church. They didn't flaunt their Jesus. And yet, *he* was there, everywhere. Any incident they seemed to see through God's eyes. Every now and again they would say "Praise God!" or "Thank you, Lord." So I took the initiative in addressing their faith, hoping to convince them how stupid and naive their trust in God was. To no avail. My mockery even seemed to strengthen them. And they displayed such confidence that in the end, we accepted their offer to pray for us – because any family faces times of trouble, and when our kids got older we faced more than one crisis. At times, we were in serious trouble. Our neighbours, with their sort of holy peace, became a safe haven for us. So today, after all those years, I know that it's their faith in Jesus Christ that has made the difference and has made them the people they are today. So in the end, it was their living testimony that intensified my interest in Christ.

Our family life has the power to convince people of the truth and the reality of the gospel – if we open our homes to the people around us. And actually, our culture gives us countless opportunities to get in contact with the neighbours living close to our homes. Certainly, we can isolate ourselves: we can invest solely in our homes and host only preferred guests – and only when our schedules and plans allow us to. But intimacy and trust are not built on schedules and programmes. Trust is grown on relationships that are authentic in real life. So to open up our homes and build good relationships with our neighbours means making ourselves available for contact beyond our schedules and investing in a "welcome culture" as a whole family.

Quite often, this happens through the children, as they quickly connect with other kids. As mentioned in previous chapters, it is easy for them to get to know each other and spend time together, as they don't hesitate to play whenever there's a chance. Once your child has made friends with the neighbour's children, it won't be long before you enter your neighbour's house. To build a good relationship, you need to open your home and allow your neighbour's children to play there. If you treat your neighbour's children kindly you will soon meet their parents. In addition, if we spend quality time with our children by playing crazy games together and letting them help in the house and garden, our home will attract other people, especially when we include the neighbour's children, and we will get known in our community very quickly. Petra, a single mother, once told me, "I'm so glad that I've got a flat close to the Müllers – otherwise, I wouldn't know how to live my life as a single mum with two children. Often I come home late and I'm really exhausted. Yet I know that my children are well. I can count on my neighbour Renate – she's such a kind person, she will have organized something fun for my children even though she's a mum of three herself. The Müllers are the greatest gift to me."

That's what I understand a true Christian testimony to be: to love our neighbour as much as we love ourselves. How easy it is to show that kind of love in our community when our neighbours need our help! When we love our neighbours, doors will open for our personal testimony and ultimately for the gospel.

Furthermore, we can adopt the same approach with the people connected to our children's kindergarten, school or the sports club around the corner; we can help out and make contact in hospitals, homes for the elderly and even when we are at a funeral; or we might simply serve our colleagues at work. There is life happening everywhere, and where there's life we find opportunities to help and get in contact with people. And where there's life, we will find family life taking place, as most people live in settings connected to the family cycle. We can hardly help living in this cycle – not even those who try to escape and renounce the institution of the family can avoid it. The stages of this cycle determine to a great extent what we've learned about life, and it's these seasons that we build our security and happiness upon. Whenever Christians make a difference in this cycle, everyone is confronted by it, and the gospel becomes very attractive. When we enjoy life instead of worrying all the time, when we handle the challenges of life better or when we solve problems and conflict in a better way than non-believers, it will naturally start a process of evangelism. But it is only when we are transparent that our lives will be attractive; only when others can see our lives will they be attracted. In a nutshell, being missional means being transparent witnesses.

Mission Needs Our Servanthood

When we truly mingle with people and when we really love our neighbours, we won't close our eyes to their challenges and needs. Besides, people will ask for our help when they see our testimony and are attracted to our lives.

Throughout church history, churches and Christians have been known for their ministries of serving the needy and the poor, and those who have followed Christ have been engaged in shaping humane societies. As societies – indeed all our lives – pass along the family life cycle, any such ministry will come across the family sooner or later. And vice versa: any family in an active missional church will be involved in serving people around them.

Supporting Children

Any mission committed to the *missio Dei* is committed to life itself – life as given by God. In this light, all human life already starts in a missionary context, so to speak, as from the very beginning we care for our babies, we raise and educate our toddlers, and we socialize and enculturate our children, thus equipping them within the family to become independent mature grown-ups, capable of managing their lives themselves one day. It was God's intention from the beginning that we should all start our lives as needy creatures, incapable of living on our own and dependent on adults to look after us. As we grow older we pass through the stages of personal development, discovering our potential and learning to use it with dignity. All of this development happens mainly within the context of the family: it is our family that shapes our personality and leaves an imprint on how we live the rest of our lives – and whether that is in a healthy way or not depends on how we've been socialized by our background.

Consequently, any family's mission task starts right at the beginning of a newborn family member's life. God gave to humankind the Cultural Mandate to be fruitful and increase in number (Gen 1:28); hence, the family has the mandate to conceive and nurture life and, even more so, to nurture what we all know as *humanity*. In other words, it is the family's assignment to make humankind truly human.

In Christian families, children are raised as Christians – that is, they are socialized according to God's will and they are supported in learning to live out of God's grace and power. In such families, the key to raising the children will be the parents' faith and their personal relationship with God. That's what the parents will speak about and what the children will observe in their parents' lives. In this way, the children learn how to deal effectively with life and how to love themselves, their neighbours and society.

Raising our children as Christians mainly means raising them to become sound and stable characters who know their own identity – because we all need to know that we are created by God and that he has a plan for us. We all need to discover our godly dignity, competence and assignment as created in God's image. In addition, we want our children to be likeable – how can they love their neighbours if they don't like themselves?

It is important to gain self-confidence by forging our identity, and therefore we need to have role models and find support in our families from parents and siblings, but also within our kinship, through our friends and in our church. It is good for parents to be open when it comes to the education of their children because in most cases, as parents, we don't have all the gifts needed to develop good character and personalities in our children. We don't always have the competence to uncover the treasures God has put in them. We sometimes fail to be role models in particular areas. But when we open up our families and homes, our children get the greatest positive influence from others as well, which they need in order to grow.

Furthermore, it is very helpful to grow up in a missional family culture. Think, for example, of a family that gives a home to an orphan or fosters a neglected child: while this family brings healing and self-esteem to a little one in need, their own children will grow and learn alongside. The children become aware of the brokenness and consequences which follow from sin and they will more likely later refrain from such sinful lifestyles themselves. In other words, to grow a healthy identity, we first need loving parents, and it's even better to grow up in a missional context where we experience the benefits of active Christianity at first hand.

A few years ago, we visited a slum in South Africa as a family, and I remember how our daughter, then five years of age, witnessed the great poverty there. We later saw the positive influence it had on her personal development. Our trip had led us to a Christian church situated in an extremely poor township on the outskirts of Pretoria. Our daughter was affected by the range of unknown smells, the omnipresent poverty and the sight of the multitudes of children playing on the streets. At around noon we visited a school for toddlers and lower grades which had no roof, no chairs or desks and no mats for the younger ones to sleep on. When we entered the building the teachers were laying the children down to sleep on the bare floor! "Why do they lie on the ground, Daddy?" my daughter asked me. I explained that they had no beds and no sheets. "And when it gets cold in winter?" she insisted. I told her what I knew: that it would get quite cold in this area and therefore in winter the people would simply stay at home. She was still not satisfied: "But why do their mummies and daddies not buy them what they need?" I had to tell her about the poverty in that country, which led to the next question: "Daddy, how much would it cost to build a roof on this school and buy beds, and how much money would they need to buy chairs and desks?" The local church's pastor knew the answer: it would cost two thousand US dollars.

Our daughter kept asking a lot more questions that day. For her, having been born in Europe and raised in a Western country, it was incomprehensible that little children should have to suffer like this. She kept talking about it. When we returned to Germany she declared she would collect money for the school, and she started this project at once. For a whole year she set aside any gifts, just accepting money as a present, which in turn she saved. In order to earn money she made hand-crafted items which she would sell. And the miracle happened: the next time I visited South Africa I withdrew two thousand US dollars from her account – she had saved exactly that sum of money! Today, our daughter is a mother herself, she knows what she wants, she is a healthy person and, above all, she is a warm-hearted Christian who loves and follows Christ. We are thankful for her great heart and character which were formed through experiences like this visit to Pretoria.

When our young people are socialized as Christians, it includes their learning to love their neighbours and serve the poor. Certainly, we raise our children as individuals, yet they shouldn't become egotistical along the lines of our individualistic society. Rather, they should learn to love their neighbour as themselves, as God commanded (Luke 10:27), in order to manifest his love and presence on earth. Their parents, friends and the church can show them how this command manifests itself in real life. Children don't learn by listening to words so much as by experience. They learn to love by dealing with real situations and real people, being confronted with needy people who are hungry for love. And they learn by observing love in practice as they experience their parents' commitment to each other or, even more so, when they get to a share in a practical serving activity.

In our family, from the time our children were little, we expected them to deal with all kinds of needy people who moved into our home to live with us. That wasn't always easy; at times, it was particularly challenging. Some of our special guests stirred our family life up. It would have been much easier and much more peaceful (and more comfortable!) to not have had them around. But that way, our children would never have got to know these people who were worse off than us. For example, we would invite a needy family to join us on our holiday trips. And it made us happy when one of our children would ask whether we could take a certain child with us on a journey, arguing "He/she has never been on holiday and has no chance of doing so – let's take him/her with us." Or "Daddy, you know I've travelled by plane quite often, but my friend has never been on a plane – why can't we take him/her next time?" This love and care demonstrated a character in line with God's command to love.

And what about those people we serve as a family? Certainly they will spend a wonderful time with a Christian family, yet to what benefit? In our experience, most of them actually heard about Jesus for the first time in their lives when they stayed with us. They overheard us pray and read the Bible together. A simple one-day trip to a lake could turn into a life-changing experience for them. And we would keep in touch after such trips; we made friends, and sooner or later their children would turn up in church on Sunday – and eventually the parents would come too. So whenever we open up our homes and families we guarantee the best Christian education for our own children by teaching them to reach out to others. They will certainly benefit from our missional lifestyle by witnessing people get to know God. And, needless to say, those people in need who get to know Christ through our family benefit from our open homes too.

What else can missional families do to practically serve others around them? They can help them raise their children according to God's good plan. I remember once, when I was teaching a seminar on education, a stressed mother came up to me complaining, "Every time my daughter returns home from the Schneiders she is so cheerful and really excited. Whenever we have problems at home, she says that she wishes she had been born a Schneider instead of belonging to our family!" The Schneiders were Christians and this mother's neighbours, and they had invited her to the seminar. Over the previous weeks they had been visiting each other more and more often – at first only the women, but then also the men. This mother went on: "I've learned so much from the Schneiders. Their lives just confirm what you are teaching here. So how can I become a biblical mother like that?"

The Schneiders had been a role model for this woman by authentically sharing their family life. So this women became a believer. In short, the missional ministry of the Schneiders started by them simply serving their neighbours. Soon these neighbours turned to them to ask for help for their colleagues in need. First, the families shared their issues on raising their children, but in the end, they all became good friends. This way, they built a family cluster – a cluster of befriended families.

Today there is a great need for such clusters because biological kinships don't live together in one place any longer due to globalization. Consequently, young parents lack natural reference points – people they can ask for advice – as their own parents live too far away. Therefore, it makes a great difference to have neighbours who happen to be experienced mothers and fathers themselves, or even substitute grandparents, to fill this gap. When such adopted family members are Christians they can be witnesses for Christ by their love that actively serves in practical ways.

Supporting People

People today face challenges not only in raising their children – there are many other issues as well. Indeed, there is hardly anything in our life cycle that does not become a problem at some point – for example, when our children leave home trying to find a good university place or quality training in order to get a good job, only to find themselves in a jungle of confusing and complex opportunities in a rapidly changing world. Our adult children cannot simply follow in our footsteps. They don't know what to choose, where to get trained or which direction in life to take. This is a vast area, and our young people need help, advice and training.

Or take another challenge: the question of whom to marry, or even whether to marry. As a young person, whom do I turn to for advice – especially if the older generation has also failed and my own parents got divorced? "Mum has navigated through three marriages. And she has never been happy. I don't want to become like her," a young woman once told me. She was accompanying a Christian friend of hers who had come to me to ask if I would give her and her fiancé marriage preparation. Having listened to our talk, the young friend said afterwards, "Wow – I think it would be a good idea to do that with my boyfriend as well." Indeed – for the happiest day of our life should be the stable base for a good life and the start of a successful marriage.

Most of us, therefore, are confronted with the same challenges: with the families we come from, with raising our children, with financing our daily lives or even building a house. We all have to deal with questions like: How do we handle all those things that cost us so much time and energy? How do we best structure and schedule our lives? How can we balance our lives and stay healthy? How can we realize our dreams?

And even when the mortgage is paid off and the children have moved out to live successful, happy lives of their own, we may struggle. For, all of a sudden, our home has turned cold and empty, and life has become too silent. The parents, left alone, go crazy. What do we do with all our extra time? Whom do we talk to when our partner falls asleep in front of the TV set every night? And when our spouse dies – what next?

All these questions of life, these challenges which we share with everybody else, can be turned into great opportunities to serve our neighbours. Any need can turn into a chance to manifest God's love in practical ways, and this may become a true mission field for a Christian family, or even a ministry of several families joining together to serve others around them.

Supporting Society

When we invest ourselves in our neighbours, we commit ourselves to society. Christian families teach their children to assume responsibility for society. This is God's Cultural Mandate (Gen 1:27–28) to all of us – Christian as well as non-Christian families. After the fall of humanity our God did nor modify or cancel this mandate. Hence, it is good for us as a family to intentionally address the concerns of our community. And serving our communities is the same as transforming our society; serving our cities means transforming our nations. How does that work in practice?

I remember when our daughter came running into the house in great agitation one day, telling us that a neighbour's daughter had hurt herself at the playground because it was always dirty and slippery there. We listened to her sadly, as we were well aware of this problem. In fact, we had already lodged a complaint with the town council, but to no avail. Our local community did not have enough money to provide public maintenance. But all of a sudden I had an idea, and I told my daughter to call together all the children in the neighbourhood for a meeting: "Go and get them together. Meet in front of the town hall and explain that you are not willing to put up with the bad condition of your playground any longer. Tell them you will gather every day until things change!" The very next day, there was a group of children meeting in front of the mayor's office. All the parents had helped them paint posters and banners and we had informed the local press. After two such public meetings a building company agreed to take charge of the playground. Our daughter was proud. She had learned that her voice could change things for the better and that her commitment had mattered to the whole community.

The Family Proclaiming the Gospel

Through manifesting an alternative lifestyle in accordance with God's will and serving the needs of their neighbourhood, missional families inspire people with confidence in active Christians again, which in turn encourages them to trust the churches to which they belong. And trust is the key door-opener for the gospel!

As we have seen in earlier chapters, the family is the most effective place to share the gospel. Throughout the world, we find outstanding examples of the success of family-centred evangelism. In his book *Evangelisation* on holistic outreach, mission authority George W. Peters explored and described mission in practice in the southern hemisphere. Again and again, he found successful methods based on family-centred evangelism.[7] The same is true in Uganda today, where a revival movement among the Umoja has also been focusing on the family, with great success.

---

7. George W. Peters, *Evangelisation: Total, durchdringend, umfassend* (Bad Liebenzell: VLM, 1977), 164.

In contrast to the southern hemisphere, the churches of the Western world do not have the family in mind when reaching out, as we have seen. Yet "there is no evangelism when there are no evangelists," as Arthur Bennett points out.[8] Therefore, whenever the family is neglected as the mission agent, evangelism misses out. Whenever churches do not reflect upon, let alone support, the family as an active missionary agent, they lose great evangelistic potential. Arthur Bennett studied outreach especially in rural areas and detected that Christians could do much more in these areas if we only revived "church in the homes" again as portrayed to be ideal in the New Testament.[9]

Yet what exactly is family evangelism? Simply put, it is proclaiming the gospel *to*, *in* and *through* our families. Any family-centred mission regards the family as the primary target of outreach, on the one hand, and the primary instrument of outreach, on the other. When we focus on mission to *and* through families our horizons widen to undreamed-of opportunities, as we can use the whole range of communication, both verbal and non-verbal, to share the gospel. We have already seen how, in contrast to all other kinds of outreach, the context of the family provides the most natural environment; also, mission in this context needs no complicated techniques of contextualizing to a foreign culture: it needs no translation processes and no laborious confidence-building measures.

We have noted how mission, according to the New Testament was family-based; Dutch missionary and minister Harry R. Boer summarizes the practice of New Testament mission by stating that the apostles always sought to convert and baptize whole families as an integral part of their method of doing mission.[10] In the early church, the home served as the gathering place for worship services, was the hostel for travelling missionaries and other ministers, and yet, at the same time, remained the most natural as well as the most immediate space to shape Christian life.[11] As the early church's position in the Roman Empire was a contested one, the private home was the best – if not the only – way to reach people for Christ. The privacy of their homes protected the early Christians from external enemies, yet at the same time through their homes they had better access to their unreached relatives.[12]

---

8. Arthur Bennett, *Rural Evangelism* (London/Oxford: A. R. Mowbray & Co., 1963), 19.

9. Bennett, *Rural Evangelism*, 24.

10. Boer, in Peters, *Evangelisation*, 170.

11. Eckhard J. Schnabel, *Urchristliche Mission* (Wuppertal: R. Brockhaus TVG, 2002), 1243–1244.

12. Schnabel, *Urchristliche Mission*, 1244.

Today, the family has not lost any of its importance for evangelism. Take Mary, a woman who got to know Christ in my church when she was already middle aged. She had lived all her life in a highly problematic environment, as she put it. Her partner Jim ended up in jail every now and then, and for longer periods of time. He was known to be a cruel and abusive man. A friend of Mary told her about Jesus and about how the Lord had totally changed her life. Mary became curious, visited our church and found a unique access to our Saviour. A few months after Mary had given her life to Jesus, she joined us as we gathered in our home one evening to read the Bible, when Jim suddenly arrived at our flat. With an axe in his hand, half naked and obviously drunk, he screamed out, "Is Mary here with you?" I tried to calm him down and to stop him from entering our home.

He challenged me, "So you're the pastor, are you?"

"Yes."

"Well, you're gonna change me like you did Mary – or else I'm gonna behead you!" he shouted.

Taking the axe off him, I invited him in. Jim joined our group and sat beside Mary. As the alcohol overwhelmed him, Jim was soon fast asleep. But he came back, joining our Bible study on a regular basis. He accompanied Mary to church and eventually gave his life to Jesus. Why? Because Mary had shown him what it meant to have a different life, and her testimony reached the heart of this hardened man, who was hungry for change.

Valeri, who used to be a notorious drunkard, got to know Christ through his colleagues at work. It wasn't easy for him to stop drinking but finally he managed to do so with the help of his friends from the local church. His life changed so radically that his wife and children became interested in these new Christian friends of his. They started a cell group at his home and soon most of his family members were following Christ too.

There are thousands of such life stories. There is hardly any missionary church without such testimonies. Other family members will notice when one of them comes to faith in Jesus and his or her life changes. That's why experts suggest that local churches should prioritize the family if they want to reach their communities. Indeed, such is the success among churches that evangelize in and through families that some rapidly growing missionary movements don't even count their individual members any longer but count only whole families. George W. Peters reports that to be true of the Japanese revival movement led by pastor Daisaku Ikeda: they counted the first convert of a family as one family. When asked by a missiologist why they counted that way, one of their pastors answered: "We won't leave this family alone until all members are part of our movement – until the whole family is won for Christ. The first person is just the door. Our goal is to enter the whole house. Our task is not fulfilled as long as we haven't won the whole family. That's Japanese culture."[13]

The Family and Discipleship

However, our mission task will only be fulfilled when the people who have got to know Christ have become responsible disciples. For God wants disciples – that's his goal for our mission to transform the world. Yet what is a disciple? In short, a disciple is a follower of Christ who lives his or her life in obedience to everything he commanded (Matt 28:19–20). To be his disciples means to trust and follow God's specific plan for our lives. And, as pastor Rick Warren states in his famous book *The Purpose Driven Life*, God's plan is essentially that Christians are created to be part of God's family.[14] Hence, discipling people means integrating them into the *familia Dei*. For God desires a family; as we have seen, he is the origin of family. So, when someone starts following Christ, we want that person to grow in faith – to become an active part of the family of God – with Christ being the "head over everything for the church" (Eph 1:22). Hence, the church is the primary family for new believers. In their book *Global Church Planting*, Craig Ott and Gene Wilson declare that the new identity of a person who has just come to faith in Christ goes hand in hand with belonging to the family of God.[15] For those who come to Christ, their relationship with God stands above all other familial, social and cultural relationships (Gal 3:26–29). And that's the key: the church is our family. Therefore, the biological family, created as a social unit of society, delineates the format of this spiritual family according to God's will. Thus, the church does not dissolve but integrates the family.[16]

Consequently, we need to learn to be such members of God's family. To become part of the church of Christ means above all to be discipled – that is, to be accompanied in a process of growing spiritually: raised like a spiritual newborn in order to "become mature, attaining to the whole measure of the fullness of Christ" (Eph 4:13). We have to keep in mind that our Lord Jesus

---

13. Peters, *Evangelisation*, 175.

14. Rick Warren, *The Purpose Driven Life: What on Earth Am I Here For?* (Grand Rapids, MI: Zondervan, 2002), 117.

15. Craig Ott and Gene Wilson, *Global Church Planting: Biblical Principles and Best Practices for Multiplication* (Grand Rapids, MI: Baker, 2011), 244.

16. For more on this, see the discussion in Rodney Clapp, *Families at the Crossroads: Beyond Traditional and Modern Options* (Downers Grove, IL: InterVarsity Press, 1993), 67–70.

Christ commanded his disciples to make disciples by teaching them to obey everything that he had commanded them (Matt 28:20).

It is clear that the early church placed this process of discipling into private homes. It was in the privacy of homes that the Christian faith grew. It was here, within the most intimate fellowship of a household, that the early Christians studied the Word of God, helped and supported each other, prayed and broke bread (Acts 2:42). In this way, in private homes, they became a fellowship. Urban church planter Robert C. Linthicum, studying church planting in cities, emphasizes that technically the Christian faith is based upon fellowship. His summary is: "No fellowship, no Christianity."[17] The church of Christ is a close collective, an intimate fellowship of connected body parts, because "we were all baptised by one Spirit so as to form one body" (1 Cor 12:13).

Certainly, each part of this body has an individual destiny, function and calling. The apostle Paul asserts that "we are God's handiwork, created in Christ Jesus to do good works, which God prepared in advance for us to do" (Eph 2:10). And for this reason, God placed people with special giftings and callings within his family "to equip his people for works of service, so that the body of Christ may be built up" (Eph 4:12). And this equipping took place where? Within private homes and within the natural community living under one roof. The apostle even compares his making disciples in Thessalonica with the role of a father or mother (1 Thess 2:1–11).

Robert Coleman, author of *The Master Plan of Discipleship*, writes that in New Testament times, the focus of mission was on the head of the family, because when the patriarch had been won for Christ he would lead the rest of his family to the Lord.[18] Indeed, our biological parents are our best mentors. This holds true even when their children reject their advice and rebel against them during their teenage years. Wise parents know that this season is normal and will pass. In general, parents are the first people their children turn to for advice when they want to learn about life.

Parents are role models from the very beginning. That's their function. Therefore, biological parents don't necessarily have to learn about the role of being "spiritual parents." They have raised their own children successfully – their children having learned to walk, speak and laugh – and they have mastered teaching them social behaviour and cultural norms. And their children trust

---

17. Robert C. Linthicum, *City of God – City of Satan: A Biblical Theology of the Urban Church* (Grand Rapids, MI: Zondervan, 1991), 26.

18. Robert E. Coleman, *The Master Plan of Discipleship* (Old Tappan, NJ: Fleming H. Revell, 1987).

them more than they would trust a stranger – even if this trust has at times been broken. Thus, it is evident that parents and close family members are best able to nurture faith, to naturally instruct and disciple others, in and outside their family (note again Timothy's family story, 2 Tim 1:5).

Christian educator Lawrence Richards claims that Christian education has to aim first and foremost at discipling children.[19] He explains that to be a disciple means to "seek to become like Jesus Christ."[20] He speaks of "the modelling method" in this context, referring to the educator being a role model.[21] Yet can we really be trained to have faith? Can we learn to believe and follow Jesus? Is it right to link our socialization within the family to a discipleship process?

If we take Christ's Great Commission seriously (Matt 28:19–20), the answer is "Yes!" For according to our Lord, teaching is a main factor in making disciples. Yet there are important criteria for this teaching. Swiss theologian David Plüss and his team examined a range of evangelistic courses to establish a list of criteria for effective teaching to grow in faith. According to Plüss, such a process has to be connected to:

- God;
- The Bible;
- A confession of faith;
- Our personal experience;
- The church; and
- The world around us.[22]

Let's apply these criteria to missional families focused on discipleship.

Connected to God – Personally and Collectively

Christian faith is a personal relationship between the believer and God. And our faith comes from God as it is a gift given by him (Eph 2:8), though we need to accept it. In order to be able to accept that offer we need examples to experience it in real life. That's why Jesus invited his first disciples to come

---

19. Lawrence Richards, *Christian Education: Seeking to Become Like Jesus Christ* (Grand Rapids, MI: Zondervan, 1975), 70.

20. Note the subtitle of Richards's book: *Christian Education: Seeking to Become Like Jesus Christ*.

21. Richards, 80.

22. David Plüss and Stephan Degen-Ballmer, *Kann man Glauben lernen? Eine kritische Analyse von Glaubenskrisen* (Zurich: TVZ, 2008), 103–112.

and see (John 1:35–42). Later, having reflected upon that theologically, the evangelist John got to the heart of observing Jesus, summarizing, "In the beginning was the Word, and the Word was with God, and the Word was God. . . . The Word became flesh and made his dwelling among us. We have seen his glory" (John 1:1, 14). Later, John wrote to the churches in Asia:

> That which was from the beginning, which we have heard, which we have seen with our eyes, which we have looked at and our hands have touched – this we proclaim concerning the Word of life. The life appeared; we have seen it and testify to it, and we proclaim to you the eternal life, which was with the Father and has appeared to us. We proclaim to you what we have seen and heard, so that you also may have fellowship with us. And our fellowship is with the Father and with his Son, Jesus Christ. We write this to make our joy complete. (1 John 1:1–4)

John and his companions believed because they had seen God manifest in Jesus's life. Their experience and what they had witnessed made them believe. Note too that John speaks collectively: "which *we* have seen." It wasn't only him, but all of the disciples together became witnesses of the same glory. And what they had seen Jesus do was soon the common experience of the whole community. As Paul says, "faith comes from hearing the message, and the message is heard through the word about Christ" (Rom 10:17). "What we hear" in this context does not mean a message uttered by words only – though words are also needed – but, as the Word becomes flesh, the message is both a verbal and a non-verbal testimony and hearing it is therefore a holistic experience. The Word has been becoming flesh ever since – it is flesh in the lives of people today. Therefore, the gospel can be heard and also seen, perceived and understood by everyone. It is in the reality of the flesh that our faith can be identified by others.

Thus children make their first steps in faith as they step into the faith of their parents by *experiencing* that faith in parallel with *hearing* what their parents believe in. Of course, it may happen the other way around: it might be the children being a living testimony and explaining their faith to their parents. But whatever the case, note that this happens within the family! It is the close fellowship of a family that best sets the stage for getting to know God.

Connected to the Bible – in Faith and Freedom

"Faith comes from hearing . . . the word about Christ" (Rom 10:17). Christian faith is, above all, biblical faith. For the Bible is the Word of God – his divine revelation. Our faith stands on what God has revealed of himself to us in Scripture. The great German Reformer Martin Luther postulated *sola scriptura* – by Scripture alone – a confession which should also be the basis for our family to grow in faith. If parents want their children to believe in God even when their testimony fails or their example is set aside, they need to make them appreciate the Bible early on. The Bible tells us our story, the story of all humankind, which is the only fundamental truth for our lives in the face of all postmodern doubts and confusion. Raising our children and making disciples draws on the Bible as the sole approach to God's promises. "It is written" is the weapon that wipes out all temptation, as we see from Jesus's example when he was tempted by Satan in the desert (Matt 4); he was able to strongly resist the enemy simply by turning to God's Word. This grounding in the Word is the only remedy for us mortals as well. When the Bible is fundamental to our lives we have a foundation that will withstand every conflict and challenge we will ever face.

Therefore, discipling within the family is closely connected to God's Word. Living our lives with our Bibles in our hands enables our faith and spirituality to grow; and at the same time, his Word will deliver us from all religious lifestyles which would quickly make us slaves again.

Catechism and Creed – Well Prepared and Clearly Understandable

Faith comes from the Word of God; however, quoting verses from Scripture is not always the best way to make the gospel accessible to unbelievers. That was clear even to the church fathers many centuries ago. Therefore they searched for simple formulas – manuals and guidelines for all believers to follow. Certainly, the different catechisms they formulated can never replace reading the Bible. Such doctrines do not live up to God's Word. Nonetheless, expressing the truth in simple sentences and everyday language does help seekers to find their way to God.

When we are trying to disciple people we need to use simple sentences that express our convictions clearly. For example, there is material that explains God as our Creator and Father, Jesus as his Son and our Saviour, and the Holy Spirit as our Helper and Comforter. There are helpful illustrations for why the cross and resurrection of Christ is of central importance to us. Such materials help us to understand. Furthermore, they knit believers together, constituting fellowships of people who share a common belief. It is then easier for new converts to lean on the faith (i.e. the convictions and creeds) of their spiritual brothers and sisters, and they can rely on their support and prayer within a clear set community. It is therefore important for families to belong to a particular fellowship and church. Such membership illustrates and underlines their belonging to the large family of Christians who have certain beliefs and convictions. Hence, it is worth learning the formulas of our confession by heart and professing the doctrines as part of the liturgy in our Sunday services.

Personal Experience – As Individuals and as a Collective Fellowship

Faith is very personal. Therefore, if we want to disciple individual family members and nurture their faith we need to adapt to their personal needs, because everybody needs to have a personal experience of God. So, the more a family includes God in real life every day, the more children learn to believe in God and have a personal relationship with him. In contrast, whenever we segregate our lives into everyday business on the one hand and spirituality on the other, our opportunities to nurture faith in others will decrease.

Yet our personal experience of God, involving him in our everyday lives, is not secret and private, because Christian faith is a collective experience too. It is within the fellowship of other believers that our faith is encouraged, prompted and supported. In short, we grow in faith when we experience God personally within the fellowship of our brothers and sisters. The closer such fellowship, the better the chances of growing in faith. Obviously, the family is the closest fellowship we can think of. When faith is real in a family it will automatically have a great impact on everybody.

Christian faith means trust that can and will be experienced in real life. Our faith is not just a way of thinking, of believing something to be true only in our minds: we must experience what we believe. If we think of God only in our minds, this image of him will have nothing to do with the reality of his existence. Faith without experience is ineffective. The apostle James brings it home by saying, "faith by itself, if it is not accompanied by action, is dead" (Jas 2:17). Yet, wherever faith manifests itself in real life, it is contagious and enables others to grow too.

Connected to a Church – Pushing Our Boundaries

Christian faith has always been a shared experience: it is a collective that *is* church. And church is, by definition, larger than our own family. Church includes other individuals and other families as well. And these other people have different lifestyles from ours and, thus, will push our boundaries by their personal experiences and distinct biographies. Therefore Christian families who want their members to grow will join a fellowship of other believers. This will support and grow their own faith, widen their horizons and enable all family members to gain new experiences.

Connected to the World around Us – Where Our Faith Is Actually Manifesting Itself

Christian faith is relevant in our everyday lives, it is empowered by real life – that is, life in our communities and the societies we actually live in. God has given us faith in order to change and serve the world around us. In other words, we can live our faith and experience heaven solely on this earth. Like our Lord, we are not *of* this world, yet we live *in* this world (John 17:11–18); furthermore, we are even sent into this world to prove and proclaim our faith.

Hence, Christian families remain open to the world around them. They don't hide their faith; in contrast, they manifest their belief by involving God in their everyday lives. Thus, they give testimony of how they manage their lives by trusting in him. In this way, faith is real and socially relevant at the same time. Note that Christ has sent us *into the world*; he did not command us to hide and live in a ghetto – escapism has never been part of his Great Commission. The dynamite (Greek *dunamis* means "power") of our faith – the power to reconcile humanity to God – will only be manifest among unreconciled people who live in this broken world without yet knowing him. It is in this darkness that our faith will shine and attract people to the Light of the world; it's here that we will get to know our potential and power in Christ.

In such circumstances, it is even more precious and effective to have families who disciple others. Mission takes place almost automatically by discipling in real circumstances. The family as a place where life is naturally shared turns into a lifelong workshop for all members to grow in following Christ. And wherever this workshop is opened up to friends and neighbours, to guests and strangers, and even to the poor and needy, outsiders will find both a home and a place to grow. That way, discipleship becomes a natural process; it doesn't need to be initiated as it already happens in real life.

Some years ago, we invited a young woman to stay at our home and live with us as she had lost her way in life. She was in great need of discipleship: she lacked someone to take her hand and help her deal with life. Later, she told us that those years under our roof were the most healing experience of her life. What was interesting was that, in stating that, she did not refer to me, her pastor and counsellor, or my wife, who had become a good friend of hers;

instead she referred to our whole family! It was our fellowship, our family life, that healed her and brought her back to life and was so convincing to her.

The Family and Church Growth

In their book *Global Church Planting*, Craig Ott and Gene Wilson write that hospitality and family-based ministries are essential for planting churches.[23] Unfortunately, this comment is left dangling in the air as Ott and Wilson dedicate only two out of their four hundred (!) pages to this topic of the private home being important for church planting, although it is clearly the object of their whole book to underline that connection. In contrast, real life and actual church planting should fill in this blank and emphasize the family and open homes: our churches must be practical experts here! Church growth must be centred around the family, as missional families are *the* appealing alternative for our society today; they are faithful partners of the needy, they are the voice and manifestation of evangelists calling people to follow Jesus, and their homes become the very places where people are discipled naturally.

Questions for Reflection

1. How do you talk about your faith and your convictions? Do you use "strange" Christian language and clichés which outsiders don't understand – and is that the reason why nobody wants to talk to you about spiritual things?

2. Is your life open and transparent? Do you let others take part in your everyday life so that they can observe the way you follow Jesus? Do others see and experience Christ in you? If so, how?

3. Do you know parents in your neighbourhood who would benefit from your being a mother/father? Do you know people who need your parental guidance, help and support in raising (or letting go of) their children? What role could you play? What might practical help look like?

4. How can you strengthen and improve the situation of the families in your community, parish or town?

5. What does your family life look like when it comes to your faith in God?

---

23. Ott and Wilson, *Global Church Planting*.

8

Family Mission in Practice (2)

Missional Character Put into Action

As we've seen, there is a missionary dimension to the very nature and calling of any family, which means that anything that happens through the family serves God's mission – even when it is not always obvious and most of it doesn't necessarily turn into an outreach event. In his booklet entitled *The Household Church* Henry L. Ellison wrote that the family is better able to connect the gospel to everyday life than any other institution of society.[1] Yet how does church, when focused on the family as God's agent of mission, turn from "being a church" to "doing life," as British missiologist and minister Michael Moynagh demands?[2] What can the church do in practice to manifest its missional character?

This chapter suggests practical examples of action that could be undertaken by missional churches with the focus on the family. Yet these are simply examples as real life, with all its creativity, has such a wide range of possibilities that no book can describe all of them. Therefore we present ways to find the right programmes in church, how to actually get practical ideas and then how to put them into practice. Our examples are taken from different cultures around the globe which means they need to be put into your context. Yet all ideas presented here focus on family mission and evangelism. Consequently, this chapter explores the less famous "door-to-door evangelization" (reaching

---

1. H. L. Ellison, *The Household Church: Apostolic Practice in a Modern Setting* (London: Paternoster, 1963), 33.

2. Michael Moynagh, *Being Church, Doing Life: Creating Gospel Communities Where Life Happens* (Oxford: Monarch, 2014).

from neighbour to neighbour)[3] approach rather than presenting the "front-door" approach[4] with which most Christians are more familiar.

Missional Programmes Respond to Needs

Missional churches bring their culture and mission into line with the desires, needs and questions of the people around them instead of aligning everything according to the needs of the church. As a rule, we could say that being missional means to mingle with the community or neighbourhood,[5] for we need to be in contact with our neighbours in order to know about their needs and concerns. Consultant professor Alan Roxburgh even demands a "radical neighborhood," that is, a church which is focused on its community.[6] To reach our community with the gospel we need to find out about our neighbours' essential issues and the challenges they cannot solve themselves, because this is exactly where they are trying to find help and where they will become open to talking, and where the good news presents practical solutions.

Therefore, we first must analyze our town and neighbourhood to discover these topics. Roxburgh even speaks of creating a "neighborhood map."[7] To map or analyse our community means to explore in detail the lifestyle, culture and environment of the neighbourhood around our local church. There is helpful material to enable you to do context analyses.[8] To use such material in the family context I recommend focusing on analysing the average family status and the family ministries offered in your community. For example, a Church of England task force undertook a survey of its parishes throughout the United Kingdom. The conclusion was that most of its churches had little or even no knowledge of the situation of the families living in their parishes that they had been trying to reach through their ministries. Consequently, the Church directed its parishes to further address and explore the situation

---

3. Elmer L. Towns, ed., *Evangelism and Church Growth: A Practical Encyclopedia* (Ventura, CA: Regal, 1995), 219.

4. Towns, *Evangelism and Church Growth*, 219.

5. Alan J. Roxburgh, *Missional: Joining the Neighborhood* (Grand Rapids, MI: Baker, 2011), 183–184.

6. Roxburgh, *Missional*, 82.

7. Roxburgh, 85.

8. Johannes Reimer, "Vision, Plan und Potenzial," in *Die Welt verstehen: Kontextanalyse als Sehhilfe für die Gemeinde*, ed. Tobias Faix and Johannes Reimer, Transformationsstudien 3 (Marburg: Francke-Buchhandlung, 2012), 37–84.

in their communities.[9] Another pastor, Joan King, even suggests doing such analysis in accordance with the life cycle of the family,[10] that is, exploring the living spaces and situations of our neighbours and community families from the cradle to the grave, focusing on their particular needs in their different seasons of life under the following key questions: what are their concerns and desires and how can our church meet their needs through our families?

The Needs of Families Today

We live in a world of rapid change, which has significant effects on families. What problems and challenges do families face today? We have touched on some of these issues briefly throughout the book, but here we look at them in more detail.

First, most families struggle with financial issues as life has become expensive. Children cost a lot of money. Nowadays, if a parent becomes unemployed his or her family soon faces such shortfalls that they have to change their whole lifestyle, perhaps even moving from where they live, which makes life difficult for them all. This daily struggle to survive leaves them with no time and energy to support the children. As a result, the children may fall behind in school, damaging their future prospects – a vicious cycle that mostly hits migrants and lower classes, the underdogs, of our society, with (at least in Europe) serious political and social consequences.[11] Our churches should meet these challenges any way they can. Yet we first need to understand the real situations of the families in our community in order to help in the right way.

The next big challenge today is the social misery of substantial parts of society. Economic problems often result from social problems. We can see the mutual effect: when poor families know they are different, they usually withdraw from the collective. Thus they avoid community fellowship out of embarrassment, especially when their neighbours belong to a very different class and culture. But, as a consequence, both the children and the parents grow increasingly lonely, and loneliness carries the great danger of letting people slide into unhealthy habits, with more children of the lower classes becoming addicted to online games and adults starting to abuse alcohol. So it

---

9. Church of England Board for Social Responsibility, *Something to Celebrate: Valuing Families in Church and Society* (London: Church House, 1995), 129, 210.

10. Joan King, "Families: Something to Celebrate," *Ministry Today* 8 (Oct. 1996): 48–51.

11. See, for example, in England: Church of England, *Something to Celebrate*, 139–140.

is right here that we as a church can come in: our support and love will open doors for Christ.

Living in a social hotspot or belonging to such troubled underclasses will always affect families in the minutiae of their lives: frequent disputes among couples, stressed-out parents who are overwhelmed by their children, and often an atmosphere of conflict and violence that is the norm. Such families are in desperate need of support, advice, mediation, therapy and consultation. Isn't the church best suited to caring, counselling and supporting them? When we know where the shoe pinches, we can develop programmes or ministries tailored to their needs and thus open doors to people's hearts.

The third greatest social emergency today is the lack of solid values and ethics. Some years ago, evangelism trainer and coach Christopher C. Walker identified five issues that are central to people today.[12] We need to know them to have the keys for sharing the gospel with non-Christians:

1. Today, people search for perfectionism. Self-fulfilment is the highest goal, overshadowing any other value in life. Everybody seems to test the limits, trying to enjoy life as much as possible and acquire the best of everything. According to Walker, this craving simply hides the search for our lost image in the likeness of God; we try (again) to become like God, and end (again) in the enemy's trap of trading transcendence for a godless existence. And we know where this path leads: humankind's search to be like God has always led us to destruction, pain and misery. The only true solution is the gospel of Christ, radically showing us that we are unable to save ourselves in our own strength.

2. People want to know where they come from and where they are going. Despite all the Cassandras today, people are trying to find their meaning in life and to orientate themselves. The theory of evolution, while seeming to explain all the questions of life, has left most people dissatisfied as it gives no real answers or solutions for our everyday life. Note how people today grab any chance to find out more about their roots. When I've come across people who were adopted as little children I've noticed how, as soon as they get the chance to find their biological parents or even meet with them, everything else in their lives becomes insignificant. They say, "I need

---

12. Christopher C. Walker, *Connecting with the Spirit of Christ: Evangelism for a Secular Age* (Nashville: Discipleship Resources, 1998), 24.

to know my biological parents" and "I must know where I come from." This is the true desire of someone searching for the meaning of life.

3. People are driven to create. And they want more. They seek challenges in life and enjoy meeting them. In any culture in this world you will find this desire, this zest for life and this search for happiness.
4. Today, most people find their identity in what they achieve. Their status has much higher value than simply who they are. Perhaps underlying this is the desire to find fulfilment in life and also to achieve maturity.
5. People long for a just and peaceful world. This desire for social justice is becoming more popular, especially among the younger generation.

Certainly, these general ideals of today's generation don't tell us what specific problems we might face within our particular community. Therefore, any churches focusing on practical solutions need to first examine their specific neighbourhood to find their missional strategy.

From Analyzing to Strategic Concepts

When we know what the people in our community are preoccupied with, we can start a strategic process to meet their needs practically, sharing the gospel in word and deed. Disciple-maker Ron Bennett argues for a paradigm shift in evangelism when it comes to reaching postmodern men and women, suggesting the following steps for changing our mission patterns: (1) from event to process; (2) from reaching out to the individual to reaching the collective; (3) from closed venues to living in the midst of life; (4) from one gifted person to the gifts of everyone; (5) from prayer for conversion to real conversion; (6) from the local to the kingdom perspective; (7) from doing sporadic outreaches to penetrating society; (8) from viewing non-believers as enemies to perceiving them as broken people.[13] Any church committed to family-focused evangelism will pay heed to Bennett's suggestions as his advice demonstrates in practice all that we have discussed so far.

---

13. Ron Bennett, "Authentic Church-Based Evangelism in a Relational Age," in *Telling the Truth: Evangelizing Postmoderns*, ed. D. A. Carson (Grand Rapids, MI: Zondervan, 2000), 275–280.

The Shift from Event to Process

Reaching out to families takes time. Evangelizing people in line with the New Testament is a process of people growing in faith – it is a gradual development rather than an event. The apostle Paul uses the metaphor of sowing and reaping (1 Cor 3:6–8), saying that we work the ground, sow the seeds and reap the harvest. And surely family life is like growing a crop: we know each other from early on as tiny seeds who need a lot of time to care. Teaching our children the essential things in life, and their growing up, takes time! If we want to pass on our faith to others, especially within our families, we need to have time and we need to let others take their time.

Churches that rely on their families as mission agents will allow for this time factor. They will support their families in any way possible without forcing conversions. Such churches will provide open spaces where families can meet, share their lives and take time to experience God. These churches will nurture parents to become role models to others in faith and in their practical way of life, and they will invest in children being raised in the fear of God. All of that supports families, and though proclamation will accompany all such ministries, preaching can never replace serving.

Note that such processes to reach families with the gospel can be planned strategically just like any other process in life. And any support is more effective when it is well targeted. So the question is, what might such a process of family evangelization look like? And how can we support churches to enable family mission?

The Shift from Reaching the Individual to Reaching the Collective

It is important for missional outreach that we aim at reaching the whole family rather than just individuals. Mission, according to the New Testament, is the task of the fellowship of all believers, who share the work: as the apostle Paul explains, there was one who planted and one who watered (1 Cor 3:8). Yet if we want the whole collective to jump into action, we also need to support the whole collective; so if the whole family is relevant for mission collectively, the church has to support and nurture the entire family.

That's why it makes sense to support and nurture fathers and mothers. Parents are vitally important for healthy families. Healthy parents will raise healthy children; parents who believe strongly will automatically pass on their faith to their children. So churches implementing family mission invest in sound ministries for mothers, fathers and parents as a whole. Whenever a father or mother becomes lost, the whole family is jeopardized and family evangelism programmes will fail.

That's also why it makes sense to invest in sound education, and why churches need to tackle all the issues around raising children and support parents every way possible. Especially in our Western world, we lack advice and support when it comes to raising our children: globalization, economic migration, prosperity and welfare have replaced the old form of kinship where several generations used to live under one roof helping each other and passing on advice. Christian churches can fill this vacuum by facilitating mentoring programmes for young parents by older, experienced parents.

The Shift from Closed Venues to Living in the Midst of Life

Family mission takes place in real life. Evangelism in the New Testament never took place in an exclusive club in a special building but in the midst of family life in private homes. Missional churches focused on the family should do the same: mingling with people and going out into all the world instead of just inviting everyone to join us. Such churches and missional families conquer the market place and public life.

The Shift from One Gifted Person to the Gifts of Everyone

Evangelizing families is a collective experience. New Testament evangelism happened through the use of the different gifts of different people: thus, it's not about the anointed evangelist, the one gifted superstar, but the Spirit moving, with his different gifts manifesting themselves through different members of the church of Christ and tailored to different occasions. Such an approach can be applied one-on-one to the family as well as to the network (cluster) of families within a local church. While an individual person may take on a special role and have the specific gifting to do so, nevertheless, it is the entire collective that is on God's mission. And ultimately, our faith and our giftings will be multiplied when we combine them for mission.

The Shift from Decision to Conversion

Christian mission aims at real transformation and change. When we make disciples, we are calling people to follow Christ – that is, to live their lives according to what he commanded all of us to do (Matt 28:19–20). We are not trying to induce a new religious conviction in people but to bring about a radical change in their lives – a genuine conversion. We can only speak of having evangelized successfully when someone has changed his or her life completely.

The Shift from the Local to the Kingdom Perspective

Family evangelism is a holistic endeavour. It is not about teaching just a few aspects of faith, building local structures for religious practice or simply moral change. Rather, family mission aims at changing lives in all aspects. It means nothing less than building God's kingdom and bringing God's reign on earth, and his kingdom will have an impact on our entire lives.

The Shift from Doing Sporadic Outreaches to Penetrating Society

Family mission relies on sustainability and does not settle for doing things only 50 percent. Missional families will never give up or abandon anyone, just as good parents would never abandon their child. Thus, setbacks will never end our relationships but will rather give greater space to God.

The Shift from Viewing Non-Believers as Enemies to Perceiving Them as Broken People

Mission is only possible when we have right ideas about people – that is, when non-believers aren't our enemies but rather our neighbours who happen to be in need of God's love and Christ's forgiveness, renewal and healing. If they provoke us with their behaviour, we will not reject them or get aggressive, but rather we will have compassion on them and love them. Family evangelism is carried out by our God, and he is the God of all hope. Thus, missional people are able to go the extra mile, reaching out in grace and mercy.

Connecting with Our Neighbours: Missional Families Are Active in Their Communities

Christian families connect with the families living around them. Like anybody else in their community, the adult family members go to work and the children go to schools and kindergartens. They buy their food at the same supermarkets. In short, missional families share the same social space as everybody else. Even if we wanted to, we couldn't withdraw completely from society or hide, unless we chose to find a community outside civilization.

Yet it is possible to live among people without being connected to them and without sharing our lives with them. It is possible to stay out of each other's way, to close our eyes to the world around us and to only see people when we receive a benefit from them. However, missional families will never want to live in such a ghetto, disappearing into a parallel universe or merging in a subculture. They mingle with their communities, they regard themselves as God's mission agents for their society! This includes joining in communal work to shape their communities and living spaces. Their mission is inspired by their community ministries and welfare programmes which set the framework for their actions in this world.[14] They will be a kind of drop-in centre for comfort and friendship, reconciliation and fellowship, counsel and support – a contact point for neighbours, colleagues and friends alike. There are hundreds of opportunities for such missional influence. The following are just a few examples.

Let's Make Friends! The First Step of Mission

Family evangelism and mission starts with friendship; thus, missional churches are hospitable and open fellowships,[15] because friendship develops where trust grows. A. Grace Wenger speaks in one of her great books about "family-to-family evangelism" (FFE),[16] simply suggesting that Christian families consciously and systematically make friends with their non-Christian neighbours. The key to building such friendships is hospitality, and we find this kind of mission by families already happening throughout the world. The Müller family, whom I got to know at a seminar in southern Germany, is one example of this. Mrs Müller shared her story with me:

> Whenever we moved into a new town [which they did quite often due to their professions], we would visit all of our neighbours first. We cannot imagine living our life alongside unknown people. And [she smiled], after having got to know us, our neighbours

---

14. For more on community work/ministry as an inspiration and basis for mission and church planting, see Johannes Reimer, *Die Welt umarmen: Theologie des gesellschaftsrelevanten Gemeindebaus*, Transformationsstudien 1, 2nd ed. (Marburg: Francke Verlag, 2013), 271–290.

15. Ross Hastings, *Missional God, Missional Church: Hope for Re-Evangelizing the West* (Downers Grove, IL: IVP Academic, 2012), 12.

16. A. Grace Wenger and Dave and Neta Jackson, *Witness: Empowering the Church through Worship, Community and Mission* (Scottdale, PA: Herald, 1989), 141–142.

couldn't imagine that either. There is so much that neighbours can do together, there is so much to share. And that's how we make friends. For instance, in this church you will meet wonderful people who happen to be our neighbours. And they first came with us only because we had been taking on half the world with them.

Talking with both the Müllers, it soon became obvious that this kind of friendship with neighbours does cost time and energy. It is straining at times. Yet, as Mr Müller commented, "Nothing ventured, nothing gained!" If we do not invest in friendships, we cannot expect much in return. "But it's always worth the effort to invest in people and in our neighbours," he said.

Friendships between families always pay off – especially in mission. Whenever we share a hobby or passion it opens up a great opportunity to invest time and energy in people, and soon we make friends with neighbours, colleagues and others who share our passions. In this context, Joe Aldrich, author of *Lifestyle Evangelism*, refers to the list of qualifications for overseers and deacons[17] that we find in 1 Timothy 3:2–3 and Titus 1:7–8. Here, the apostle Paul mentions hospitality as one of the key prerequisites for leaders in the church. The Greek word *philoxenos* literally means "to love strangers." Hence, this hospitality isn't about inviting friends and acquaintances, but is explicitly about welcoming strangers – or people who don't yet know Christ – into our homes.

FFE lives on such hospitality. The LOP 36 report gives the example of a local church in the United Kingdom that encouraged its member families to make friends with the families whose children went to the same school. At the same time, this local church became the official sponsor of the school, supporting it in every way. This way, they strengthened the friendships among their children, and people also lost their fear of church, and consequently of church members, as they naturally got to experience Christian faith.[18]

Other ideas along these lines can easily be imagined. For example, a local church situated in a rural part of central Germany became the official sponsor of the local football club; an association of local churches in southern Germany organized and financed a public playground for their community; another church started to run a ballet dance school for children; some churches have

---

17. Joseph C. Aldrich, "Lifestyle Evangelism," *Christianity Today*, 7 January 1983, 13–15.

18. Lausanne Committee for World Evangelization, "Non-Traditional Families: Reaching Families with the Good News," Lausanne Occasional Paper (LOP) 36, in *A New Vision, a New Heart, a Renewed New Call: Lausanne Occasional Papers*, ed. David Claydon (Pasadena, CA: William Carey Library, 2005), 478.

sponsored local health care centres; and so on. All these initiatives open doors to making friends with other families and to building family clusters, which in turn opens the door to naturally evangelizing friends who don't yet know Christ. The common care for children and the shared hobbies and interests build the trust that is necessary for successful and effective mission.

Let's Have a Party!

Any relationship gets better when we not only share but enjoy our lives together. Enjoying and celebrating life makes room for fellowship and friendship. And there is nothing on earth as effectual and easy as celebrating a party together. Our neighbours love having coffee and cake at our house and enjoy our barbecue parties. We have friends who even turned part of their estate into a coffee house for their neighbourhood. They renovated their old workshop and invited their friends and neighbours to join them in decorating the place in order to turn it into a party venue for all. They were overwhelmed by the excited response. Asian Reverend Alfred Yeo recommends holding family parties for colleagues at work and neighbours,[19] and to organize activities for the whole family.

As we've said already, children make friends easily. Whenever we organize games for them, we will win their parents too, even if they don't usually play with their children at home. Then, whole families also have fun, fellowship and make new friends. You may overhear children saying things like, "Daddy, for my birthday I want to have a party like this!" And your work colleagues may say to you, "It was really cool at your party yesterday." When another party comes up, your family will be invited. Never turn such invitations down. After several parties and get-togethers you will form a family cluster which is the best foundation for family mission and evangelism, especially when such a cluster becomes closer to your local church.

Pastor David Young, who is growing a church in a rural part of the United Kingdom, had a fascinating idea: his church encouraged its families to open their homes and invite their neighbours for a "spiritual" afternoon, a kind of "church afternoon," on Sundays. They advertised this action as "Church among Neighbours," telling the people in their community that Sunday services didn't necessarily need sermons and liturgies, so how about some fun, food and fellowship? Each family would invite six to ten people from

---

19. Alfred Yeo, "The Local Church Reaches Its Neighbourhood," in *The Church: God's Agent for Change*, ed. Bruce J. Nicolls (Exeter: Paternoster, 1986), 143.

their neighbourhood. And these people would come – especially if there had already been positive previous contact. David told me that this way, they grew neighbourhood clusters which met on a regular basis and ultimately turned into cell groups of their church.[20]

Let's Assist Our Neighbours!

There is a Russian saying, "Find a common task for two friends and their friendship will get closer." That's so true for mission through families! If we have connected with our neighbours or thrown parties for our work colleagues, why not build welfare task forces to serve our communities as well? Any community and society lives on volunteer work, as every neighbourhood or town faces problems that need to be dealt with, yet quite often municipal budgets lack the money or local authorities simply don't know how to solve them. That's why politicians count on volunteer public welfare programmes to positively influence and shape our living together. Missional families find many opportunities to engage in such programmes to care for their communities. So why not join with family friends and do such work as a cluster together? This is particularly effective as family mission is mission *with* families not (only) *for* families. Serving together to meet needs will strengthen our friendships and build trust, both of which open the door for sharing the gospel. Mrs Müller, already mentioned above, told me,

> We had been inviting our neighbours for barbecues every now and then. There was a family called Huber, an inconspicuous couple with two lovely little children, who always came round. Yet, this particular time, it was just the two kids. When we asked about his parents, little Fritz's answer came right out: "They don't want to come because there is so much windfall in our garden. And they need to collect the fruit to make juice. Otherwise we won't have any juice for winter. We cannot buy any because Daddy has lost his job." Everybody heard his loud voice and heard about the Huber family's situation. Then my husband had this brilliant idea: "Why don't some of us go over to the Hubers to help them collect the fruit? More helping hands means we'll finish quicker and the couple can still join us. Meanwhile, the others can stay here –

---

20. David Young, "Mission in Rural Community," in *Local Church Evangelism*, ed. David Wright and Alastair Gray (Edinburgh: Saint Andrew Press, 1987), 67.

prepare the food and lay the tables. Let's go!" Almost everybody joined to help and it was only an hour later that we sat at the table together. One of our neighbours commented, "We should do this more often. Tidying up is more fun together." And this is how our small neighbourhood service got started. And we still tidy up gardens. The other day, we cleaned the courtyard of our church and all the neighbours were there to help! It's really cool to eat, drink and even work together!

Certainly, there are other possibilities in addition to helping clean up our neighbourhoods; for example, you could provide a space for children to play. Some churches offer playgrounds even indoors during the cold season, turning the church venue into a kind of games park. This way, people get to know the church building from the inside without having to visit a Sunday service first, which is a wonderful side benefit.[21] I came across another example of such public community service in Brüchermühle, a little town in central Germany.[22] In order to do something for their environment, families join together to tidy up their village once a year. The whole neighbourhood is invited to tidy up and decorate, and nobody is excluded because of a different religious belief; thus Christian, Muslim and atheist families join in a common target and to share fellowship.

Some public welfare programmes in eastern German cities[23] run public kitchens where children get a warm lunch for free plus centres where they can get help to do their homework and have space to play. While their parents go to work, other parents who have the time look after these children voluntarily. These municipal ventures gladly welcome the help of Christian family clusters.

Again in Germany, some families in the small town of Olpe founded a non-profit initiative with the official name Families Help Families (Familien

---

21. Examples include "FeG Church" in Schwelm, "Winterspielplatz im Gemeindehaus," accessed 10 May 2015, http://feg-schwelm.de/wp-content/uploads/2014/12/20130207_WP0001.pdf; City Mission in Berlin, Berliner Stadtmission, accessed 10 May 2015, http://www.winterspielplatz.de; and others.

22. For the story of the Free Evangelical Church of Brüchermühle, see Martin Schulten, "Gesellschaftstransformativer Gemeindebau am Beispiel der Evangelischen Freien Gemeinde Brüchermühle und deren Sozialprojekt für Hartkernarbeitslose in der Christlichen Beschäftigungsgesellschaft Brüchermühle (CBB) (unpublished MTh diss., University of South Africa, 2011), http://uir.unisa.ac.za/bitstream/handle/10500/8630/dissertation_schulten_m.pdf.

23. For example, Kindertafel Lüneburg, http://kindertafel.de; Düsseldorfer Kindertafel, http://www.duesseldorfer-kindertafel.de; accessed 10 May 2015.

helfen Familien). They organize and sponsor holiday trips and leisure activities for families in need.[24] Such initiatives exist in other areas as well.

There are abundant examples of men and women, indeed whole families, joining together to engage in caring for their neighbours' needs, making their world a better place. They serve each other, they serve others who are in need together, and all the while their friendships get stronger and closer. This is our great chance, a big opportunity for missional families to join such initiatives. When we as Christians engage in welfare in our communities and for the people around us, when we meet our neighbours' needs and serve the poor, our testimony will attract people. And it will lead them to ask questions about why we commit ourselves, resulting in interesting conversations – including conversations about Jesus.

Let's Pray, Act and Believe for Miracles!

Families are best suited to assist other families in need or in times of trouble. We all at times welcome neighbourly help. It's not only the typical poor and lower-class families who need our help today. There are many young families raising their children without the assistance of grandparents or the wider family. Even though they are average, "normal" families, they can feel overwhelmed at times and they certainly welcome experienced (grand)mothers and (grand)fathers dropping by once in a while to check that everything is OK. They certainly will not reject a helping hand, a good piece of advice or reliable babysitting. And again, this may lead to the establishing of long-term good friendships.

The opportunities to help are innumerable, depending on our life stage: whether it is an unplanned pregnancy, the birth of a newborn child within a family lacking the assistance of a wider family, a stressed family with more than one or two children, the care of a disabled family member or elderly parents, the death of a close relative – anything can throw us off track in our normal family lives and we can find ourselves in trouble. When we have to face extraordinary situations, we more readily welcome the help of kind neighbours and compassionate church folk – especially when there are no conditions attached to their help.

It is worth joining in with public, private and church initiatives to be better able to help families facing crises. Our world is full of failure – broken people, broken homes and broken families. Thousands upon thousands of children live in precarious family situations. There is not only trauma caused by the

---

24. http://www.kolping-ms.org/de/spenden-und-helfen/familien-helfen-familien.php.

divorce of parents; many single parents are then overburdened by having to raise their children alone. There are parents of children with disabilities who long for one single day off their daily routine and care. There are so many blows of fate, so many unhappy stories of people who need our love and care. It is such a treasure when Christian families are able to reach out and meet these needs. In this way, they are unique witnesses to God's love and compassion and become a blessing to their neighbourhoods,[25] especially when they are able to bring their family clusters along.

There are even some initiatives that cross national borders. The German Families Help Families association was founded to help families in need in the ex-Soviet republic of Ukraine.[26] Some friends of mine collect Christmas boxes each year throughout their neighbourhood and drive them to Romania, distributing the parcels to the poorest people. They always take their family with them. They say:

> These journeys have changed our neighbourhood. For example, some of our neighbours have witnessed being an answer to the prayers of these poor families. There are stories like of a family, having run out of coal, crying out to God for help together, and then we arrived with the necessary money. No one can explain such a situation – but you should have seen the faces of our neighbours witnessing this joy and praise, and they were not yet believers!

Furthermore, initiatives offering assistance to the critically ill or dying are very appealing to families. I witnessed the great impact on an usually grumpy man when several of our families offered to keep watch at the deathbed of his dying father. I joined the watch as well. We sang songs, we prayed or we sat in silence beside the dying man, who had shown few signs of life for months. Yet, just before he died, he uttered a clear sentence to his son: "Thank you for bringing these nice folk." This was a father who had never said "Thank you" to his son in all his life! Our neighbour had known his father only as a harsh man. I remember having a long conversation with him after his father's death; he shared about his awful childhood and how difficult it had been to care for his grumpy father during his last days, more or less involuntarily. He told me, "I have often been angry at you guys and your church. But what you did for

---

25. For more on this, see Wenger and Jackson, *Witness*, 45; Church of England, *Something to Celebrate*, 170–173.

26. See "Familien helfen Familien," http://www.kolping-ms.org/de/spenden-und-helfen/familien-helfen-familien.php.

me and my father. . . . I can hardly believe this has happened. I'm speechless. Please forgive me." No, this man did not give his life to Christ instantly; I don't even know whether he has become a Christian yet. However, I do know that his view of Christians and Christianity changed radically during that time. He would come and offer us help whenever he saw someone working in the church yard. He would join us at our events every now and then. I'm convinced that his father died in peace, and his formerly bitter son is on the best path to follow in his father's footsteps in finding that same peace.

All this is also likely to bring in families from our neighbourhood if they are interested in helping with us. They don't have to be born-again Christians to be able to help people in need. And by serving and doing something good, we all get closer to the One who really is good, the One who is love – we draw close to God, who wants the best for all of us. In addition, when outsiders experience Christians turning to God in those situations when only miracles can help, and when they witness how we receive this help, they experience God in reality.

Connecting Them with People from Our Church

Making friends and joining in family clusters is the first and best step to evangelize our community. Certainly, holistic family mission wants to bring people to Jesus Christ. Yet it is important to realize that our friendship with people – those we know individually or with their families – is something we can invest in without the pressure of having to preach the gospel in a certain way to them.[27] Actually, for a missional family, it is more important that their new friends share everyday life with them. As no area is left out, trust will grow. Just as true friends will say, "We talk about anything with our friends," so missional families will share naturally about their faith and their church.

But this might not be one evangelistic conversation – quick and strategic as we may have learned to do in street outreaches. Friends don't try to indoctrinate each other, they don't impose their opinions on others. When friends talk and share things, it's done naturally. When we have real long-term friendships we will share our faith from our everyday life situations without being compelled to convert the other person.

Therefore, if we want to stay authentic yet at the same time talk about the specific things we believe in, we need to get our family cluster closer to

---

27. John Hattam, *Families Finding Faith: Reaching Today's Families with the Gospel* (Milton Keynes: Scripture Union, 2000), 26.

our local church. Whenever our new friends meet our brothers and sisters in faith naturally – that is, at our parties, leisure activities and welfare work – conversations will automatically turn to spiritual things; and we get the chance to share more about our faith, which makes every evangelistic heart happy. Opportunities to connect new friends with our church folk are bountiful; let's see just a few examples.

The Friend of My Friend Is My Friend Too

There is nothing more natural than to introduce our new friends to our old friends. When missional families are part of a church that understands church as family and true fellowship, such families do have real friends in church. Whenever they take initiatives to make new friends, such as by inviting their neighbours to a party, they will surely invite their friends from church as well. That's no big deal; it's not an official church event. It is logical to invite your children's friends to his or her birthday party, whether they are friends from the neighbourhood or good friends from church. The same is true for your own birthday party – even when this includes a secret missionary strategy. Just don't forget to prepare your church friends to mingle naturally with your cluster! There's nothing worse than parties where people are split into spiritual and secular groups; then you may forget the reason for connecting your neighbours with your church friends. When you are the host and they are all your guests, you can encourage all your friends to mingle together.

Hey, I Know Somebody Who...

Every now and then, we all face unexpected emergencies when we urgently need the help of experts, and so do our friends within our family clusters. In such situations, it is valuable to know the right experts and specialists or to have qualified friends from church who know what to do. And it's only natural among friends and neighbours to call when we hear of an incident and say, "Hey, I know someone who might be able to help." When our brother or sister does us the favour and comes over to assist our neighbour in need, it's another excellent opportunity to get our cluster friends in contact with our church friends – provided we have people in our church who really know how to handle the emergencies, for it's only good assistance that will be remembered well. In addition, we should not hand out calling cards from our church or tracts on such an occasion. This is simply our brother or sister's living testimony – nothing more or less – that is, to create a good image of

Christ's church (kingdom). And next time, when we hold a neighbourhood barbecue, we might invite our "church and specialist" friend too, and we will see our family cluster welcoming him or her with open arms. Your neighbours might say to you, "These are nice folk in your church." And you could reply nonchalantly, "Our church is open for anybody. You might fit in well too! Why don't you come over some time?"

Some Hours without the Children

All of us would like to go out as a couple from time to time, and so do our friends within our family clusters: we all want to have some time without the kids to go to the movies, to listen to a concert or even to participate in a seminar. But do we always have qualified babysitters at hand, or can we even afford good babysitters? Here's another possible opportunity for missional families to jump at, depending on the situation where you live: ". . . and when you need babysitters for the kids, we can ask someone from church – they're involved in children's ministry anyway, and just the other day, they held a wonderful party for our kids." Get excited about the actions they do with your children at church, yet without getting religious or spiritual, as some parents might refuse your offer for fear of getting religious instruction instead of babysitting. We must bear in mind that some people have consciously turned away from Christianity or even profess another faith.

Or why not offer games afternoons or football matches in church instead of only Sunday school? Parents will be thankful if they have time as a couple without the children, if their kids are well taken care of.

The benefit will be double: while you serve the parents, you do something positive for their marriage; and you serve their children, who spend a wonderful time that they will surely want to repeat! If such good experiences happen more often, your neighbours might say "yes" when you invite their children to a Bible adventure camp the next summer. Maybe they will even join the staff themselves for such activities. Thus, positive contacts have the potential to develop into friendships and ultimately to their becoming a part of a local church.

Our Church Needs Your Help

It is usual to ask friends to give a hand when their assistance is needed, and the same is true for our clusters in our neighbourhoods, even when it's our church that needs the helping hand. I'm sure the friends within your family cluster would love to assist as long as it is not the worship service we need help with but some particular event, activity or project. For example, a church in central Germany has been offering several projects with the help of people who are good friends with church families but haven't yet set foot in the church. For example, they run a ballet school for children and aerobics classes for women with staff who aren't Christians yet, but who signed up to assist.

Or why not organize a concert at your church, inviting your musician friends to play there? In our church, we have held such concerts regularly, inviting professional artists who were part of friendship clusters of our church families. Events like Christmas, when the whole world joins in celebrating anyway, have been good occasions, and our friends still remember the way we welcome people at church – the kind and loving atmosphere of an authentic "welcome culture" before and after such an event. Again, this leads to a more positive image and interesting conversations within our neighbourhood; thus, you might get the same feedback we did when we overheard our friends telling their cluster folk, "The other day I got invited to play at their church. You know what, it was really cool! I'm not a believer, to be honest, but they are such nice people I'll gladly come again."

Yes, We Can Offer a Location for Free

Families, including our family clusters, at times need extra space for their activities – to celebrate parties, have a barbecue or some other particular leisure activity as whole families together. But there is not always enough space or the right venue to easily do that. Think of a whole cluster, which means several families including their children: it's not always easy to find a good location to fit them all in. When they are planning actions like a neighbourhood convention, where can they go? This again becomes a great opportunity for local churches to support their missional families by (building and) offering club rooms for family activities. Imagine a multifunctional venue offering a modern canteen kitchen plus a recreation ground to be used by children, youngsters and adults at the same time – would anyone refuse the offer to use such a location for free? On the contrary, such venue turns to gold whether it's just open for families to meet for fellowship and games or whether it's used for special occasions like anniversaries, weddings and funerals. When our friends and neighbours know we have room for them at our church venue for free, they won't be able to resist the temptation. Yet their passing the threshold of our church building once makes it easier for us to invite them to other events as well – maybe even for church on Sunday, as happened to Victor and his family.

Victor was a construction worker who had become friends with a church family. As the church were planning to expand their building, the family asked Victor for his advice. Victor had never had anything to do with church, but he would never say "No" when asked for help by a good friend. Thus, one day, he turned up at the construction site, and his counsel was much appreciated and praised. He even came back and checked the work again. When the church's new centre was eventually finished, Victor and his wife joined the opening ceremony. And later, when he asked this church whether he could use their building for a family celebration, no one denied him his request. Victor's family was then spotted at events at the church again and again. And today, the whole family are members of this church.

Some of our church buildings are only used on Sundays, but they could easily become meeting places during the week. When they are changed into multifunctional rooms, we can offer this space to our neighbours for their use or even to our missional families to have a centre for their cluster's activities.

Even churches with smaller rooms and less suitable facilities may offer an infrastructure which is convenient for families, for churches often have better access to public venues.

Connecting Them with Our Church Ministries

Connecting our neighbour family clusters with our church clusters will build trust. When our neighbours trust people at our church they may trust our invitations as well. And they will make use of our programmes and ministries if they are tailored to their desires and needs – the next step towards belonging to Christ and his local church. These further steps depend on what our church has to offer, otherwise any preparatory work of the family clusters will miss the mark. For, as we mentioned earlier, missional families need missional churches behind them.

As we saw earlier, missional churches shape their church life and activities according to the needs of the people around them. And as no one community resembles the next, so no programme or ministry offered by one local church will resemble those offered by the next church.

Obviously the gospel still runs the agenda of all the different churches and ministries. Though context and culture and programmes and events may differ, their content and values are similar: the gospel of Christ works to bring reconciliation, Jesus renews our everyday lives, the Father heals our identity and the Spirit leads us into meeting our responsibility for our world. Hence, any church programme or project will have to be in line with these characteristics and goals.

Mediation Offered in or for Our Community

The church is Christ's ambassador for reconciliation (2 Cor 5:18–20), hence to reconcile people with God and with one another is our core task.[28] There is no other institution in society better suited to settle disputes – to confront problems and to help solve conflict.[29] Note that family life will hardly ever avoid conflict. Even "perfect" couples have arguments at times, sparks fly in even the best relationships between parents and their children, and even more so between families living side by side. It is the local churches who are able to – and are obliged to – bring reconciliation. In short, the church is the best mediator in any conflict. Thus, it is here that people find a helpful place to turn to, learning to overcome disputes and to live as good neighbours in spite of different opinions and their massive issues. Our ministry of reconciliation makes church the best partner for any community or town to offer professional counsel and mediation.

In order to offer a competent ministry of reconciliation, mediation and support in conflict we need to have appropriate centres and people: we need to offer competent counsel and knowledgeable coaching within a clear infrastructure so the parties in conflict know where to turn in their community. When they have gained trust in church folk, when they are our friends, they will follow our advice and recommendation to turn to such help. Also bear in mind that people will only rely on the competence of those we recommend as mediators if they see the results of their peacemaking in our lives, as it is not what we recommend but what they see in our lives which will attract them. In this way, our communal mediation is advertised by the missional families living in our community. As a friend of mine, Margret Hirschler, once told me,

> When we got to know our new neighbours we were having a really rough time as a couple. They had invited us to a garden party, and it was so good to meet and be around such nice people. Our children made friends too; and so we kept hanging out together

---

28. For more about our calling to reconcile, see Johannes Reimer, "Der Dienst der Versöhnung – bei der Kernkompetenz ansetzen: Zur Korrelation von Gemeinwesenmediation und multikulturellem Gemeindebau," *Theologisches Gespräch* 1 (2011): 19–35.

29. Church of England, *Something to Celebrate*, 173–176.

while I observed them closely as a family. I would watch how they treated each other. They were so different from us in every way. They were a lot more at peace than us, they seemed to be totally reconciled with themselves, with each other and the world around them. Even my husband noticed the difference. Therefore one day, we dared to question them and we were surprised by their answer. They said, no, they weren't like that all the time; on the contrary, they had recently been about to divorce. However, they had received an invitation by a local church offering family and marriage training. As they had had nothing to lose, they went; and since that seminar things completely changed. They told us they had just become members of that church although they had been convinced that church was antiquated. On hearing this my husband and I did not run there immediately. It took a few months, but finally, we decided to go there too. Our neighbours suggested they accompany us so that we would not feel like strangers. And I'm so glad we went. Our lives have completely changed. And yes, we visit the same church as well – we go there every Sunday.

It was the kindness and friendship of their neighbours that made Margret and her husband find hope for a positive change, yet the church ministry of marriage training was what made the difference. Friends had become mentors and fellowship turned into evangelism and discipleship.

Life Counselling and Coaching Offered in and for Our Neighbourhood

Missional family-centred churches need to turn into drop-in centres for families where they can receive good counsel, helpful advice and true support in times of trouble. No, we Christians do not have all the answers and solutions to all the problems of the world, yet we dare to tackle any question and challenge for we know that we ourselves are carried by a God who ultimately does have all the answers. And even when we don't find the right answers we can still offer comfort and support. In church we don't abandon people.

There are many examples of churches running such family centres. The Fountain of Live Covenant Church in Long Beach, CA defines the vision of their Family Centre as follows: "The Family Center seeks to serve and benefit our community by offering a variety of programs and services. Our primary effort is to provide tutoring and art classes for youth and English as a Second Language classes for adults. We also network with the City of Long Beach's community resources to provide food distribution, shelter, medical, and other low-cost or free services."[30]

Indeed, we read about the successful work of such family centres. As a general rule, such local ministries focus on issues relevant to the families in their vicinity. These drop-in centres are the first port of call for church people to get support and counsel, yet, as such family centres offer mediation and coaching to anybody in need, non-church families can seek help there too. Support is tailored to the life stages of the family, ranging from various seminars to counsel and support children, parents and the elderly, to other topics that may arise from the cradle to the grave: prenatal classes, raising toddlers and teens, marriage courses, caring for the elderly, how to care for sick and dying family members, and so on. Seminars on how to raise children are commonly the most popular. In Germany, churches also book professional counsellors and coaches for special workshops and seminars at their centres. Furthermore, all kinds of leisure activities are offered at the centres, which is also very supportive. It is amazing how many such offers exist even just in Germany.[31] Interestingly, Christians have often thought that non-believers won't accept such offers by church ministries, yet on the contrary, we find a strong tendency among non-believers to turn to such centres for help today.

Here is an example of how such a work can change the life of a whole family.

A girl named Julia became friends with Mareike in school and they got on like a house on fire. As summer approached, Mareike told Julia about their exciting church camp. Every year, some parents from her church would build a camp in the woods and the children would stay there for two whole weeks. It was called SOLA.[32] "Why don't you just come with us?" Mareike asked her best friend. She had a flyer which Julia showed to her parents, but they were hesitant and even called Mareike's parents to find out more. Mareike's father in turn suggested, "Why don't you join us and see for yourselves? We are just going to meet as a staff to plan and organize. I'm a carpenter, so I'm in charge of building the huts together with some other fathers." Julia's father went to this staff meeting so that he could help them build the camp – and he got excited.

---

30. http://www.folcov.org/family-center/, accessed 24 January 2020.

31. http://www.kircheborby.de/index.php?page=1017448096; and Murrhard, http://www.evangelisch-in-murrhardt.de/familienzentrum/familienzentrum/.

32. SOLA – Sommer Lager (summer camp) for kids and teens. This programme is offered throughout Germany by Forum Wiedenest, https://www.wiedenest.de/kidsteens/veranstaltungen/kids-teens/sola?MP=242-40.

The two fathers started to meet every now and then, and then the two families had barbecues together on a regular basis.

A wonderful friendship was developing between the families when they faced some unexpected challenges: Julia's father lost his job and Julia's grandmother, who had dementia, had to move into their house to be cared for, all of which made their life difficult. It might have ended badly if not for these new friends and their church's offer to help. And Julia's parents were open to receiving assistance. The problems did not disappear, yet they dealt with the challenges. When the next summer approached, Julia's father went to an official meeting of school parents and persuaded them to send their children to SOLA: "You won't regret it, believe me! I was very sceptical too. If you had told me a year ago that I would advertise this camp, I would never have believed you. But you are my witnesses: our lives have changed for the better ever since we went to SOLA." In short, the family ministry of that church had changed the life of his family completely.

From Sharing Our Lives to Having Profound Conversations

There certainly is a lot of talking within our family clusters. Otherwise we wouldn't be true friends, would we? Imagine friends who don't share anything or speak about anything. Imagine a barbecue party or outdoor activity with no word spoken – it is impossible! Friends talk to one another. And the closer their friendship becomes, the more personal their conversations will get. The more they trust each other, the more private the things they will share. So it is only logical that neighbours who casually encounter each other may become close friends who meet to talk deeply about everything and anything. And this is exactly what missional families do. Yet they will not force an artificial conversation about God; rather they live their faith for all to see, and this automatically leads to conversations about it. At first there may be only casual comments and remarks as questions pop up in everyday life or when stories are shared. Later, this may become more structured as serious discussions are provoked. In an ideal case, it will be our friends who ask to talk about topics of faith and who suggest reading the Bible together. That way, we can start a cell group, a Bible study group or home church naturally. It doesn't matter what you call such a meeting, the key is that your group evolves organically and meets authentically. It is important that your friendship stays the same; there is just a new level of spirituality added, which should never displace the fellowship and social life you have come to cherish. And yet you take a bit of additional time now to explicitly share your faith, to read the Bible and to support each other in prayer, and so on.[33]

Such cell groups usually meet in private homes. This way, interested guests and curious outsiders are less scared of coming, especially when they know the host personally. I advise evangelistic house groups to meet in the homes of families who have a large circle of friends and who are well known for their hospitality by friends and neighbours alike. Who the host will be is the key factor when founding a new cell group. I even recommend special training for such hosts in order to reach out effectively. Yet I doubt such hosts need to have a lot of theological knowledge and special evangelistic gifting, as evangelist Shirley Fraser points out.[34] It is important, though, that some members of the group are competent in sharing their faith and that you have good leadership (which might be a different role from hosting the group).

Another evangelistic practice in this context is when a missionary visits a home – a method which has been applied effectively over many centuries. Christians who are gifted in evangelism enter the private homes of families they want to reach. One of the best-known examples of such a conversion is Dwight L. Moody, who was visited by the evangelist Edward Kimball in his home and was led to Jesus this way.[35] In Nigeria, such evangelistic home visits started a great revival movement there, known as "New Life for All," with millions being saved.[36] Pastor Ajith Fernando (Sri Lanka) reports on the tribe of Malros in India (known as a people who would never wash, thus they smelled bad), who have seen 34,000 conversions since 1996.[37] Church-planting specialist Robert Bolton reports a similar dynamic in Taiwan. Summarizing his studies on church growth on this island he writes that one of the strengths of these churches – whether big or small – is their fellowship groups.[38]

---

33. There are dozens of books on how to start a cell group or initiate a Bible study group; see, for example, David Watson, *I Believe in Evangelism* (London: Hodder & Stoughton, 1976), 147–150.

34. Shirley Fraser, "House Groups and Church Organizations," in *Local Church Evangelism*, ed. David Wright and Alastair Gray (Edinburgh: Saint Andrew Press, 1987), 30.

35. Ajith Fernando, *Checkliste Glaube: Dienen wie Jesus* (Marburg: Francke Verlag, 2011), 278.

36. Eileen Lageer, *New Life for All: True Accounts of In-Depth Evangelism in West Africa* (Chicago: Moody, 1970), 68–69.

37. Fernando, *Checkliste Glaube*, 278.

38. Robert J. Bolton, *Sons of Han: Strategies for Urban Church Planting and Growth among Chinese in East Asia* (Haverton, PA: Treasure Island, 2002), 37.

Church-planting projects in Europe have also had positive experiences of mission through home groups and family cell groups. For example, Howard Astin, an expert in church growth in the UK, confirms that success, describing his experiences within the Anglican Church throughout the UK.[39] No matter which nation, no matter whether it's a church planted in the country or in a big city, we need above all to invest in good fellowships, as fellowship is the linchpin in founding and growing churches, especially in towns. Fellowship in urban settings can be nurtured by "primary groups," as Kofi Manful calls them.[40] Such groups may have different forms and settings but they will always live on in family-like structures.[41]

In short, it is in the home group, initiated and nurtured by missional families, that friends and neighbours find opportunities to talk about their faith in Jesus.

From Good Conversations to a Decision for Christ

The ultimate goal of family-focused church ministries is to call people to follow Jesus Christ. Even when some ministries seem to have no evangelistic approach at all, everyone in a missional church ultimately works towards this one goal to make disciples – missional families really want to transform their neighbourhoods.

Admittedly, the time and place are not always right for our friends to take the decision to follow Christ right here and now. And remember that as Christians we do not convert them; we lead people to God with the help of the Holy Spirit. It is his job to speak to them about sin, righteousness and judgment, and to show that there is forgiveness only in Jesus Christ (John 16:8–10). He may do this through some of our private conversations, within our home group or in an evangelistic event at church. Yet, in addition to that, people need to hear about our own conversions to become familiar with the idea that it's necessary to make a clear decision for Christ. Hence, I suggest we share our testimony casually on special family occasions, such as when other family members have given their lives to Jesus. Hold a party on such an occasion and invite all your friends – for they should see how Christians

---

39. Astin, in Michael Eastman and Steve Latham, *Urban Church: A Practitioner's Resource Book* (London: SPCK, 2004), 132.

40. Cited in Eastman and Latham, *Urban Church*, 16.

41. For more on how to build cell groups in church and how to grow faith, see Wilhelm Faix, *Wo zwei oder drei . . .* (Wuppertal: R. Brockhaus, 1997).

celebrate being born again! Invite your family cluster to the baptisms of your children. Soon, you will be in the midst of interesting conversations triggered by the question: "Why do you do that?" This way, we share our testimony just by answering their questions instead of starting contrived conversations that try to indoctrinate our friends.

If you and your friends already meet to study the Bible, you may choose "How to give my life to Jesus" as a topic for one evening, yet only if they bring it up as an item on the agenda. Don't force either your sharing or their decision making! Rather, it is about our openness to a seeker who has been hit by God's Word; it is about honestly answering the question "And what do I do now?"

Furthermore, special services for families have great potential to lead whole families to Jesus.[42] These are great opportunities to invite our friends as a whole family to come with us and experience our fellowship at church. Special occasions like Christmas, Easter, Thanksgiving and Mother's Day are good dates to invite our friends.[43] No matter what the event, pay attention to arrange such services so that they are interactive and to make the message clear yet not too plain and confrontational.

At a Christmas service in Brüchermühle, Germany, all the children of the community attending the church's dance school performed a Christmas ballet which they had put together. All the parents had been invited, and of course they all came to see their children perform. I will never forget one grandfather who came to me after the performance; he said that he had never believed in God or evil, but added, "Pastor, now I've understood what you Christians really believe in." I dug deeper and soon we had a rich conversation about all kinds of faith issues. I did *not* ask him to pray the Prayer of Salvation with me, I did *not* tell him to get right with God. However, as we said goodbye, his words to me were: "Now I know that I have to make a decision for Jesus, and I haven't got much time left." And it wasn't long before he came to my office to officially start his life with the Lord.

In a nutshell, no pressure or persuasion should be put on people to make this decision, yet missional churches will create the opportunities for clear conversations.

---

42. See Watson, *I Believe in Evangelism*, 145–147; Wright and Gray, *Local Church Evangelism*, 171–172.

43. Wright and Gray, 71.

From Conversion to Becoming a Missional Family

As soon as people start to follow Christ, they need to be taught to become missional families themselves. Missional churches will offer such training even when new believers have already seen the missional lives of their friends and families whose ways of life are certainly encouraging and motivating examples. It is good that these new disciples are already part of a family cluster in their community; they are part of common projects and belong to a prepared structure of fellowship and ministry – therefore they need not become members of anything new. They are already part of a missional culture and they even had missional training there before they were converted. The newly converted don't need to end their contacts and friendships; missional churches regard this as a great advantage as friendships are the first step of family mission anyway. In short, a missional church's training to grow faith and character in their disciples aims at transforming their hearts and not at changing their social networks.

Questions for Reflection

1. What impulses and ideas do you take practically from this chapter – for your own life and for your church?
2. Do you know the needs and concerns of people living in your vicinity, in your community?
3. How can you naturally build friendship with your neighbours, acquaintances and work colleagues?
4. What are the occasions when your family could extend an invitation to other families or to people in need?
5. Would it be possible to initiate a kind of neighbourhood service in your community? What could you do? What is needed?
6. Which family could you personally assist and help? How?
7. With whom could you join to have a small group for people to share their questions, concerns and needs?

9

Families in World Mission: A Unique Challenge

Being Called into Mission Abroad

There are missionaries serving on all continents of the world. We even find mission taking place on our doorstep. But it is a different dimension and a greater challenge to be called as a missionary abroad. Yes, it's true that we find foreign cultures living just around the corner these days, a phenomenon caused by today's globalization. However, even when we live in a multi-ethnic neighbourhood, we ourselves are still at home. We know the ropes of our own culture and need not go far to find familiar ground. All this changes when we live in a foreign country. Families who go into mission abroad soon find themselves confronted by challenges they wouldn't even think of at home. That's why it makes sense to have a whole chapter about this unique setting in a book about family and mission.

As we've argued so far, no Christian family needs a special calling into mission, as the family is called by God already. It is the nature of any family to be his missionary agent on earth. Any Christian family is already part of God's great mandate, otherwise we are not being faithful to his calling to follow him. However, in the special case that God calls us to serve him abroad, we need to listen carefully to his specific calling to us as individuals or as whole families. Remember the calling of Paul and Barnabas. They had been active in spreading the gospel from Antioch via Cyprus up to Derbe. Their ministry had been blessed and fruitful, indeed, a success in evangelism, when one day they were called more specifically:

> Now in the church at Antioch there were prophets and teachers: Barnabas, Simeon called Niger, Lucius of Cyrene, Manaen (who

had been brought up with Herod the tetrarch) and Saul. While they were worshipping the Lord and fasting, the Holy Spirit said, "Set apart for me Barnabas and Saul for the work to which I have called them." So after they had fasted and prayed, they placed their hands on them and sent them off. (Acts 13:1–3)

This special calling would change their lives for ever. Now, as they left to go out into the world, they had to face grave dangers, even to the point of nearly being killed at times. The apostle Paul later reflected on those times:

I have worked much harder, been in prison more frequently, been flogged more severely, and been exposed to death again and again. Five times I received from the Jews the forty lashes minus one. Three times I was beaten with rods, once I was pelted with stones, three times I was shipwrecked, I spent a night and a day in the open sea, I have been constantly on the move. I have been in danger from rivers, in danger from bandits, in danger from my fellow Jews, in danger from Gentiles; in danger in the city, in danger in the country, in danger at sea; and in danger from false believers. I have laboured and toiled and have often gone without sleep; I have known hunger and thirst and have often gone without food; I have been cold and naked. Besides everything else, I face daily the pressure of my concern for all the churches. Who is weak, and I do not feel weak? Who is led into sin, and I do not inwardly burn? If I must boast, I will boast of the things that show my weakness. The God and Father of the Lord Jesus, who is to be praised for ever, knows that I am not lying. (2 Cor 11:23–31)

Mission is never easy when we live in territories foreign to us. Thus, missionaries leave their comfort zones as they risk being challenged, confined or even rejected in hostility by their new habitat and its foreign culture. And foreign mission becomes even more challenging when we go abroad as a whole family. That's why it's crucial that all family members are sure of their family's calling. A family is a collective unit, and God will call them together by speaking to all of them about leaving their home. In short, any family sensing God's calling on their life to become missionaries needs to check this impression together before their Lord. All too often it's only the men or husbands who feel called and thus mission becomes only their business, which the family has to support whether they feel the same calling or not, as J. D. Payne says is common in the US.[1] Yet it is not just the man who carries the burden and consequences of God's calling; his family is affected too! And it is never only the man or husband who serves on the mission field; his whole family either supports his mission or is an obstacle to his ministry, depending on the degree to which he involves them. Certainly, the same holds true for any woman who senses a special calling by God on her life. Our God, who is the inventor of the family, will always call the whole family into his ministry. Hence, it's best to involve the whole family in the process of taking such a life-changing decision and the preparations to go abroad.

Christhart, a good friend of mine, is a missionary and an outstanding example to me. Many years ago, God gave him a burden for Africa. His wife Sarah, however, could not imagine ever living in Africa, and certainly not in a Muslim African context. Christhart didn't try to persuade her or force any decision. He kept praying, while Sarah avoided talking about anything that had to do with Africa. Christhart was convinced that it was up to God: if it was really his will to send them there as a family, it was up to him to warm Sarah's heart for the African continent. And finally the day came when the Holy Spirit overwhelmed Sarah, speaking to her heart about Africa. Unexpectedly for her, she was filled with overflowing love for the African people. Instantly, she approached her husband, telling him to restart his thoughts of leaving for Africa. Today, the whole family, including their children, serves together in Zanzibar. Christhart's patience and waiting paid off.

Furthermore, each Christian family is an integral part of God's family, the *familia Dei*: all families belong to the one body of Christ. Therefore, whenever we feel called abroad, it should be the result of a collective listening to the voice of the Holy Spirit and not just our individual decision. For God calls us while we are part of his church. Hence, it is important to take any individual sense we have about God commissioning us to God in collective prayer too. Either we will have it confirmed or we won't – the Lord wants to speak through the church. I've come across situations, even in my own church, where couples were convinced they were being called abroad, yet the church prayed about it and reached a different conclusion, and so tried to keep them from leaving. In some cases, these couples still went into mission, only later to mourn their work

---

1. J. D. Payne, *Discovering Church Planting: An Introduction to the Whats, Whys, and Hows of Global Church Planting* (Colorado Springs/Milton Keynes/Hyderabad: Paternoster, 2009), 297–299.

that had borne no fruit. Other families simply left their churches to look for new congregations, until someone commissioned them to where they wanted to go. There are apparently some churches and ministries that have turned their backs on mission altogether; in such cases, the wise thing to do might well be to take an individual decision and go abroad. Yet that ought not to be the rule. The biblical example of Paul and Barnabas tells us they were commissioned by the church they were accountable to; and they shared all the blessings they experienced with their brothers and sisters on their return.

As we have seen, missional families are sent into God's mission field right where they live, yet, in the special case of going into foreign mission, we need to listen carefully and we ought to be sensitive to God's specific directions and words to us as a family; we will receive confirmation through the unanimity of family members and from our church. This way, we will be confident of our calling; also, while living abroad we can rely on the support of our brothers and sisters in faith for any of our concerns.

Being Well Prepared Is the Key
Mission Starts Right on Our Doorstep

Mission work abroad is distinct, yet at the same time it is not so different from our experience at home. Consequently, serving abroad is easier for those families who have already played an active part in the mission work of their local churches, who have experienced the Holy Spirit using their potential and who have seen miracles happen as God has restored people's lives. The opposite is also true: mission abroad will be more difficult for those families who have not spread the gospel at home among their relatives, friends and neighbours even though they speak the same language and know the same challenges in life. It is a myth that sharing the gospel is easier somewhere other than at home. Even if it's true that a prophet is not without honour except in his home town, certainly he is understood by his own people there. But in a foreign country, he doesn't even speak the language! When abroad, you have to learn the ropes of all aspects of life. Therefore, anything we have discussed so far is true for families in foreign mission as well: the most important prerequisite for potential missionaries is that they minister to people in their vicinity at home first, before they leave to engage in mission abroad. Also, they need to learn everything about the family in ministry and mission, and they need to know about the possible joys and tensions, the opportunities and the challenges, mission life might hold for them as a family, before they leave their home.[2]

---

2. Payne, *Discovering Church Planting*, 298–299.

And yet it is true that anyone ministering in a foreign country needs to have a greater passion for mission than those staying at home. Donna S. Thomas calls such families who serve in mission abroad the "Great Commission families"[3] – that is, families who have a heart for the world[4] and for mission, who love the Lord and who are focused on spreading his kingdom on earth.[5] If we want to become such families, we have to start early in preparing our spouses and children for foreign mission – not only ourselves. Donna Thomas gives good advice for parents seeking to raise a heart for mission abroad in their children, including the following:

- Look for contacts and invest strategically in friendships with people in your neighbourhood, school and community who belong to cultures that are different from your own.
- Seek contact and make friends with other missionaries and their families.
- Talk as a family about what is happening in countries around the world.
- Take holiday trips to foreign countries and get to know their cultures.
- Learn a foreign language together.
- Go on short-term outreaches as a whole family and support your children in joining evangelistic outreaches.
- Support children in other countries financially and through family prayer.
- Talk about money and how to spend it – decide as a family which missionary to support personally or support a mission project or ministry.
- Pray and intercede as a family for mission, missionaries and the needs of unreached peoples.
- Meet as a family to talk about any problems or challenges you face and work out and pray for solutions together.
- Develop a "welcome culture" so that people are always welcome in your family.
- As parents, engage in evangelistic projects to be a living testimony to your children.[6]

---

3. Donna S. Thomas, *Becoming a World Changing Family: Fun and Innovative Ways to Spread the Good News* (Grand Rapids, MI: Baker, 2004), 29.

4. Thomas, *Becoming a World Changing Family*, 32.

5. Ann Dunagan, *The Mission-Minded Family: Releasing Your Family to God's Destiny* (Downers Grove, IL: InterVarsity Press, 2007), 2.

6. Thomas, *Becoming a World Changing Family*, 3.

There are countless more ideas in Donna's book for how to learn about world mission as a family while still living at home, including how to invest in your children to expand their five senses for world mission.[7] Like all of us, children will enjoy things only when they can see, hear, touch, smell and taste them first. Thus, they will be willing to stretch their boundaries if they have been trained to do that from early on. So families with a heart for foreign mission open the window wide for their children to experience the world, for example, with the help of pictures, movies and books, or even by going on trips with them. Such missional parents enable their children to make contact with other languages, the laughter of other people groups and the sounds of celebration and mourning of other cultures. They expose them to different kinds of music, songs and melodies from around the world. Their children get the chance to literally touch other people: they may play with toys from foreign cultures and enjoy hugging and kissing friends from a different ethnic background. They are exposed to the smells of a totally different culture, having the strange ingredients of foreign cuisine explained as they are served exotic foods by their multi-ethnic friends for dinner. Certainly, their parents avoid making judgmental or negative comments about other cultures. In fact, they would rather increase and support their children's joy of discovery, curiosity and excitement in light of cultural diversity.

My family has always sought to live out Donna's ideas in practice. We've read books and watched video clips about missionaries. We've played geography games with our children in which we all expanded our knowledge about nations, capital cities, rivers or different kinds of food just for fun. And today, it is not difficult to find true stories about missionaries by searching the Internet together with our children.

In similar vein to Donna Thomas, missionary trainer Ann Dunagan gives a number of helpful ideas on how to raise a missionary family.[8] One idea is especially intriguing: Ann suggests making a family calendar on which we highlight dates of famous personalities and events in mission history alongside the usual family birthdays and anniversaries.[9] For example, we could highlight the date of birth or death of missionaries like Hudson Taylor (1832–1905), William Carey (1761–1834), David Livingstone (1813–1873), Gladys Aylward (1902–1970) and many other brave men and women of God. This gives us an opportunity to talk about their lives and ministries. And don't forget to

---

7. Thomas, 39–43.
8. Dunagan, *Mission-Minded Family*.
9. Dunagan, 89–103.

specially mark the birthdays of the missionary family sent out by your own church! Such a calendar also reminds us to pray for mission and unreached peoples. The ministry of Youth With A Mission even provides intercession material for world mission.[10]

Such a calendar would certainly also include all the main Christian holidays – Christmas, Easter, Pentecost, and so on – as most of us celebrate these special occasions. It is easy to add aspects of world mission to these special celebrations by integrating the world into our rituals; for example, we could sing Christmas songs from other countries, we could try recipes from foreign cuisine along with our Thanksgiving turkey (each year trying another nation or continent) or we could invite people to join our Easter breakfast at home. Once you start with a few simple intercultural ideas, you will quickly find many more. Yet in this way, the whole family becomes aware of the concerns of world mission and the local church's missionaries.

Donna Thomas calls children who are raised in such an approach the "Great Commission kids"[11] – these are children who naturally talk about God in any context, who are sensitive to injustice and suffering, and who are willing, and prepared, to go the extra mile and help those in need, even when this means overcoming obstacles and losing time, energy and money. We find such children in families with a heart for mission. If such missional families receive a special calling to go into mission abroad, they are not taken by surprise but rather see God's calling as his gift and as a privilege. While they are certainly launching into a new adventure, for them it will be just a change of scenery within God's mandate, and as far as their heart for mission is concerned, if they are wholehearted missionaries at home, it will be easy for them to serve abroad.

Missional churches know their task to reach out to the world, taking the gospel "to the ends of the earth" (Acts 1:8). Hence, world mission is natural to them. When you visit such a church, you will come across signs of foreign mission everywhere: walls will be covered with pictures of their missionaries and ministries around the globe, there will be maps with little flags of world regions they pray for, and so forth. You will find articles on mission in their newsletters and brochures, calling people to specific outreaches. A friend of mine who visited our church centre told me afterwards, "I could even smell world mission at your place" – probably referring to the smells from our church kitchen which used to serve Asian food back then! In a nutshell, our families

---

10. For an overview, see Dunagan, 215–216. Other ideas can be found in Michelle Drake, *Walking with God: The Young Person's Diary* ([n.p.]: YWAM, 2005).

11. Thomas, *Becoming a World Changing Family*, 36.

develop a heart for world mission when we as churches breathe mission and world mission ourselves.

Let's Leave Our Homes Tidied Up

Obeying God's call to mission abroad marks a radical turning point in any family's life, because when we start something new we need to leave something behind. We need to have settled our previous lives in order to be able to let go of things and say goodbye. Studies on the reasons why missionaries return home without success have shown that the primary reason for ending mission ministry is that the missionaries had unresolved issues which they had brought from home; it was not because of the problems they were facing abroad.[12] It is a common (and big) misconception to think that our personal issues and the problems in our marriages and families will automatically disappear once we've surrendered everything to the Lord and his mission. In her book on how to prepare potential missionaries for their ministry abroad, Marion Knell points out that any unsettled issues in our personal relationships will significantly reduce our capability to start our lives in a new context. In other words, we don't leave our troubles behind but we export them to the new environment.[13]

This is true for both the parents and the children in such a family. Therefore, it is vital that we deal with any problems and settle any issues. David Pollock developed the "RAFT" strategy to prepare potential missionaries for the mission field: "Reconciliation, Affirmation, Farewells, and Think Destination."[14]

Applying this preparation strategy, we need first to reconcile with all those we are about to leave at home – our work colleagues, school friends, relatives, including our wider family, friends and neighbours, and people in our church – thus following the Lord's advice: "[when] your brother or sister has something against you, . . . first go and be reconciled to them" (Matt 5:23–24); "if your brother or sister sins against you, rebuke them; and if they repent, forgive them" (Luke 17:3). It is crucial not to leave any bitterness behind – otherwise we will suffer from it sooner or later.

Furthermore, it is crucial to close the chapters of our previous life in a positive way. Certainly, not all of them have contained "peace, love and chocolate," yet we might have tried our best and now we are able to accept the

---

12. Marion Knell, *Families on the Move: Growing up Overseas – And Loving It!* (Grand Rapids, MI: Monarch, 2001), 48.
13. Knell, *Families on the Move*.
14. Pollock, in Knell, 56–59.

unhappy times in our lives as part of our story. We are able to look forward to opening the next chapters. Marion Knell encourages parents to take stock in this positive way first, and then to encourage their children to do the same.[15]

Only when we are reconciled with everybody and with our past can we prepare ourselves to say goodbye. We should choose our farewell rituals and strategies carefully; we might even follow a kind of liturgy. For example, we might plan last visits to people, places and even pets. Remember that it is normal, and even healthy, to shed some tears saying goodbye to them. If we plan carefully, we can make sure not to forget anyone. This way, we let our friends and family members share in a positive experience too, and everything is settled between us. If anything should happen to them afterwards – for example, if somebody should die during our stay abroad – we have comfort knowing that we clarified and settled everything between us. Conversely, if we forget to celebrate our goodbye we might feel bad, and we might even struggle with self-reproach, depression and other negative emotions, which do not lessen the challenges of missionary life.

Only when we have made our farewells can we start to think about life in our new home abroad and imagine in detail how it will be. Beware of becoming too romantic; it is better to stay realistic about our new home. Of course, we should be excited enough to look forward to living there for a season. Modern media is helpful because you can easily look up any place on the planet, for example, on Google, and explore it before actually arriving. Besides, most mission ministries have websites where they may provide film footage of their outreach locations. We may even find people in our own neighbourhoods – such as international students – who originate from the country we are going to. We could invite them for dinner and ask questions about their culture and local customs in their home countries, perhaps prepare their traditional food together, and so on.

Through these means, we can find out which house or flat we might live in, how to travel and use public transport, whether and where there are schools and hospitals, and which leisure opportunities we will find there or where to go on family trips. For now, it is best to make the first specific plans – indeed, it's good to make plans. That way, we spur on our anticipation as a family, and everyone becomes more excited and willing to adapt to the new circumstances well.

---

15. Knell, 57.

We've Got to Prepare Our Actual Move

Moving our household to another country is a challenge, especially as a whole family. There are hundreds of details we need to think of unless we want to risk a nasty surprise on the day of our arrival. Many mission ministries provide checklists which we are advised to work through. The most frequent questions you find are the following:

- Where are you going to live?
- Who is going to help you during the first days of arrival?
- How are you going to travel in the country?
- How do local people travel in general?
- What are you going to eat?
- Where are you going to take language classes?
- Where are your children going to go to school?
- Is there a nursery school available?
- Which doctors and hospitals can you turn to in case you need medical help?
- Where is your embassy or agency abroad and how will you get there quickly?
- Where will you get legal assistance if you face legal issues?
- Are there any other foreigners living there?
- Where do they come from?
- What languages do they speak?
- Should you make friends with local people first or rather connect with the other foreigners living there?
- What do you need to bring?
- What are the must-haves to take, and what are the nice-to-haves?
- What behaviour will cause positive reactions, and what behaviour will be offensive?
- How can you make friends, and what are the obstacles to friendships in that culture?
- How can you make local people curious and how do you risk making them jealous?

These questions, and many more, should be pondered well. Talk about these details together as a family. Usually, mission ministries provide experts who assist this preparation process. Alternatively, you could try to get in touch with former missionaries or even with the staff of the culture's agency or embassy in your home country. If you seek professional help and assistance for both the actual move and the preparation on-site, it will make it a lot easier to start your new life. And don't forget the practical details of your future spiritual and church life. The following questions may be helpful:

- Are there any churches there? Which ones?
- What do their Sunday services look like?
- What needs to be considered if you don't want to offend local believers?
- Is there a dress code?
- Are there any rules on what to eat – is anything forbidden?
- Is there a children's ministry?
- What is expected of your children – how should they behave?
- What do your children need to know?

In general, the mission ministry you serve will provide this kind of information as well. If not, I recommend contacting the churches there directly. Usually it's not only our wish to get integrated in a local church there, but the hosting church is also concerned to have their ministering missionaries integrate well. The earlier you can make personal contact, the better. At the same time, such contacts will strengthen your relationship with the local Christians even before you arrive. And don't forget your children in that respect, either! If you can connect your children in advance with local kids of about the same age there, it'll be a great help in preparing them for their new life. Why not let your kids write a letter together in Sunday school, adding some photographs, and send it to the children's group there? In this way, you might get to know the needs and concerns of the local children, which you can turn into prayer as a family. Imagine beginning as a new missionary family and your children bringing with them exactly the things that these kids have been praying for and in need of! There are many countries where children lack things that we can get at home very easily.

I remember the story of a little boy named Jens who bought crayons as a gift for his new children's group abroad. New pencils were the greatest wish of the children there. And Jens had written all their names on the crayons; thus, each child not only got a new colour pencil, but a special personal one! They were really excited, and instantly Jens was the hero of every single boy and girl there.

A German missionary girl named Tina asked the children's group of their new church in South Korea what souvenir gift it would be best to bring along, and they all chose German chocolate. So Tina brought chocolate from Germany. Again, the children's group were really excited. The Sunday school teacher in Korea installed a video for them to talk to Tina's children's group in Germany who had bought the chocolate, and the friendship between the Koreans soon extended to the church who had commissioned Tina's family.

Jens and Tina are good examples of how we can make it easy for our children to gain ground in a foreign country. We just need to prepare for our new home enough time ahead.

How to Organize Our Support at Home

Missionaries are usually commissioned by their local churches. That is the ideal (and I believe it should be the rule). There, in their home church, they find their practical, financial and spiritual support. Yet, in most cases, people think only of the parents when it comes to supporting their missionaries from home. Whenever families are commissioned, there should be families at home who will actively support them as a whole family. The missionaries could even be supported by their family clusters, who might become sponsors to a certain extent. Ideally, the commissioned family will have been an integral part of such a cluster, and that way the children know each other too. In such cases, the parents are supported or sponsored, but the children at home also commit themselves to the commission of their friends abroad. And if we are the ones staying at home and supporting missionaries and our kids have committed themselves as sponsors, it's up to us as parents to remind them to think of the mission and family abroad.

Missional churches are likely to display pictures of their missionary children on the walls of the children's ministry rooms, keep praying for them and seek direct contact, talking with the children abroad via Skype or FaceTime. Some churches even let their missionaries report on their life and ministry by having the whole family present live for such video calls.[16] Such a structure of direct support and close contact needs to be prepared prior to leaving, though. Note that there's nothing as harmful to a mission's ministry than the lack of relationships, and such contacts need to be well established at home before the missionaries leave the country. After they have left, the commissioning church and the family abroad both need to invest in keeping in contact, even when they obviously can't stay as close as they were now that they are living so far apart. But any relationship will languish if it is not cultivated.

It is also crucial that the parents and grandparents at home support their relatives abroad. In their book on parents of missionaries, Cheryl Savageu

---

16. For example, this is common practice at the Anglican All Souls Church in London. Documented in interview with Anna Bishop.

and Diane M. Stortz describe the conflicting emotions when parents or grandparents watch their children or grandchildren leave for foreign mission: it is a painful experience to let them go that far, yet at the same time they know that supporting them is an essential blessing to them, both personally and for their ministry.[17] Hence, whenever possible, it is good to gain the support of the whole of our wider family. Foreign mission bears greater fruit when there are commissioning families as well as commissioning churches backing their missionary families abroad.

We Need to Discover Our New Home

When we actually arrive at our new home, there might be a few surprises. In spite of our best preparation we eventually realize what it means to live in a completely different culture. Be prepared for the unexpected! People forgot to pick you up from the airport? Don't panic; it is just the first lesson of your learning-by-doing programme. Your accommodation falls short of your family's expectations? That's no tragedy; their mission training has just started. Your children may not go to school at once? Enjoy your extra time with them to explore your environment.

There might be countless things you haven't expected and manifold situations you have not (been) prepared for, which might stir up your fear and anger or simply confuse you. If you take such challenges as chances to learn you will progress more quickly and you will stay healthier. If you grumble and focus on the problems, you will postpone your real arrival in the foreign culture. Note that things that take us Westerners aback are quite normal or even standard for people in most other parts of the world. It can be bewildering at times, yet that's the reality of our new home, and we had better get used to it if we want to stay living there. Even if we have prepared ourselves well we will face culture shock, but we may soften its after-effects. We might even enjoy the challenge as an adventure we take together, and watch our family become stronger and more resilient on this journey.

Actually, we need to undertake an expedition: we need to discover and explore our new home. This process of acculturation that has to take place is both a learning process about a new way of life and a letting go of old things. Forget sentences that start with "But at home . . ." The sooner you understand

---

17. Cheryl Savageu and Diane M. Stortz, *Parents of Missionaries: How to Thrive and Stay Connected When Your Grandchildren Serve Cross-Culturally* (Colorado Springs, CO: Authentic, 2008).

that principle the better. Our children will most likely adapt more quickly than we do as it's the nature of children to learn quickly.

The Family as an Outreach Base

Mission is only possible within and through the social structures of a culture. In most cases, the family provides this structure; that's why the family is central to mission. Successful mission must focus on the families, especially in cultures that live in larger collectives, as is the case in Africa and Asia. John E. Apeh, who studied mission among the Igala tribes in central Nigeria, is convinced that evangelism and church planting is about households. And a household consists of the head of the family, his wife and their children. No matter what role any receiver of the gospel has, it is always the family structure that sets the context of evangelism. Any church founder must pay attention to the importance of family structures and life at home. It is important to comprehend how family is constituted (how family is structured, what it looks like) within a certain culture, and the social dynamics within the target families.[18]

Therefore, it is necessary to explore the specific structures of the families, kinships and clans we want to reach. There is great variety within the different cultures of the world when it comes to the ways in which a family is defined, distinguished and organized. In John Apeh's helpful book for mission practice he lists some areas to explore that might help us to understand family structures in our mission field:[19]

- How people organize family and how they sustain these structures;
- What roles are assigned to family members and what happens if these roles are neglected;
- Which of these structures are problematic when tested against God's Word, and which are wise to adopt.

As a missionary of Christian Mission in Many Lands (CMML), Apeh put his advice into practice when church planting among the Igala in Nigeria.[20] During the last decades, ten thousand people have come to believe in Jesus Christ there. According to Apeh, the main reason for this overwhelming

---

18. John E. Apeh, *Social Structure and Church Planting* (Shippensburg, PA: Companion Press, 1989), 13.

19. Apeh, *Social Structure*, 14–15.

20. Apeh, 15–105.

success was the strategic focus on evangelizing families and kinships. This is why he strongly recommends such family-focused mission anywhere in Africa.

The same is true of Buddhist cultures or parts of Asia. Alex G. Smith, a missionary to Buddhists, writes that working within social and familial structures provides the best opportunity for an effective testimony.[21] Equally, David Lim demands a paradigm shift concerning the conventional methods of mission, demanding a change from the individualistic method to the family-focused approach.[22] In his view, this is the only way to reach Asians, as they are family people. Others confirm Lim's assessment.[23]

This focus on the family is both a gift and a challenge for missionaries who serve as whole families on the mission field. On the one hand, they can simply continue the missional lifestyle they used to live as a family at home; for there, they learned to be a living testimony and to witness together as family. They made friends with their neighbours and joined neighbourhood family clusters. They learned how to build trust and to be patient. Hence, for such families it is releasing and relaxing to follow the same approach in their new environment. On the other hand, they are only able to do that (i.e. to connect and communicate) when they manage to integrate their family lives into the host culture. This might require massive adjustments. My friend Helga said of her struggle as a missionary in a Muslim country: "After all this time I still struggle when my husband walks two steps in front of me when we go for a walk in town. It would cause real offence if I walked beside him or even first. Also, men and women always eat in separate rooms here. While the men are served the best parts of the meat, the children have to wait to eat only when the men have had enough. It's horrible." Yet Helga had to adjust to these conventions, some of which she felt humiliated by. She added, "When the people saw me recognize, and even respect, their local customs, they started asking how we live life at home."

At the same time, it can be a fascinating experience to adjust to a foreign culture. It might make our mission task even more interesting. And if we are able to share the gospel biblically, yet at the same time in line with the way the local people think and the customs they live by (without imposing or currying favour), we will have undreamt-of opportunities to evangelize. Helga

---

21. Alex G. Smith, "Family Networks: The Context for Communication," in *Family and Faith in Asia: The Missional Impact of Social Networks*, ed. Paul H. De Neui (Pasadena, CA: William Carey Library, 2010), 71.

22. David Lim, "Catalyzing 'Insider Movements' in Buddhist Contexts," in De Neui, *Family and Faith*, 34–37.

23. For more voices, see the essay collection in De Neui, *Family and Faith*.

continued: "After all those years, we meet as couples at our church today. We meet in one room, men and women together, and we even share dinner at one table. Indeed, we are witnesses of the change that is taking place in this patriarchal culture. If we had rebelled against this system at first, we would still be in the place where we started years ago – or, more probably, we would have returned home." In this way, a Western family has influenced culture by being a role model to the local people.

Sadly, we are seeing the collapse of the family today, not only in the US and in Europe but also in Asia, Africa and Latin America, because of globalization's negative effects on all cultures worldwide. However, people are seeking alternative solutions. What a great opportunity for any Christian family to be God's answer in flesh and blood to the cravings of this world! What a chance to let our light shine, to be an authentic testimony with our very lives!

Epilogue

The Family Is the Path of the Church

In 1994, on the occasion of the Year of the Family, Pope John Paul II stated that "The family is the path of the church."[1] Pondering on the family in light of this quote, German Roman Catholic Cardinal Walter Kasper postulated that "The future of mankind depends on the family [i.e. the family is crucial, it is the guarantee for the future of mankind]. No family, no future – or rather ageing societies, the very danger we already face in today's Western societies."[2] This man of God, and obviously also his church, seems to have recognized the importance of the family for the future of the church – indeed, for the future of the whole world. As Donna S. Thomas says, it is families who understand their mandate and commission by God who will change the world. It is missional families who will shape the world's transformation – families where faith is nurtured and carried out into the world.[3]

In this book we have explored the interrelationship between the family and mission. It is clear that God created the family, and that he did so in order to manifest his will and to implement his mission on earth. We need to not only comprehend this close connection between the family as a social institution and God's mission, but also realize that the family is at the very heart of God's divine plan. Therefore, the family must become the primary target of all evangelism, as Pope John Paul II rightly claimed.[4] So why don't we talk more about the family in our churches? Why do we invest so little effort and energy in nurturing and supporting our families? The reason for this lack of investment might be the fact that we take the family – and the families in our

---

1. Quoted in Walter Kasper, *Das Evangelium von der Familie* (Freiburg: Herder, 2014), 10.

2. Kasper, *Das Evangelium von der Familie*, 26.

3. Donna S. Thomas, *Becoming a World Changing Family: Fun and Innovative Ways to Spread the Good News* (Grand Rapids, MI: Baker, 2004).

4. Ralph Weimann, "Die Familie als Keimzelle der Erneuerung des Glaubens," in *Ehe und Familie: Wege zum Gelingen aus katholischer Perspektive*, ed. George Augustin and Ingo Proft (Freiburg: Herder, 2016), 465–477.

churches – for granted, for example, in counting the families of our members as automatically being church members. Such at least is the assessment of family-centred church growth expert Gerald Foley.[5]

Actually, hardly anyone denies the importance of the family. But why, then, is the family seldom a central issue that we talk about? Why is the family seldom a primary concern in church, let alone seen as a, if not *the*, mission agent? That's preached hardly anywhere. Do we neglect the family because we have been focusing on our churches as such? That's what Pope John Paul II assumed to be true for the Roman Catholic Church. Therefore, he demanded a radical reorganization of the church into one based on the family.[6] It was clear to him that "as soon as family collapses, the world will vanish" and therefore "Church . . . the future of our church . . . depends on the family."[7]

It is up to our churches to find the right answers to the questions above. It is my prayer that this book will contribute to our journey into the future God intended. Please take time to reflect. And don't believe those voices of the zeitgeist proclaiming that the times of the traditional family belong to the past. Don't be disturbed when society praises alternative forms of living together – forms of sharing life that imitate family without being a family. The history of humankind has seen such elations pass that represented the periods of decadence in our history, marking the decay of cultures parallel to the self-idolization of humankind. The church must take a stand against such trends by being the witness of the living God – Father, Son and Holy Spirit. And yes, it will be our living testimonies – the testimonies of how we live our lives as fulfilled, happy families – that will in the end be most convincing anyway.

---

5. Gerald Foley, *Family-Centred Church: A New Parish Model* (Kansas City, MO: Sheed and Ward, 1995), 12.

6. FC 70; Foley, *Family-Centred Church*, 5, 19.

7. FC 3, 75.

Bibliography

Abraham, William. *The Logic of Evangelism*. Grand Rapids, MI: Eerdmans, 1989.
Aldrich, Joseph C. *Life-Style Evangelism: Crossing Traditional Boundaries to Reach the Unbelieving World*. Portland, OR: Multnomah, 1981.
———. "Lifestyle Evangelism." *Christianity Today*, 7 January 1983.
Allensbach Institut. *Familienstudie 2013*. Wuppertal: Vorwerk, 2013.
AOK. *Familienstudie 2014: Forschungsbericht des Sinus-Instituts*. Berlin: AOK, 2014.
Apeh, John E. *Social Structure and Church Planting*. Shippensburg, PA: Companion Press, 1989.
Apfelbacher, Karl-Ernst. *Selig die Trauernden: Kulturgeschichtliche Aspekte des Christentums*. Regensburg: Friedrich Pustet, 2002.
Baker, Dwight P., and Robert J. Priest, eds. *The Missionary Family: Witness, Concerns, Care*. Pasadena, CA: William Carey Library, 2014.
Balswick, Jack O., and Judith K. Balswick. *The Family: A Christian Perspective on the Contemporary Home*. Grand Rapids, MI: Baker, 1989.
Banks, Robert, and Julia Banks. *The Church Comes Home*. Claremont, CA: Albatros, 1986.
Barna, George. *Transforming Children into Spiritual Champions: Why Children Should Be Your Church's #1 Priority*. Ventura, CA: Regal, 2003.
Barrett, David. "Defining Missional Church." In *Evangelical, Ecumenical and Anabaptist Missiology in Conversation: Essays in Honor of Wilbert Shenk*, edited by James Krabill, Walter Sawatsky and Charles E. Van Engen, 177–183. Maryknoll, NY: Orbis, 2006.
Barrs, Jerram. *The Heart of Evangelism*. Wheaton, IL: Crossroads, 2001.
Barth, Karl. *Church Dogmatics* IV/3. Edinburgh: T&T Clark, 1962.
Barton, Stephen C. *Life Together: Family, Sexuality and Community in the New Testament and Today*. Edinburgh/New York: T&T Clark, 2001.
Becker, U. "Seligkeit." In *Theologisches Begriffslexikon zum Neuen Testament*, ed. L. Coenen et al. II/2 (1971), 1133–1135.
Becker, Uwe, ed. *Perspektiven der Diakonie im gesellschaftlichen Wandel*. Neukirchen-Vluyn: Neukirchener Verlag, 2011.
Beinert, Wolfgang. "Seligkeit." In *Lexikon für Theologie und Kirche*, Vol. 9, 437–442. 3rd ed. Freiburg: Herder, 2000.
Bennett, Arthur. *Rural Evangelism*. London/Oxford: A. R. Mowbray & Co., 1963.
Bennett, Ron. "Authentic Church-Based Evangelism in a Relational Age." In *Telling the Truth*, edited by D. A. Carson, 275–280. Grand Rapids, MI: Zondervan, 2000.

Betz, H. D. "Die Makarismen der Bergpredigt (Mt 5,3–12): Beobachtungen zur literarischen Form und theologischen Bedeutung." *Zeitschrift für Theologie und Kirche* 75 (1978): 1–19.

Beyerhaus, Peter. *Er sandte sein Wort: Theologie der Christlichen Mission, Vol. 1: Die Bibel in der Mission*. Wuppertal: R. Brockhaus TVG, 1996.

Böhm, Karsten, and Jonathan Bauer. *Denk orange! Für eine Generation voller Glaube, Hoffnung und Liebe*. Asslar: Gerth Medien, 2013.

Bolton, Robert J. *Sons of Han: Strategies for Urban Church Planting and Growth among Chinese in East Asia*. Haverton, PA: Treasure Island, 2002.

Bonhoeffer, Dietrich. *Letters and Papers from Prison*. Enlarged edition. London: SCM, 1971.

Bosch, David J. *Ganzheitliche Mission*. Marburg: Francke Verlag, 2011.

———. *Mission im Wandel: Paradigmenwechsel in der Missionstheologie*. Gießen: Brunnen Verlag, 2012.

———. *Transforming Mission: Paradigm Shifts in Theology of Mission*. Maryknoll, NY: Orbis, 1991.

Bosse, Michael. "Ehrenamtliche Helfer für Sterbenskranke." *Die Welt* online, 10 January 2013. http://www.welt.de/regionales/duesseldorf/article112669104/Ehrenamtliche-Helfer-fuer-Sterbenskranke.html.

Brind, Ian, and Tessa Wilkinson. *Creative Ideas for Whole Church Family Worship*. London: Canterbury Press Norwich, 2011.

Broer, Ingo. *Die Seligpreisungen der Bergpredigt: Studien zu ihrer Überlieferung und Interpretation*. Bonner Biblische Beiträge 61. Bonn: Hanstein, 1986.

Brown, P. *The Making of Late Antiquity*. Cambridge, MA: Harvard University Press, 1978.

Brunner, Emil. *Die Christliche Lehre von der Kirche, dem Glauben und der Vollendung*. Zurich: Zwingli, 1964.

Caaps, Donald. "Erikson's Life Cycle Theory and the Local Church." *Pastoral Psychology* 27, no. 4 (1979): 223–235.

Carson, D. A., ed. *Telling the Truth: Evangelizing Postmoderns*. Grand Rapids, MI: Zondervan, 2000.

Cha, Peter, and Greg Jao. "Reaching out to Postmodern Asian Americans." In Carson, *Telling the Truth*, 224–241.

Church of England Board for Social Responsibility. *Something to Celebrate: Valuing Families in Church and Society*. London: Church House, 1995.

Clapp, Rodney. *Families at the Crossroads: Beyond Traditional and Modern Options*. Downers Grove, IL: InterVarsity Press, 1993.

Cloutier, Mary Carol. "'Family Problem': Challenges in Balancing Maternity and Mission in Nineteenth-Century Equatorial Africa." In Baker and Priest, *Missionary Family*, 79–97.

Coleman, Robert E. "The Lifestyle of the Great Commission." In Carson, *Telling the Truth*, 255–269.

———. *The Master Plan of Discipleship*. Old Tappan, NY: Fleming H. Revell, 1987.
———. *The Master Plan of Evangelism*. Grand Rapids, MI: Revell, 2006.
———. *Des Masters Plan für Evangelisation*. Neunhausen-Stuttgart: Hänssler Verlag, 1978.
———. *The Master's Way of Personal Evangelism*. Wheaton, IL: Crossway, 1997.
Covey, Stephen R. *7 Habits of Highly Effective Families*. London: Simon & Schuster, 1998.
Das, Man Singh, and Panos D. Bardis. *The Family in Asia*. London: George Allen & Unwin, 1979.
Dawn, Marva J. *Sexual Character: Beyond Technique to Intimacy*. Grand Rapids, MI: Eerdmans, 1993.
Dawson, Scott, ed. *The Complete Evangelism Guidebook: Expert Advice on Reaching Others for Christ*. Grand Rapids, MI: Baker, 2006.
De Neui, Paul H., ed. *Family and Faith in Asia: The Missional Impact of Social Networks*. Pasadena, CA: William Carey Library, 2010.
Dobson, James. "Keys to a Family Friendly Church." *Leadership* 7, no. 1 (1986): 19.
Dorr, Donal. *Mission in Today's World*. Maryknoll, NY: Orbis, 2000.
Drake, Michelle. *Walking with God: The Young Person's Diary*. [n.p.]: YWAM, 2005.
Drane, John. *Evangelism for a New Age: Creating Churches for the Next Century*. London: Marshall Pickering, 1994.
Dunagan, Ann. *The Mission-Minded Family: Releasing Your Family to God's Destiny*. Downers Grove, IL: InterVarsity Press, 2007.
Eastman, Michael, and Steve Latham. *Urban Church: A Practitioner's Resource Book*. London: SPCK, 2004.
Ellison, H. L. *The Household Church: Apostolic Practice in a Modern Setting*. London: Paternoster, 1963.
Escobar, Samuel. *A Time for Mission: The Challenge for Global Christianity*. Leicester: Inter-Varsity Press, 2003.
Evans, David. "Evangelism with Theological Credibility." In Wright and Sugden, *One Gospel, Many Clothes*, 29–38.
Faix, Wilhelm. "Familie heute: Zwischen Anspruch und Wirklichkeit." *JETh* 9 (1995): 116–145.
———. "Familie im Wandel: Gesellschaftliche Bedingungen heutigen Familienlebens als Herausforderung für die christliche Familie." In *Theologische Wahrheit und die Postmoderne*, edited by H. H. Klement, 378–411. Wuppertal: SCM Brockhaus, 2002.
———. "Die individualisierte Familie: Familie mit Zukunft? Eine Lebensform im Umbruch." *JETh* 27 (2013): 187–215.
———. "Kinder im Glauben erziehen." In *Mündiger Glaube*. Witten: SCM R. Brockhaus, 2015.
———. *Wo zwei oder drei . . .* Wuppertal: R. Brockhaus, 1997.
———. *Zinzendorf: Glaube und Identität eines Querdenkers*. Marburg: Francke Verlag, 2012.

Fernando, Ajith. *Checkliste Glaube: Dienen wie Jesus*. Marburg: Francke Verlag, 2011.
Fiddes, Paul S. *Participating in God: A Pastoral Doctrine of the Trinity*. London: Darton, Longman & Todd, 2000.
Finley, Mitch. "A Family Ecclesiology." *America* 149 (30 July 1983).
Finney, John. *Wie Gemeinde über sich hinauswächst: Zukunftsfähig evangelisieren im 21. Jahrhundert*. Neukirchen-Vluyn: Aussaat, 2007.
Fitts, Robert. *The Church in the House: Return to Simplicity*. Salem, OR: Preparing the Way, 2001.
Fleming, Dean. *Recovering the Full Mission of God: A Biblical Perspective on Being, Doing and Telling*. Downers Grove, IL: IVP Academic, 2013.
Foley, Gerald. *Family-Centred Church: A New Parish Model*. Kansas City, MO: Sheed and Ward, 1995.
Fong, Kenneth. *Insights for Growing Asian-American Ministries*. Rosemead, CA: EverGrowing Publications, 1990.
Fowlkes, D. W., and P. Verster. "Family (*oikos*) Evangelism for Reaching Forward Caste Hindus in India." *Verbum et Ecclesia* 27, no. 1 (2006): 321–338.
Fraser, Shirley. "House Groups and Church Organizations." In Wright and Gray, *Local Church Evangelism*, 29–34.
Frazee, Randy. *The Connecting Church*. Grand Rapids, MI: Zondervan, 2001.
Frey, Jörg. "Die Ausbreitung des frühen Christentums: Perspektiven für die gegenwärtige Praxis der Kirche." In *Kirche zwischen postmoderner Kultur und Evangelium*, ed. Martin Reppenhagen, Beiträge zu Evangelisation und Gemeindeentwicklung 15, 86–112. Neukirchen Vluyn: Neukirchener Verlag, 2010.
Gibbs, Eddie. *Winning Them Back: Tackling the Problem of Nominal Christianity*. Tunbridge Wells: Monarch, 1993.
Giesekus, Ulrich. *Familien leben: Spielregeln für Eltern und Kinder*. Wuppertal: RB Brockhaus, 1994.
Gitari, David. "Kenya: Evangelism among Nomadic Communities." In Wright and Sugden, *One Gospel, Many Clothes*, 60–70.
Gornik, Mark. *To Live in Peace: Biblical Faith and the Changing Inner City*. Grand Rapids, MI: Eerdmans, 2002.
Gourdet, S. "Identification in Intercultural Communication." *Missionalia* 24, no. 3 (1996): 399–409.
Green, Bryan. *The Praxis of Evangelism*. 4th ed. London: Hodder & Stoughton, 1958.
Green, Michael. *Evangelisation zur Zeit der ersten Christen: Motivation, Methodik und Strategie*. Neuhausen-Stuttgart: Hänssler, 1970.
———. *Evangelism through the Local Church*. London: Hodder & Stoughton, 1990.
Greenlee, David. "Growing Churches in Resistant Areas." In *Extending God's Kingdom: Church Planting Yesterday, Today, Tomorrow*, edited by Laurie Fortunak Nichols, A. Scott Moreau and Gary R. Corwin, 215–221. Wheaton, IL: Evangelism and Mission Information Service, 2011.

Grigorenko, Donald and Margaret. "Experiencing Risk: Missionary Families in Dangerous Places." In Baker and Priest, *Missionary Family*, 25–43.

Grimshaw, Patricia. *Paths of Duty: American Missionary Wives in Nineteenth-Century Hawaii*. Honolulu: University of Hawaii Press, 1989.

Gronemeyer, Reimar, and Hans-Eckehard Bahr, eds. *Nachbarschaft im Neubaublock: Empirische Untersuchungen zur Gemeinwesenarbeit, theoretische Studien zur Wohnsituation*. Weinheim: Beltz, 1977.

Groß, Walter, Joseph Ernst et al. "Gottebenbildlichkeit." In *Lexikon für Theologie und Kirche*, Vol. 4, 871–878. 3rd ed. Freiburg: Herder, 1995.

Guder, Darrell. *Missional Church: A Vision for the Sending of the Church in North America*. Grand Rapids, MI: Eerdmans, 1998.

Gundry, Robert H. *Matthew: A Commentary on His Handbook for a Mixed Church under Persecution*. 2nd ed. Grand Rapids, MI: Eerdmans, 1994.

Hagner, Donald H. *Matthew 1–13*. Word Biblical Commentary 33a. Nashville: Thomas Nelson, 1993.

Hammond, Peter. *Cultural and Social Anthropology: Selected Readings*. New York: Macmillan, 1964.

Hardmeier, Roland. *Geliebte Welt: Auf dem Weg zu einem neuen missionarischen Paradigma*. Schwarzenfeld: Neufeld Verlag, 2012.

———. *Kirche ist Mission: Auf dem Weg zu einem ganzheitlichen Missionsverständnis*. IGW 2. Schwarzenfeld: Neufeld Verlag, 2009.

Harnack, Adolf. *Die Mission und die Ausbreitung des Christentums in den ersten drei Jahrhunderten*. 4th ed. Leipzig: J. C. Heinrichs'sche Buchhandlung, 1924.

Hastings, Ross. *Missional God, Missional Church: Hope for Re-Evangelizing the West*. Downers Grove, IL: IVP Academic, 2012.

Hattam, John. *Families Finding Faith: Reaching Today's Families with the Gospel*. Milton Keynes: Scripture Union, 2000.

Hays, G. H. "Christian Evangelism and the Japanese Family." *Review & Expositor* 49, no. 2 (1952): 179–186.

Hedlund, Roger E., and Paul Joshua Bhakiaraj. *Missiology for the 21st Century: South Asian Perspectives*. Delhi: ISPCK/MIIS, 2004.

Herbst, Michael. *Deine Gemeinde komme: Wachstum und Gottes Verheißungen*. 2nd ed. Holzgermingen: Hänssler, 2008.

Hesselgrave, David. *Communicating Christ Cross-Culturally: An Introduction to Missionary Communication*. Grand Rapids, MI: Zondervan, 1991.

Hiebert, Paul G. *Cultural Anthropology*. Grand Rapids, MI: Baker, 1983.

Holl, Karl. "Die Missionsmethode der alten und der mittelalterlichen Kirche." In *Kirchengeschichte als Missionsgeschichte, Vol 1: Die Alte Kirche*, edited by H. Frohnes and U. W. Knorr, 3–17. Munich: Chr. Kaiser, 1974.

Howel, Richard. *Transformation in Action: A Case Study of India*. Thailand: Forum for World Evangelization, 2004.

Hunter, George G., III. *How to Reach Secular People*. Nashville: Abingdon Press, 1992.

Hunter, Jane. *The Gospel of Gentility: American Women Missionaries in Turn-of-the-Century China*. New Haven: Yale University Press, 1984.

Hvalvik, Reidar. "In Word and Deed: The Expansion of the Church in the Pre-Constantinian Era." In *The Mission of the Early Church to Jews and Gentiles*, edited by Jostein Adna and Hand Hans Kvalbein, 265–288. Wissenschaftliche Untersuchungen zum Neuen Testament 127. Tübingen: Mohr Siebeck, 2000.

Jamison, Todd. "House Churches in Central Asia: An Evaluation." In *Extending God's Kingdom: Church Planting Yesterday, Today, Tomorrow*, edited by Laurie Fortunak Nichols, A. Scott Moreau and Gary R. Corwin, 222–230. Wheaton, IL: Evangelism and Mission Information Service, 2011.

Jinadu, Philip, and David Lawrence. *Winning Ways: Creating a Culture of Outreach in Your Church*. London: Authentic, 2007.

Joiner, Reggie. *Lebe orange! Gemeinde und Familie – gemeinsam stark*. Asslar: Gerth Medien, 2012.

Joiner, Reggie, and Carey Nieuwhof. *Gemeinsam Kinder stark machen: Wie Freunde, Familie und Gemeinde sie in der Erziehung unterstützen können*. Asslar: Gerth Medien, 2012.

Käser, Lothar. *Fremde Kulturen: Eine Einführung in die Ethnologie*. Nuremberg: VTR, 2014.

Kasper, Walter. *Das Evangelium von der Familie*. Freiburg: Herder, 2014.

Killinger, John. *Letting God Bless You: The Beatitudes for Today*. Nashville: Abingdon Press, 1992.

King, Joan. "Families: Something to Celebrate." *Ministry Today* 8 (Oct. 1996): 47–53.

Klaiber, Walter. *Ruf und Antwort: Biblische Grundlagen einer Theologie der Evangelisation*. Stuttgart: Christliches Verlagshaus, 1990.

Klassen, Heinrich. *Mission als Zeugnis zur missionarischen Existenz in der Sowjetuinon nach dem Zweiten Weltkrieg*. Nuremberg: VTR, 2003.

Knell, Marion. *Families on the Move: Growing up Overseas – And Loving It!* Grand Rapids, MI: Monarch, 2001.

Kolbell, Erik. *What Jesus Meant: The Beatitudes and a Meaningful Life*. Louisville/London: Westminster John Knox, 2003.

Köstenberger, Andreas J., and David W. Jones. *God, Marriage, and Family: Rebuilding the Biblical Foundation*. 2nd rev. ed. Wheaton, IL: Crossway, 2010.

Lageer, Eileen. *New Life for All: True Accounts of In-Depth Evangelism in West Africa*. Chicago: Moody, 1970.

Lausanne Committee for World Evangelization. "Christian Witness to Muslims." Lausanne Occasional Paper (LOP) 13. 1980. Accessed 19 January 2015. http://www.lausanne.org/content/lop/lop-13.

———. "Non-Traditional Families: Reaching Families with the Good News." Lausanne Occasional Paper (LOP) 36. In *A New Vision, a New Heart, a Renewed Call: Lausanne Occasional Papers*, edited by David Claydon, 437–493. Pasadena, CA: William Carey Library, 2005.

Leman, Kevin, at al. *The Family Matters Handbook.* Nashville: Thomas Nelson, 1994.
Lim, David. "Catalyzing 'Insider Movements' in Buddhist Contexts." In De Neui, *Family and Faith*, 31–46.
Lindner, Herbert. *Kirche am Ort: Gemeindetheorie*, Praktische Theologie heute 16. Stuttgart: Kohlhammer, 1974.
Linthicum, Robert C. *City of God – City of Satan: A Biblical Theology of the Urban Church.* Grand Rapids, MI: Zondervan, 1991.
Loewen, Jacob A. *Culture and Human Values: Christian Intervention in Anthropological Perspective.* Pasadena, CA: William Carey Library, 1977.
Luhmann, Nicklas. *Soziale Systeme: Grundriß einer allgemeinen Theorie.* Berlin: Suhrkamp, 1987.
Lukasse, Johann, and Ted Kamp. *Divide and Multiply.* Hasseln: European Church Planting Consultation, 2010.
Lutzbetak, Louis J. *The Church and Cultures: New Perspectives in Missiological Anthropology.* Maryknoll, NY: Orbis, 1988.
Mack, Ulrich. *Ehrenamtliche Hilfe für Familien mit schwerbehinderten Kindern.* Göttingen: Vandenhoeck & Ruprecht, 2011.
MacMullen, R. *Christianizing the Roman Empire (100–400).* New Haven/London: Yale University Press, 1984.
———. *Roman Social Relations, 50 BC to AD 284.* New Haven/London: Yale University Press, 1974.
Malphurs, Aubrey. *The Nuts and Bolts of Church Planting: A Guide to Starting Any Kind of Church.* Grand Rapids, MI: Baker, 2011.
———. *Planting Churches for the 21st Century.* 3rd ed. Grand Rapids, MI: Baker, 2004.
Manchini, Will. *Church Unique: How Missional Leaders Cast Vision, Capture Culture, and Create Movement.* San Francisco: Jossey-Bass, 2008.
Marshall, Michael. *The Gospel Connection: A Study in Evangelism for the Nineties.* London: Darton, Longman & Todd, 1991.
Mayers, Marvin K. *Christianity Confronts Culture.* Grand Rapids, MI: Zondervan, 1981.
McFarland, Andrew D. "William Carey's Vision for Missionary Families." In Baker and Priest, *Missionary Family*, 98–115.
McNeal, Reggie. *Missional Communities: The Rise of the Post-Congregational Church.* San Francisco: Jossey-Bass, 2011.
———. *Missional Renaissance: Changing the Scorecard for the Church.* San Francisco: Jossey-Bass, 2009.
———. *The Present Future: Six Tough Questions for the Church.* San Francisco: Jossey-Bass, 2003.
Moe, O. *Kristendom ok slegskap: Familiens beydning for troens utbredelse i den forste krestenhet.* Kristiania: Lutherstiftelsens Boghhandel, 1915.
Moreau, A. Scott, Gary R. Corwin and Gary B. McGee. *Introducing World Mission: A Biblical, Historical and Practical Survey.* Grand Rapids, MI: Baker, 2004.

Motz, Arnell. "How Churches Are Doing Evangelism." In *Reclaiming a Nation: The Challenge of Evangelizing Canada in the Year 2000*. Richmond, BC: Church Leadership Library, 1990.

Motz, Arnell, with Donald Posterski. "Who Responds to the Gospel and Why?" In *Reclaiming the Nation: The Challenge of Evangelizing Canada in the Year 2000*, edited by Gerald Kraft et al. Richmond: Church Leadership Library, 1990.

Moynagh, Michael. *Being Church, Doing Life: Creating Gospel Communities Where Life Happens*. Oxford: Monarch, 2014.

Mühlan, Eberhard. *Familien-Strukturen in Indien: Fremden Kulturen eine christliche Familienlehre bringen*. Mission Academics 33. Nuremberg: VTR, 2011.

Nazir-Ali, Michael. *From Everywhere to Everywhere: A World View of Christian Mission*. London: Collins, 1990.

Neill, Stephen, Niels-Peter Moritzen and Ernst Schrupp. *Lexikon zur Weltmission*. Wuppertal: R. Brockhaus, 1975.

Newbigin, Lesslie. *The Open Secret: An Introduction to the Theology of Mission*. Grand Rapids, MI: Eerdmans, 1995.

Nida, Eugene. *Message and Mission: Communication of Christian Faith*. New York: Joanna Cotler Books, 1960.

Niejahr, Elisabeth. "Nachbarschaftshilfe: Das Netzwerk nebenan." *Die Zeit*, 9 August 2012. http://www.zeit.de/2012/33/Netzwerk-Nachbarschaft.

Ott, Craig, Stephen J. Strauss and Timothy Tennent. *Encountering Theology of Mission: Biblical Foundations, Historical Developments and Contemporary Issues*. Grand Rapids, MI: Baker Academic, 2010.

Ott, Craig, and Gene Wilson. *Global Church Planting: Biblical Principles and Best Practices for Multiplication*. Grand Rapids, MI: Baker, 2011.

Payne, J. D. *Discovering Church Planting: An Introduction to the Whats, Whys, and Hows of Global Church Planting*. Colorado Springs/Milton Keynes/Hyderabad: Paternoster, 2009.

Peters, George W. *Evangelisation: Total, durchdringend, umfassend*. Bad Liebenzell: VLM, 1977.

———. *Missionarisches Handeln und Biblischer Auftrag: Eine Theologie der Mission*. 1st ed. Bad Liebenzell: VLM, 1977.

Petersen, Jim. *Living Proof: Sharing the Gospel Naturally*. Colorado Springs, CO: NavPress, 1989.

Pilkinton, Ross. *Evangelistischer Lebensstil*. Marienheide: Bibellesebund, 1979.

Piper, John. *Let the Nations Be Glad: The Supremacy of God in Missions*. Grand Rapids, MI: Baker, 2004.

Plüss, David, and Stephan Degen-Ballmer. *Kann man Glauben lernen? Eine kritische Analyse von Glaubenskrisen*. Zurich: TVZ, 2008.

Pope John Paul II. "Apostolic Exhortation *Familiaris Consortio* of Pope John Paul II to the Episcopate, to the Clergy and to the Faithful of the Whole Catholic Church on the Role of the Christian Family in the Modern World." 1981. http://

w2.vatican.va/content/john-paul-ii/en/apost_exhortations/documents/hf_jp-ii_exh_19811122_familiaris-consortio.html.

———. "Brief Papst Johannes Pauls II. an die Familien" (Letter to Families by Pope John Paul II). 1994. Accessed 1 September 2016. http://w2.vatican.va/content/john-paul-ii/de/letters/1994/documents/hf_jp-ii_let_02021994_families.html.

Pope Paul VI. "*Evangelii Nuntiandi*: Apostolic Exhortation of His Holiness Pope Paul VI to the Episcopate, to the Clergy and to All the Faithful of the Entire World." 1976. http://w2.vatican.va/content/paul-vi/en/apost_exhortations/documents/hf_p-vi_exh_19751208_evangelii-nuntiandi.html.

———. "Pastoral Constitution on the Church in the Modern World *Gaudium et Spes* Promulgated by His Holiness, Pope Paul VI on December 7, 1965." http://www.vatican.va/archive/hist_councils/ii_vatican_council/documents/vat-ii_const_19651207_gaudium-et-spes_en.html.

Powell, Mark A. "Matthew's Beatitudes: Reversals and Rewards of the Kingdom." *Catholic Biblical Quarterly* 58 (1996): 460–479.

Pritchrad, John. *Living Faithfully: Following Christ in Everyday Life*. London: SPCK, 2013.

Rankin, Jerry. "The Family and Mission: Reflections from the Life of a US Missionary." In Baker and Priest, *Missionary Family*, 45–59.

Ratzinger, Joseph. "Diener euer Freunde." In *Gesammelte Schriften*, Vol. 12, edited by G. L. Müller. Freiburg: Herder, 2010.

Reifler, Hans Ulrich. *Handbuch der Missiologie: Missionarisches Handeln aus biblischer, historischer und sozialwissenschaftlicher Perspektive*. Nuremberg: VTR, 2009.

Reimer, Johannes. *Aufbruch in die Zukunft: Geistesgaben in der Praxis des Gemeindeaufbaus*. 3rd ed. Hammerbrücke: Conception Seidel, 2005.

———. "Der Dienst der Versöhnung – bei der Kernkompetenz ansetzen: Zur Korrelation von Gemeinwesenmediation und multikulturellem Gemeindebau." *Theologisches Gespräch* 1 (2011): 19–35.

———. *Gott in der Welt feiern: Auf dem Weg zum missionalen Gottesdienst*. 2nd ed. Schwarzenfeld: Neufeld Verlag, 2011.

———. *Hereinspaziert: Willkommenskultur und Evangelisation*. Schwarzenfeld: Neufeld Verlag, 2013.

———. *Leben, Rufen, Verändern: Theologie der gesellschaftstransformierenden Evangelisation*. Marburg: Francke Verlag, 2013.

———. "Vision, Plan und Potenzial." In *Die Welt verstehen: Kontextanalyse als Sehhilfe für die Gemeinde*, edited by Tobias Faix and Johannes Reimer, 37–63. Transformationsstudien 3. Marburg: Francke-Buchhandlung, 2012.

———. *Die Welt umarmen: Theologie des gesellschaftsrelevanten Gemeindebaus*. Transformationsstudien 1. 2nd ed. Marburg: Francke Verlag, 2013.

Reuter, Wilfried. . . . *Und bis ans Ende der Welt: Beiträge zur Evangelisation; Eine Festschrift zum 60. Geburtstag von Gerhard Bergmann*. Neuhausen-Stuttgart: Hänssler, 1974.

Richards, Lawrence O. *Christian Education: Seeking to Become Like Jesus Christ*. Grand Rapids, MI: Zondervan, 1975.

Robert, Dana L. *American Women in Mission: A Social History of Their Thought and Practice*. Macon, GA: Mercer University Press, 1997.

———. "The 'Christian Home' as a Cornerstone of Anglo-American Mission Thought and Practice." In *Converting Colonialism: Visions and Realities in Mission History, 1706–1914*, edited by Dana Robert, 134–165. Grand Rapids, MI: Eerdmans, 2008.

Roenfeld, Peter. *Handbuch für Gemeindegründer*. Lüneburg: Advent Verlag, 2003.

Roxburgh, Alan J. *Missional: Joining the Neighborhood*. Grand Rapids, MI: Baker, 2011.

Roxburgh, Alan J., and M. Scott Boren. *Introducing the Missional Church: What It Is, Why It Matters, How to Become One*. Grand Rapids, MI: Baker, 2009.

Runyon, Robert D. "Principles and Methods of Household Evangelism." In *Vital Missions Issues: Examining Challenges and Changes in World Evangelization*, edited by Roy B. Zuck. Grand Rapids, MI: Kregel, 1998.

Ruthe, Reinhold. *Familie – Oase oder Chaos: Wege aus der Familienkrise*. Moers: Brendow Verlag, 1991.

———. *Spielregeln für die Familie: 30 praktische Vorschläge wie wir besser miteinander auskommen*. 4th ed. Moers: Brendow Verlag, 1992.

Savageu, Cheryl, and Diane M. Stortz. *Parents of Missionaries: How to Thrive and Stay Connected When Your Grandchildren Serve Cross-Culturally*. Colorado Springs, CO: Authentic, 2008.

Schaeffer, Edith. *Lebensraum Familie*. Kassel: Oncken Verlag, 1976.

Schäfer, Klaus. "Lernort Gemeinde." *Zeitschrift für theologische Praxis* 2 (2003): 24–29.

Schäfer, Paul Walter. *Evangelisation: Viele Wege – ein Ziel*. Wuppertal and Zürich: R. Brockhaus, 1989.

Schlottoff, Bernd. *Ein Traum von der Gemeinde: Mut zum missionarischen Gemeindebau*. Wuppertal: SCM Brockhaus, 2011.

Schnabel, Eckhard J. *Urchristliche Mission*. Wuppertal: R. Brockhaus TVG, 2002.

Schulte, Anton. *Evangelisation – praktisch: Mit Anmerkungen zu einer deutschen "Theologie der Evangelisation."* Moers: Brendow, 1979.

Schulten, Martin. "Gesellschaftstransformativer Gemeindebau am Beispiel der Evangelischen Freien Gemeinde Brüchermühle und deren Sozialprojekt für Hartkernarbeitslose in der Christlichen Beschäftigungsgesellschaft Brüchermühle (CBB). Unpublished MTh diss., University of South Africa, 2011. http://uir.unisa.ac.za/bitstream/handle/10500/8630/dissertation_schulten_m.pdf.

Schumacher, Michelle M. *A Trinitarian Anthropology: Adrienne von Speyer und Hans Urs von Balthasar in Dialogue with Thomas Aquinas*. Washington, DC: Catholic University of America Press, 2014.

Schütz, Paul. *Zwischen Nil und Kaukasus*. Munich: Kaiser, 1930.

Schwark, Christian. *Gottesdienste für Kirchendistanzierte: Auf dem Weg zum missionalen Gottesdienst*. Schwarzenfeld: Neufeld Verlag, 2006.

Schweizer, Eduard. *The Good News According to Matthew*. London: SPCK, 1984.

Seelbach, Larissa Carina. "Das weibliche Geschlecht ist ja kein Gebrechen, sondern Natur: Augustins Wertschätzung der Frau" ("The Female Sex Is No Illness But Nature: St Augustine's Appreciation of Women"). Lecture, Augustine Study Day, Würzburg, Germany, 2004. Accessed 1 June 2015. http://www.augustinus.de/bwo/dcms/sites/bistum/extern/zfa/texteueber/vortragbeitrag/wertschaetzung.htm.

Sills, David. *The Missionary Call: Find your Place in God's Plan for the World*. Chicago: Moody, 2008.

Simson, Michael L. *Permission Evangelism: When to Talk, When to Walk*. Colorado Springs, CO: NexGen, 2003.

Simson, Wolfgang. *Häuser die die Welt verändern*. Emmelsbühl: C&P, 1999.

Smith, Alex G. "Family Networks: The Context for Communication." In De Neui, *Family and Faith*, 47–76.

Stasson. Anneke. "Walter and Ingrid Trobisch and a Missiology of 'Couple Power.'" In Baker and Priest, *Missionary Family*, 5–20.

Stott, John R. W. "Evangelism through the Local Church." In Wright and Sugden, *One Gospel, Many Clothes*, 13–28.

———. *Gesandt wie Christus: Grundfragen christlicher Mission und Evangelisation*. Solingen: Bernhard, 1976.

Strak, R. *The Rise of Christianity: A Sociologist Reconsiders History*. Princeton, NJ: Princeton University Press, 1996.

Strange, W. A. *Children in the Early Church: Children in the Ancient World, the New Testament and the Early Church*. London: Paternoster, 1996.

Strübind, Kim. "Missionstheologie und missionarische Praxis der Baptisten im ökumenischen Kontext." *Zeitschrift für Theologie und Gemeinde* 12 (2007): 287–293.

Stückelberger, Alfred. *Der Erzieher als Seelsorger*. Zürich/Leipzig: Gotthelf Verlag, 1939.

Sundermeier, Theo. "Konvivenz als Grundstruktur ökumenischer Existenz heute." *Ökumenische Existenz Heute* 1 (1986): 49–100.

Tennent, Timothy C. *Invitation to World Mission: A Trinitarian Theology for the Twenty-First Century*. Grand Rapids, MI: Kregel, 2010.

Teplitzkaja, Nina. *Zerkov sluzhit ljudjam Istoria zerkvi "Svet Miru" v gorode Kischineve*. Kishinev: Svet Miru, 2015.

Thiessen, Elmer. *The Ethic of Evangelism*. London: Paternoster, 2011.

Thomas, Donna S. *Becoming a World Changing Family: Fun and Innovative Ways to Spread the Good News*. Grand Rapids, MI: Baker, 2004.

Towns, Elmer L., ed. *Evangelism and Church Growth: A Practical Encyclopedia*. Ventura, CA: Regal, 1995.

Van Engen, Charles. *Mission on the Way: Issues in Mission Theology*. Grand Rapids, MI: Baker, 1996.

Van Vonderen, Jeff. *Familien: Von Gott getragen*. Asslar: Projektion J., 1996.

Vance, Barbara. *Planning and Conducting Family Cluster: Education for Family Wellness*. Newbury Park, CA: Sage, 1989.

Vorwerk. *Vorwerk Familienstudie 2013*. Wuppertal: Vorwerk, 2013.
Walker, Christopher C. *Connecting with the Spirit of Christ: Evangelism for a Secular Age*. Nashville: Discipleship Resources, 1988.
Walrond-Skinner, Sue. *Family Matters: The Pastoral Care of Personal Relationships*. London: SPCK, 1988.
———. *The Fulcrum and the Fire: Wrestling with Family Life*. London: Darton, Longman & Todd, 1993.
Ward, Ted. *Values Begin at Home: Parents Provide the Most Important Moral Influences Children Ever Encounter*. Wheaton, IL: Victor, 1989.
Warren, Rick. *The Purpose Driven Life: What on Earth Am I Here For?* Grand Rapids, MI: Zondervan, 2002.
Warren, Robert. *Signs of Life: How Goes the Decade of Evangelism?* London: Church House, 1996.
Watson, David. *I Believe in Evangelism*. London: Hodder & Stoughton, 1976.
Wegner, Rob, and Jack Magruder. *Missional Moves: 15 Tectonic Shifts That Transform Churches, Communities and the World*. Grand Rapids, MI: Zondervan, 2012.
Weimann, Ralph. "Die Familie als Keimzelle der Erneuerung des Glaubens." In *Ehe und Familie: Wege zum Gelingen aus katholischer Perspektive*, edited by George Augustin and Ingo Proft, 465–477. Freiburg: Herder, 2016.
Wenger, A. Grace, and Dave and Neta Jackson. *Witness: Empowering the Church through Worship, Community and Mission*. Scottdale, PA: Herald, 1989.
Werth, Martin. *Theologie der Evangelisation*. Neukirchen-Vluyn: Neukirchener Verlag, 2004.
Wimber, John R., and Kevin Springer. *Power Evangelism*. San Francisco: Harper & Row, 1996.
Wolf, Thomas. "Oikos Evangelism: The Biblical Pattern." Accessed 24 January 2020. https://studyres.com/doc/12847558/oikos-evangelism---grace-family-church---pearland—tx.
Wright, Christopher J. H. *The Mission of God: Unlocking the Bible's Grand Narrative*. Downers Grove, IL: InterVarsity Press, 2006.
———. *The Mission of God's People: A Biblical Theology of the Church's Mission*. Grand Rapids, MI: Zondervan, 2010.
Wright, Chris, and Chris Sugden, eds. *One Gospel, Many Clothes: Anglicans and the Decade of Evangelism*. London: Regnum, 1990.
Wright, David, and Alastair Gray. *Local Church Evangelism*. Edinburgh: Saint Andrew Press, 1987.
Yates, John and Susan. *Character Matters! Raising Kids with Values That Last*. Grand Rapids, MI: Baker, 1992.
Yeo, Alfred. "The Local Church Reaches Its Neighbourhood." In *The Church: God's Agent for Change*, edited by Bruce J. Nicolls, 140–148. Exeter: Paternoster, 1986.
Young, David. "Mission in Rural Community." In Wright and Gray, *Local Church Evangelism*, 65–71.

Zdero, Rad. *The Global House Church Movement*. Pasadena, CA: William Carey Library, 2004.

Zunkel, C. Wayne. *Church Growth under Fire*. Scottdale, PA: Herald Press, 1987.

Zweininger, Jakob. "Allah oder Christus? A Missiology Case Study on the Reasons Why Kyrgyz People Convert from Islam to Christianity." Unpublished DTh diss., University of South Africa, 2009.

Index of Names

A
Aldrich, Joe 192
Anderson, Rufus 8
Apeh, John E. 3, 224
Astin, Howard 208

B
Balswick, Jack and Judith 121
Barna, George 109
Barth, Karl 154
Bennett, Arthur 172
Bennett, Ron 187
Bolton, Robert 207
Bonhoeffer, Dietrich 154
Bosch, David J. 6, 105
Brunner, Emil 91

C
Carey, William 10, 216
Cha, Peter 99
Cloutier, Mary C. 9
Coleman, Robert E. 31, 37, 175
Covey, Stephen 117, 119, 151–153

D
Dawson, Scott 99
Dobson, James C. 96

E
Ellison, Henry L. 183

F
Faix, Wilhelm x, 14
Fernando, Ajith 45, 207
Finney, John 8
Foley, Gerald 68, 88–90, 228

G
Gibbs, Eddie 4

Giesekus, Ulrich 107
Gitari, David 2
Gornik, Mark R. 98
Gourdet, S. 65, 155
Green, Bryan 3, 11, 12, 162
Green, Michael 54
Grigorenko, Donald and Margaret 61
Guder, Darrell 71
Gundry, Robert H. 126

H
Hagner, Donald A. 127, 128
Hardmeier, Roland 18, 24, 92
Hartenstein, Karl 106
Hunter III, George G. 154, 159–161

K
Killinger, John 156
King, Joan 75, 185
Klassen, Heinrich 2
Knell, Marion 109, 218, 219
Kolbell, Erik 126, 130

L
Lim, David 225
Lindner, Herbert 76
Linthicum, Robert C. 175
Lukasse, Johan 99
Lutzbetak, Louis J. 65

M
Malphurs, Aubrey 87
Marshall, Michael 102
Mayers, Marvin 63
McNeal, Reggie 4, 72, 79, 83, 86
Moody, Dwight L. 207
Motz, Arnell 2, 98
Moynagh, Michael 183

N
Nazir-Ali, Michale 61

O
Ott, Craig 174, 181

P
Payne, J. D. 87, 212
Peters, George W. ix, 25, 60, 105, 171, 173
Pollock, David 218

R
Rankin, Jerry 62
Richards, Lawrence O. 71, 176
Robert, Dana 8, 9
Ruthe, Reinhold 96

S
Samuel, C. B. ix, 2
Savageu, Cheryl 222
Schaeffer, Edith 72
Schäfer, Klaus 12
Schlottoff, Bernd 86
Schwark, Christian 86
Simson, Michael L. 101
Smith, Alex G. 225
Spurgeon, Charles 11
Stasson, Anneke 6, 9
Stott, John R. W. 91
Stückelberger, Alfred 109
Sundermeier, Theo 154

T
Tennent, Timothy C. 17
Teplitzkaja, Nina 113, 114
Thomas, Donna S. 215
Towns, Elmer L. 2, 59

U
Ubejvolk, Vladimir 114

V
Van Vonderen, Jeff 80, 99
von Harnack, Carl G. A. 106

W
Walker, Christopher 5, 186
Warren, Rick 174
Watson, David 11, 93, 94
Wenger, A. Grace 191
Werth, Martin 7
Wilson, Gene 174, 181
Wimber, John 8

Y
Yates, John and Susan 124, 125
Yeo, Alfred 62, 193
Young, David 193

Z
Zunkel, C. Wayne 78
Zweininger, Jakob 2

Index of Subjects

A
acculturation 68, 223

C
calling 26, 27, 36, 70, 72, 78, 89, 105, 109, 113, 140, 142, 144, 175, 183, 211, 212, 214, 217
   to mission 69
church growth 2, 83, 88, 98, 181, 207, 208
Church of England 184
communication 21, 154, 161, 162
   cultural methods 65
   effective 162
   evangelistic 6, 66
   human 75
   intentional 21
   natural 66
   successful 162
confrontation (with faith) 82
cross, the 47, 100, 144, 178
culture
   and civilization 25
   Buddhist 225
   church 81, 83, 92, 93, 114, 184
   collapse of 56
   familial 27, 28, 35, 67, 121, 150
   foreign 10, 68, 172, 183, 211, 212, 216, 223, 225
   German 28
   Jewish 53
   missional 81, 93, 108, 118, 147, 156, 167, 210
   of God's kingdom 68
   of relationships 93
   shame-oriented 34, 102
   societal 28, 29, 33, 34, 224
   western 35
culture shock 223

E
education, for children 110, 166, 169, 176, 189
enemies, love for 136, 150, 187, 190
ethnos 77
evangelism, permission 101
evangelization
   door-to-door 183
   family ix, 188

F
familia Dei 41, 69, 75, 92, 102, 121, 160, 174, 213
family academy 113, 114
family cluster 15, 97, 169, 193, 195, 197–202, 206, 209, 210, 222, 225
family night 96
family services 108

G
grace, God's 45, 54, 80, 83, 84, 102, 141, 166

H
holiness 123
home church 54, 120, 149, 156, 206, 222
home visits 207

I
image of God 17, 25, 124, 127
injustice 30, 140, 217
integrity 125

J
justice 30, 140–142
justification 37, 139

245

K
kingdom of God 47, 48, 91, 129, 130

L
Lausanne Occasional Paper (36) Report 192
light of the world 81, 126–129, 141, 144, 163, 180
Light of the World Church 113

M
meekness 136, 138
membership culture 81
ministry
  children's 81, 109, 200, 222
  family x, 14, 61, 81, 100, 110, 206, 214
  Jesus's 42, 44, 45, 48
  mission 221
  missional 169
  of compassion 142
  of peacemaking 144
  of reconciliation 203
  teenage 81
missia ecclesiae 93
missio Christi 42
missio Dei 17, 68
missio familiae 68
mission
  foreign 212, 214–217, 223
  neighbourhood 62
  missional families 71, 72, 76, 99, 100, 110, 117, 119, 121, 123–127, 135, 138, 141, 142, 146, 148–150, 156, 169, 171, 190, 196, 199, 208, 210, 227
mission field 9, 59, 87, 108, 170, 213, 214, 224, 225
missio patri 24
missio Spiritus 50

N
neighbour
  love for 100, 143, 151, 165, 168, 199

neighbourhood(s)
  mission to 75, 78, 89, 171, 193, 195, 197, 200
  service to 70
  transformation of 208
notae ecclesiae 7

O
oikos 54, 98
oikos evangelism 54, 59

P
preaching
  evangelistic 9, 51, 64, 65, 82
  missional 106, 161

R
reconciliation 34, 64, 80, 144, 202, 203
responsibility for the world 150

S
salt of the earth 39, 126
salvation 43, 45, 50, 77, 127, 159
salvation plan 5, 40, 41, 67
single parent(s) 97, 197
socialization 176
  religious 31, 36
social justice 187
spiritual education, for children 109
spiritual growth 89, 109
spiritual maturity 40, 84
strategy
  Holy Spirit's 55, 57
  mission 42, 63, 187, 199

T
theosis 60
Trinity, the 13, 17–22, 41, 56, 151, 159

W
Willingen 1952, missions conference 71
Word of God 52, 81, 104, 106, 175, 177, 178

Index of Scripture

OLD TESTAMENT

Genesis
1:26–28 25
1:27–28 .... 18, 60, 170
1:28 .... 27, 166
2:24 .... 19, 122
4:1–16 40
6:5 142
8:21 142
12:1–3 38
12:15–18 40
26:7–10 40
35:29 29
37:12–27 40

Exodus
3 26
3:6 26
30:35 127
34:6 141

Leviticus
2:13 127
19:18 143
25 .... 44, 68
25:8 26

Deuteronomy
6:4–7 35
6:5 143

Joshua
1 26
24:15 26

1 Samuel
2 30
8:3 30

2 Samuel
11:1–17 40

1 Kings
3:12 142

2 Kings
2:19–22 127

Ezra
6:9 127
7:22 127

Job
29:12–16 142

Psalms
1:1 129
14:1–3 139
37:1–11 136
41:1–3 142
51:10 143

78:3–4 36
103:8 141
127:1 68

Proverbs
4:23 143
11:25 142
14:21 141
20:9 143
25:21–22 137
29:18 119

Isaiah
32:17 144
46:13 139
51:4–5 127
61:1–2 .... 43, 128
61:1–3 133
65:19 44

Jeremiah
33:14–16 139

Ezekiel
43:24 127

Malachi
3:18 139
4:6 64

NEW TESTAMENT

Matthew
1:1–17 26
1:4 178
5:3 129
5:3–12 128
5:6 138
5:7 141
5:8 142

5:9 144
5:10 146
5:10–12 140
5:11–12 146

5:13–15 .... 5, 39, 69, 163	**Luke**	14:9 .... 18, 42
5:13–16 126	2:49 46	14:26 134
5:20 138	4:16–22 43	14:27 144
5:23–24 218	4:18 .... 68, 128	15:13 100
5:27–31 45	4:19 26	15:20 146
5:38–39 135	6:20 129	15:26 134
5:44 136	6:24 129	16:8 134
6:1 138	6:25 132	16:8–10 208
6:5–13 82	7:34 45	16:13 50
6:9–10 130	8:1–3 46	16:14 50
6:10 144	8:15 143	17:11–18 180
6:33 130	8:39 46	17:16–21 163
8:20 .... 131, 150	9:1–6 46	17:21 .... 78, 146
9:9–13 45	9:57–62 47	20:21 .... 24, 42, 49
9:18–20 45	10:1–12 47	
9:35–38 134	10:25–37 141	**Acts**
10:5–15 49	10:27 168	1:8 .... 22, 50, 53, 61,
11:4–6 136	12:51–53 47	163, 217
11:27–30 151	14:26–27 47	2:42 175
14:21 43	15:11–32 141	2:42–47 53
15:19 143	17:3 218	3:1 51
19:1–9 45	18:15–17 48	4:23–31 52
27–29 48	19:9 45	6:1–6 53
22:34–40 143	22:25–30 135	13:1–3 .... 51, 212
28:18–20 77		15:28 145
28:19–20 .... 5, 68, 81,	**John**	16:31–34 55
174, 176, 189	1:1 177	
28:20 175	1:1–2 42	**Romans**
	1:4–5 127	3:10 .... 40, 139
Mark	1:9 127	3:23 40
1:14–15 130	1:12 5	3:26 139
1:29–31 44	1:14 .... 42, 177	4:3–5 139
1:32–33 44	1:29 43	5:1–5 103
1:34 44	1:35–42 177	10:9 143
2:1–12 45	1:40–42 .... 44, 64	10:17 177
3:31–35 46	2:11 45	12:2 123
3:31–36 46	3:16 .... 41, 42, 100	12:10 39
6:3 43	7:38 138	12:13 39
7:9–13 46	8:12 127	12:16 39
9:49 127	8:50 145	12:18 146
10:28–31 46	11 48	14:19 146
10:29–30 46	12:46 127	15:5 39
12:26 26	13:34–35 39	15:7 39
16:10 132	13:35 61	15:33 144
	14:8 22	16:14–15 55

Index of Scripture

16:16 39

1 Corinthians
1:10–12 145
1:30 139
3:6–8 188
3:8 188
5:1–2 132
7:1 51
7:14 54
12:3 50
12:4 .... 50, 51
12:4–6 70
12:4–7 155
12:7 77
12:13 .... 39, 50, 69, 155, 175
16:15 55

2 Corinthians
3:2–9 61
3:17 .... 57, 80, 134
4:4 127
5:17 .... 103, 139, 143
5:18 .... 42, 80
5:18–20 .... 39, 69, 144, 203
5:18–21 68
5:20 24
5:21 .... 39, 69, 139
11:23–31 212
12:9 130
12:21 132
13:12 39

Galatians
1:19 43
3:26–29 174
3:28 39
4:4 22
5:13 39
5:16 140
5:16–23 145
5:19–21 145
5:23 136

6:2 .... 39, 134

Ephesians
1:12 69
1:18 141
1:22 174
1:23 23
2:4–5 141
2:8 176
2:10 .... 69, 77, 140, 175
2:14–19 64
2:16 144
2:19 39
3:14–15 .... 38, 60, 68, 72, 140
3:14–17 69
3:14–19 19
3:14–20 124
3:15 23
3:18 23
3:19 60
4:2 39
4:11–12 .... 70, 82, 140
4:12 175
4:13 174
4:13–17 84
4:22–25 123
4:32 39
5:8 127
5:21 39
5:21–32 138
6:1–4 36
6:4 32
6:6 143

Philippians
2:1–4 145
2:5 .... 131, 151
2:5–11 131
2:6 42
2:9–10 151
3:12–17 124
4:13 130
4:19 142

Colossians
3:13 39

1 Thessalonians
1:9 85
2:1–11 175
4:9 39
5:5 127
5:11 39

1 Timothy
1:5 143
3:2–3 192

2 Timothy
1:3–5 11
1:5 .... 36, 176

Titus
1:7–8 192

Hebrews
1:1–2 22
3:13 39
4:12–13 104
4:15 .... 43, 151
11:1–3 37
12:14 146
13:2 .... 39, 61

James
1:2–4 146
2:17 .... 139, 179
3:18 144
5:16 39

1 Peter
1:22 39
3:1–4 54
4:9 39

2 Peter
1:4 141

1 John
1:1 85
1:1–4 177
1:5 127
1:7 143
3:11 39
4:7 .... 20, 100, 141
4:18 60

2 John
7–11 55

Jude
1 43

Revelation
18:7 132

ALSO BY JOHANNES REIMER

MISSIO POLITICA

The Mission of Church and Politics

9781783683512 | November 2017

GBP £10.99 | USD $19.99

www.langhampublishing.org | literature@langham.org | +44 (0)1228 592033

Free international shipping on all orders

He has shown you, O man, what is good. And what does the Lord require of you? To act justly and to love mcery and to walk humbly with your God. Micah 6:8

Micah's Vision
Communities living life in all its fullness, free from poverty, injustice and conflict.

Micah's Mission
Rooted in the Gospel we become agents of change in our communities by being:

- **Catalysts** for transforming mission by promoting and living out **integral mission**
- A **movement** that advocates for poverty reduction, justice, equality, reconciliation and safety and wellbeing for all
- A **network** providing a platform for shared learning, collective reflection and action, inspiration and mobilisation of the Church, and the demonstration of Integral Mission.

Why Does Micah Exist?
Micah exists to be a catalyst, a movement and a network for **transforming mission**, with a special focus on enabling a united response to reducing poverty, addressing injustice and enabling reconciliation and conflict resolution.

We believe that Jesus came to give life in all its fullness (John 10:10). We believe that God has called out his church (*ecclesia*) to be his body, his representatives, his servants and demonstrate the new Kingdom in word and deed. We call this **integral mission**.

To learn more about Micah Global see: www.micahglobal.org
Find us on Facebook: www.facebook.com/MicahNetwork
Follow us on Twitter: @MicahGlobal
Enjoy our Instagram: www.instagram.com/micahglobal

Micah Global Secretariat
c/o Christ Church, Christchurch Road, Winchester, SO23 9SR, United Kingdom
Email: info@micahglobal.org
Phone: +44 16974 75369

Langham Literature and its imprints are a ministry of Langham Partnership.

Langham Partnership is a global fellowship working in pursuit of the vision God entrusted to its founder John Stott –

> *to facilitate the growth of the church in maturity and Christ-likeness through raising the standards of biblical preaching and teaching.*

Our vision is to see churches in the Majority World equipped for mission and growing to maturity in Christ through the ministry of pastors and leaders who believe, teach and live by the word of God.

Our mission is to strengthen the ministry of the word of God through:
- nurturing national movements for biblical preaching
- fostering the creation and distribution of evangelical literature
- enhancing evangelical theological education

especially in countries where churches are under-resourced.

Our ministry

Langham Preaching partners with national leaders to nurture indigenous biblical preaching movements for pastors and lay preachers all around the world. With the support of a team of trainers from many countries, a multi-level programme of seminars provides practical training, and is followed by a programme for training local facilitators. Local preachers' groups and national and regional networks ensure continuity and ongoing development, seeking to build vigorous movements committed to Bible exposition.

Langham Literature provides Majority World preachers, scholars and seminary libraries with evangelical books and electronic resources through publishing and distribution, grants and discounts. The programme also fosters the creation of indigenous evangelical books in many languages, through writer's grants, strengthening local evangelical publishing houses, and investment in major regional literature projects, such as one volume Bible commentaries like *The Africa Bible Commentary* and *The South Asia Bible Commentary*.

Langham Scholars provides financial support for evangelical doctoral students from the Majority World so that, when they return home, they may train pastors and other Christian leaders with sound, biblical and theological teaching. This programme equips those who equip others. Langham Scholars also works in partnership with Majority World seminaries in strengthening evangelical theological education. A growing number of Langham Scholars study in high quality doctoral programmes in the Majority World itself. As well as teaching the next generation of pastors, graduated Langham Scholars exercise significant influence through their writing and leadership.

To learn more about Langham Partnership and the work we do visit **langham.org**

www.ingramcontent.com/pod-product-compliance
Lightning Source LLC
Chambersburg PA
CBHW070729160426
43192CB00009B/1371